CW00408255
Aug 1999

Breakthrough Language Series

JAPANESE

Noriko Takada and Hiroki Kato

General editor Brian Hill
Professor of Modern Languages, The University of Brighton

Acknowledgements

Actors: Tatsuyuki Ayoki, Keiko Tanabe, Ken'ichi Miura, Noriko Takada
Audio producer: Gerald Ramshaw, MAX II.
Illustrations: Ken'ichi Miura

We are grateful to the Japanese National Tourist Organization, USA, for permission to reproduce photos on the following pages: x, 3, 19, 21, 39, 41, 49, 58, 69, 81, 83, 85, 86, 95, 97, 109, 119, 129, 139, 153, 157, 159, 162, 167, 172, 173, 175, 209.

First published 1994 by NTC Publishing Group, USA.
This edition first published 1995 by
MACMILLAN PRESS LTD
Houndmills, Basingstoke, Hampshire RG21 2XS
and London
Companies and representatives
throughout the world

ISBN 0–333–54183–9 paperback
ISBN 0–333–59804–0 cassettes
ISBN 0–333–59805–9 book and cassette pack

A catalogue record for this book is
available from the British Library

Printed in Great Britain by
Biddles Ltd, Guildford and Kings Lynn

10 9 8 7 6 5 4 3 2 1
04 03 02 01 00 99 98 97 96 95

Contents

HOW TO USE THIS COURSE

Following this course will help you understand and speak the kind of Japanese that you are likely to need on vacation or business trips. The course is based on recordings made in Japan of ordinary people in everyday situations. Step by step you will learn first to understand what they are saying and then to speak in similar situations yourself.

Before producing the course, we talked to hundreds of people about why and how they learn a language. We know how important it is for learning to be enjoyable—and for it to be usable as soon as possible. Again and again people told us that there was not much point in knowing all the grammar if they were unable, for example, to exchange simple greetings at different times of the day. Therefore, the only explanations of grammar in this course will be ones that actually help you understand and use the language.

Our main goal is to help you speak and communicate in Japanese. Since Japanese is very different from most languages, we will demonstrate how some conversations can be simplified and still convey the same idea. When you arrive at Narita Airport and hear Japanese spoken by Japanese people, you will be glad that you had familiarized yourself with native speaker conversations as you prepared yourself for the trip by studying this course.

General hints to help you use the course

- Have confidence in us! Real language is complex, and you will find certain things in every unit which are not explained in detail. Don't worry about this. We will build up your knowledge slowly, selecting only what is most important to know at each stage.
- Try to study regularly, but in short periods. 20–30 minutes each day is usually better than 3½ hours once a week.
- To help yourself learn to speak, say the words and phrases out loud whenever possible.
- If you don't understand something, leave it for a while. Learning a language is a bit like doing a jigsaw or crossword puzzle: there are many ways to tackle it, and it all falls into place eventually.
- Don't be afraid to write in the book and add your own notes.
- Revise frequently.
- It helps to get somebody to test you—even someone who does not know Japanese.
- If you can study with someone else, you will be able to help each other and practise the language together.
- Learning Japanese may take more time than you thought. Just be patient with yourself.

Suggested study pattern

Each unit of the course consists of approximately 14 pages in the book and 12 minutes of recording. The first page of each unit will tell you what you are going to learn and suggest what we think is the best method for going about it. As you progress with the course, you may develop a method of study which suits you better—that's fine, but we suggest you keep to our pattern for at least the first two or three units, or you may find you are not taking full advantage of all the possibilities offered in the material.

The book contains step-by-step instructions for working through the course: when to use the book on its own, when to use the recording on its own, when to use them both together, and how to use them. On the recording our presenter Aoki Tatsu will guide you through the various sections. Following is an outline of the study pattern proposed.

Dialogues

Listen to any dialogue first without stopping the recording and get a feel for the task ahead. Then go over it again in conjunction with the vocabulary and the notes. Items marked with an arrow are most important and you should concentrate on these particularly. Stop the recording to give yourself time to think, and don't hesitate to go back to listen to the dialogue a number of times. Don't leave a dialogue until you are confident that you have at least understood it.

Practise what you have learned

This section contains a selection of exercises which focus your attention on important phrases in the dialogue. You will need to work closely with the book and often use the recording. Sometimes you are asked to do a short writing exercise and check your answers. Some exercises require that you listen to the recording and fill in the answers in the book. In other exercises you will be given opportunity to practise speaking what you have learned, aided by prompts and directions on the recording.

Key words and phrases

Study this list of the most important words and phrases from the dialogues. If possible, try to learn them by heart. They will be practised and used throughout the book.

Grammar

Since Japanese grammar is very different from English, it will be helpful for you to read through this section, even if you don't particularly care for grammar as a subject of study. Only the most important points are explained, and the explanations have been kept as simple and pertinent as possible.

Read and understand

Since the Japanese writing system is very different from the English alphabet, you will not learn to read or write Japanese in this course. However, in this section you will become familiar with signs, menus, etc., that you might come across in Japan and that it will be helpful for you to recognize.

Did you know?

In this section you will be given practical background information on Japanese customs and culture.

Answers

The answers to all the exercises (except those given in the recording) can be found on the last page of each unit.

If you haven't learned a language using a recording before, just spend a few minutes on Unit 1 getting used to the mechanics: practise stopping the recording and see how long it takes to recap different-length phrases, and so forth.

Don't be shy—take every opportunity to speak and listen to the Japanese language. Try talking to any Japanese people in your area, and watch any TV programmes about Japan.

Ganbatte!

You will find...

- a pronunciation guide for learning the sounds of Japanese and how they are written in the Roman alphabet in this unit and at the end of Unit 1. (pp. ix, 13 and on the recording at the end of Unit 1);
- a simple overview of the basics of Japanese grammar (pp. 11, 31, 43, 57, 74, 103, 117, 131, 145, 159, 173, 185, 199 and 213);
- an introduction to the Japanese writing systems (p. 13);
- a concise listing of Japanese numbers and special "counters" (pp. 216–218);
- an index of the grammar principles taught in the course and where to find them in the text (pp. 219 and 220);
- a Japanese–English vocabulary list containing all the words presented in the text (pp. 221–232).

Symbols and abbreviations

If you have a counter, set it at zero at the beginning of the recording. Check the counter at the beginning of each dialogue and write that number in the rectangle beside the number of that dialogue in the book. This will help you find the right place quickly when you revise.

m. masculine speech
f. feminine speech

Japanese nouns are not divided into masculine, feminine and neuter groups as those in some European languages are. However, certain vocabulary and verb forms are commonly used primarily by men or primarily by women. These are noted by (*m.*) or (*f.*) wherever appropriate.

pol. polite
inf. informal/casual

Japanese speech patterns change according to the formality or informality of the occasion, the relative social status of the speaker and listener, and the relationship between them. These differences are noted by (*pol.*) or (*inf.*) where appropriate and necessary.

humb. humble verb
norm. normal-polite verb
exal. exalted verb

Similarly, certain verbs require that the subject be the person speaking; these are noted as "humble" (*humb.*) verbs. Others require that someone other than the speaker be the subject; these are noted as "exalted" (*exal.*) verbs. In between these two types of verbs are verbs in the "normal-polite" (*norm.*) level of speech, which can have either the speaker or someone/something else as the subject. These verbs are noted only when the differentiation is deemed necessary.

dic. the dictionary form of a verb or adjective
eq. equivalent (another way of saying the same thing)
or. origin (of a word borrowed from another language)
lit. literally (a more literal translation of the same phrase)
col. colloquial form
dim. diminutive (endearment) form

Pronunciation Guide

Japanese is fairly easy to pronounce. Unlike Chinese and some other Asian languages, it has no "tones" that change the meaning of a word. It also does not have accented syllables like English and other Western languages. Sometimes accent or emphasis may be put on a syllable or a word, but this is simply to convey feeling or to give emphasis and does not change the basic meaning.

There are only 5 vowel sounds in Japanese, pronounced as follows:

A as in FATHER
I as in MACHINE
U as in TUTU
E as in SET
O as in DOG

With few exceptions, a consonant is always followed by a vowel. The charts below show the basic Japanese "syllabary"—the Japanese equivalent of an alphabet.

BASIC SYLLABARY

A	I	U	E	O
KA	KI	KU	KE	KO
GA	GI	GU	GE	GO
SA	SHI	SU	SE	SO
ZA	JI	ZU	ZE	ZO
TA	CHI	TSU	TE	TO
DA	JI	ZU	DE	DO
NA	NI	NU	NE	NO
HA	HI	FU	HE	HO
BA	BI	BU	BE	BO
PA	PI	PU	PE	PO
MA	MI	MU	ME	MO
YA		YU		YO
RA	RI	RU	RE	RO[2]
WA				(w)O[3]
				N[4]

COMBINATION SYLLABLES[1]

KYA	KYU	KYO
GYA	GYU	GYO
SHA	SHU	SHO
JA	JU	JO
CHA	CHU	CHO
(JA	JU	JO)
NYA	NYU	NYO
HYA	HYU	HYO
BYA	BYU	BYO
PYA	PYU	PYO
MYA	MYU	MYO
RYA	RYU	RYO[2]

Pronunciation of these syllables is presented on the tape at the end of Unit 1.

[1]These are called "combination syllables" because they are written in the Japanese script by combining the character for YA, YU or YO with a character that represents a syllable that includes the vowel "I" (i.e., KI, GI, SHI, CHI, etc.). The "Y" sound in the middle of these syllables is not a separate vowel sound, but a soft sound connected with the consonant that precedes it. In other words, the word KYAKU ("guest/customer") is two syllables (KYA-KU), not three (KEE-YA-KU).

[2]Although the letter R is used to romanize these syllables, the Japanese "R" sound is nothing like the English "R" of "rat", "rabbit", etc. It is the same as the single-tap "R" of Spanish and some other languages (NOT the trilled"RR") and is made by placing the TIP of the tongue at the top of the mouth and flipping it downward. It occurs in American English in the middle of words like "better", "little", "paddle", etc.

[3](w)O This sound sometimes is given the slightest hint of a "W" in front of it as in the Irish pronunciation of "what" and "whether". This is not crucial, however, and you will not go wrong if you always pronounce it "O". In the text it will be represented simply as O.

[4]N This is a soft, nasal sound, and it is the only consonant sound that is considered a syllable by itself (except for double consonants, as noted below). Occasionally it will be followed by a vowel or YA, YU or YO as a separate syllable. When that occurs, it will be written as N' to distinguish it from NA, NI, NU, NE, NO and NYA, NYU, NYO. (*Ex.*: HON'YA—pronounced HO-N-YA.)

Other points to remember:

"Long" or multiple words

Every sound/syllable of Japanese, as written in the Roman alphabet, is pronounced. That means that when two or more vowels come together, each is pronounced. For example, the word NAMAE ("name") is pronounced NA-MA-E; OTOOSAN ("father") is O-TO-O-SA-N; ONEESAN ("older sister") is O-NE-E-SA-N; etc. In this book, long vowels are doubled in their written form (OHAYOO, SAYOONARA), except in proper names where they are indicated by a vowel with a bar above (TŌKYŌ, KYŌTŌ, SHŌDA).

Double consonants

Only certain consonant sounds ever occur as doubles in Japanese. They are romanized as KK, SS, SSH, TT, TCH, PP, NN. When a word includes a double consonant sound, both consonants are pronounced, and each is considered a separate syllable or part of a separate syllable. For example, KEKKOO is four syllables (KE-K-KO-O), ISSHO is three (I-S-SHO), KONNICHI is four (KO-N-NI-CHI), etc.

Note: To represent foreign words in Japanese-style romanization, some other consonants may be doubled: BEDDO (bed), HOTTO DOGGU (hot dog), etc.

Unstressed vowels

The vowels I and U are often unstressed, which makes them nearly silent, especially when they come between two "voiceless consonants" (k, s, t, f, p) or at the end of a word, as in the following sentences:
(Underlined vowels are nearly silent.)

1. Ohayoo gozaimasu.
2. Watakushi wa Shōda to mooshimasu.

Japan Rail Travel Service Centre in Tokyo Station

1 TALKING ABOUT YOURSELF

You will learn

- to exchange greetings
- to observe basic courtesies in addressing people
- to introduce yourself and your friends
- to answer simple questions about yourself
- something about the Japanese writing system and Japanese sounds

Before you begin

Read the introduction that begins on page vi. This gives some useful advice on studying alone and details of a specific study pattern recommended for this course.

Look at the **Study guide** below. It has been designed to help you make the most effective use of the unit, so that you will progress from understanding the gist of the recorded dialogues to understanding them in detail and finally to being able to speak a number of key words, phrases and sentences yourself.

We will work to develop your ability to *follow the gist* of spoken Japanese right from the start. Begin by listening to the first dialogue on the recording without using your book and without worrying about the details of what is being said.

Study guide

Keep tabs on your progress by checking off each task as you complete it.

	Dialogue 1 + Practise what you have learned
	Dialogue 2 + Practise what you have learned
	Dialogue 3 + Practise what you have learned
	Dialogue 4 + Practise what you have learned
	Study: Key words and phrases
	Study: the Grammar section
	Read and study: Introduction to Japanese writing
	Read: Did you know?

If you have a recorder with a counter, set it at zero and write the counter reading for each dialogue in the rectangle. This can help you find a dialogue more quickly when you want to listen to it a second time.

Dialogues

1 *Hello, my name is...*

Miki Konnichiwa.
Shōda Konnichiwa.
Miki Boku no namae wa Miki to mooshimasu.
Shōda A, watakushi no namae wa Shōda to mooshimasu.

boku I (*m./inf.*)
namae name
Miki Japanese surname
watakushi I (*eq.* watashi)
Shōda Japanese surname

Konnichiwa Hello. This greeting is used in the daytime.

boku no namae my name (*m./inf.*) See the Grammar section at the end of this unit for more on the grammar marker **no**.

____ **to mooshimasu**. I am called ____. Note that you normally only use your surname when introducing yourself in Japanese.

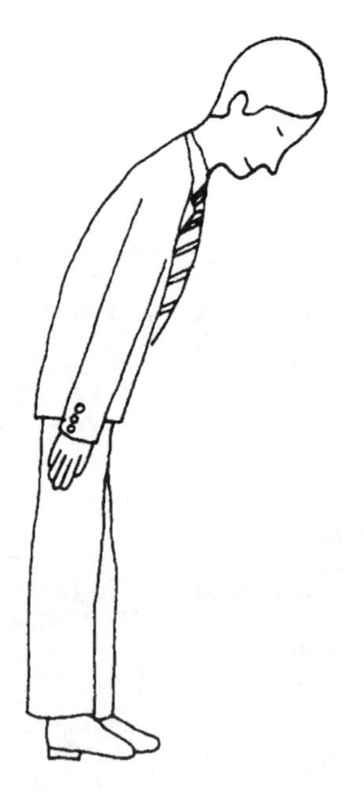

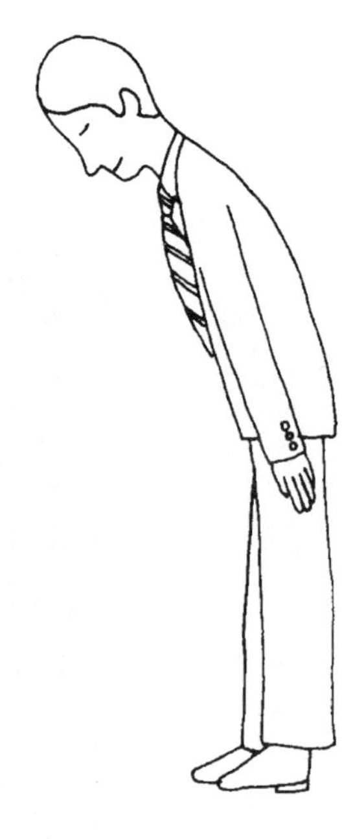

Practise what you have learned

1 Listen to the recording to hear how people introduce themselves and exchange greetings. See if you can catch their names, and check them off the following list as you hear them. (Answers p. 14)

______✓ Mori

______✓ Nakagawa

______ Yamamoto

______✓ Tanaka

______✓ Nakayama

2 Listen to the recording. Tanabe san will greet you and introduce herself to you. Say hello and introduce yourself to her. (Answers p. 14)

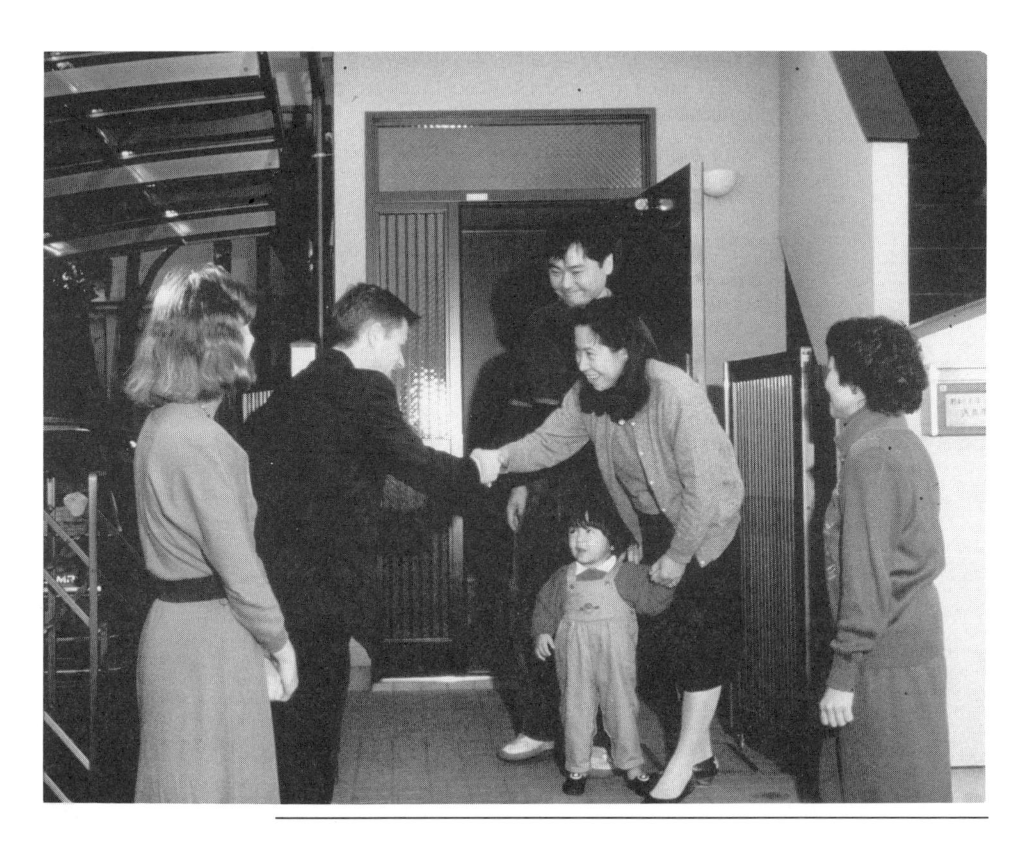

Dialogues

2 *Greetings and goodbyes*

Miki Kyoo wa ii o-tenki desu, ne.
Shōda Honto desu, ne. Atatakakute...
Miki Sore dewa, chotto shitsurei itashimasu.
Shōda A, sayoonara.
Miki Sayonara.

kyoo today
ii o-tenki good weather
honto true (*eq.* **hontoo**)
atatakakute warm (and...) (*dic.* atatakai)
sore dewa well, then
chotto a little bit
Shitsurei itashimasu. Excuse me for being rude. (*humb.*) (*eq.* **Shitsurei shimasu.**)
Sayoonara./Sayonara. Goodbye. (The latter is more common.)

Kyoo wa... The word **wa** is one of a number of grammar markers sometimes called "particles" or "postpositions". This one means that the word kyoo is the topic of the sentence—what you are talking about. **Kyoo wa** means "as for today" or "I am talking about today". See the Grammar section at the end of this unit for more about particles.

Ii o-tenki desu, ne. It's a nice day, isn't it? The Japanese verb always comes at the end of the sentence, with few exceptions. One such exception is the tag question **ne**, meaning "right?" or "isn't it?" It is often used as much to soften a sentence (make it less abrupt) as to ask for confirmation.

The Japanese often exchange small "weather talk" instead of "Hello, how are you?" or other greetings.

See the Grammar section at the end of this unit for more on the verb **desu**.

Atatakakute... It is warm and... The **-kute** at the end of this adjective indicates that the thought is not complete. The implication is that the weather is, perhaps, "warm, and that's good". The Japanese often leave a sentence incomplete, assuming that the listener can complete the thought himself.

shitsurei shimasu Excuse me. (*lit.*, "I am going to do something rude [by leaving].") The implication is that the speaker is about to end the conversation by leaving. The use of **chotto** here does not indicate that the departure is temporary, but is only to make the apology less abrupt. **Chotto** is frequently used as a softener.

Practise what you have learned

3 Complete the sentences below with the appropriate numbered phrases. (Answers p. 14)

(a) Watakushi no namae wa __________ **(1)** desu, ne.

(b) Ii o-tenki __________ **(2)** Miki to mooshimasu.

(c) Sore dewa, __________ **(3)** shitsurei shimasu.

4 Read the ten phrases listed below, then listen to the conversation on the recording. You will hear six of these phrases in the conversation. Put a tick next to the phrases that you hear. (Answers p. 14)

___**(a)** Konnichiwa

___**(b)** Kyoo wa

___**(c)** Sore dewa, chotto

___**(d)** Kinoo wa

___**(e)** Smith desu.

___**(f)** Shōda to mooshimasu.

___**(g)** Sayonara.

___**(h)** Samukatta desu, ne.

___**(i)** Shitsurei shimasu.

___**(j)** Ii o-tenki desu, ne.

5 On the recording you'll be invited to participate in a conversation using the main words and phrases from the dialogues that you have learned. You will introduce yourself and respond to small "weather talk", then say goodbye. Aoki-san will guide you through the conversation. There are, of course, no answers for this exercise. Now, enjoy speaking Japanese!

Dialogues

3 *Good morning*

Shōda Ohayoo gozaimasu.
Miki A, ohayoo gozaimasu.
Shōda Mada, asa wa samui desu, ne.
Miki Soo desu, ne. Kyoo wa chotto samui desu, ne.
Shōda Ee. A, dochira ni o-dekake desu ka?
Miki Chotto kaisha no hoo e..., shigoto de.
Shōda A soo desu ka. Itte irasshai.
Miki Hai, itte kimasu.

Ohayoo gozaimasu. Good morning.
mada still, yet
asa morning
samui cold (weather)
hai yes (*pol.*)
ee yes (*inf.*)
dochira? where? (*pol.*) (*eq.* **doko?**)
o-dekake departure (*pol.*)
kaisha company
hoo direction
shigoto work, job

Soo desu, ne. That's right, isn't it? This phrase of agreement is frequently used to make conversation flow smoothly.

Dochira ni o-dekake desu ka? Where are you going? (*lit.*, In what direction is your departure?) (*eq.* **O-dekake desu ka?**) This is a greeting, rather than a serious question, but the appropriate response is a simple answer, such as the one given here. (See the Grammar section at the end of this unit for more on **ka** and other grammar markers.)

Chotto kaisha no hoo e..., shigoto de. To the company...on business. **Kaisha e** would also indicate "to the company", but the longer phrase, along with the word **chotto** again, is yet another way to make a sentence less abrupt and, therefore, more polite.

A soo desu ka? Oh, really? / Is that right?

Itte irasshai. Hurry back. (*lit.*, "Go and come back".)

Itte kimasu. I'll be back. (*lit.*, "I will go and come back".) These are standard phrases used when someone parts company with someone else temporarily, particularly when leaving one's home or neighbourhood.

Practise what you have learned

6

Weather-related phrases are an important part of everyday life in Japan. Some useful phrases are listed below. Listen to the recording and repeat after Miura-san until these phrases become familiar to you.

(a) It's warm, isn't it? **Atatakai desu, ne.**

(b) It rains/snows a lot, doesn't it? **Yoku furimasu, ne.**

(c) It's hot, isn't it? **Atsui desu, ne.**

(d) It's cool, isn't it? **Suzushii desu, ne.**

(e) It's terrible weather, isn't it? **Henna o-tenki desu, ne.**

(f) It's cold, isn't it? **Samui desu, ne.**

Now, as prompted by Aoki-san, greet people appropriately during the rainy season and on a beautiful October morning.

7

As in English, Japanese phrases such as **Soo desu ka** and **Hontoo desu ka** can be taken as questions or as simple response statements, depending on intonation. Rising intonation on **ka** indicates a question, and the listener may respond with **Hai, soo desu**. Falling intonation indicates that no response is expected.

Read the following short phrases through first, then listen to the recording and write Q (for a question) or S (for a statement) in the blank. (Answers p. 14)

(a) Hontoo desu ka. 

(b) Samui desu ka. 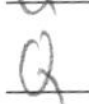

(c) Mada desu ka. 

(d) Hontoo desu ka. 

(e) Atsui desu ka. 

(f) Mada desu ka. 

Dialogues

4 *Good evening, I want to introduce my friend.*

Miki A, konbanwa.
Shōda A, konbanwa.
Miki Kyoo wa atarashii yuujin o shookai shimasu. Yoshida-kun to mooshimasu.
Shōda Yoshida-kun desu ka. Yoroshiku onegai shimasu.
Yoshida Yoroshiku onegai shimasu.
Shōda Hajimemashite.
Yoshida Hajimemashite. Konbanwa.

Konbanwa Good evening.
atarashii new
yuujin friend (*eq.* **tomodachi**)
shookai shimasu introduce, make an introduction
Yoshida Japanese surname
-kun honorific suffix (*m./inf.*)

Atarashii yuujin o shookai shimasu. I will introduce (my) friend. The grammar marker **o** here indicates that the word **yuujin** is the object of the verb **shookai shimasu**. That is, the friend is what is being introduced. For more on this grammar marker, see the Grammar section at the end of this unit.

Yoshida-kun The suffix **-kun** is a casual way of showing respect for a friend. In more polite or formal situations, or when talking with a stranger or superior, the suffix **-san** would be used. This is part of the concept of "honorifics", which is simply a way of giving respect to others by the selection of words or the addition of prefixes (**o-** and **go-**, for example) and suffixes (**-kun**, **-san**, **-sama**) to names or things belonging to people other than oneself. (Never add **-kun**, **-san** or **-sama** to your own name!)

Yoroshiku onegai shimasu. Happy to meet you. This phrase defies direct translation into English, but more literally means something like "Please accept my regards". The implication is that the speaker expects this new relationship to continue and hopes that the listener agrees. (*eq.* **Doozo yoroshiku.**)

Hajimemashite. How do you do? (*lit.* "for the first time") This word indicates that a new relationship is just beginning.

Unlike Western custom, the Japanese do not consider it necessary to introduce people to others. You should not feel offended if your Japanese friend does not formally introduce you to someone. You will soon be included in the conversation without an introduction.

Practise what you have learned

8 Look at the illustrations and decide which phrase or greeting is best suited for each one. (Answers p. 14)

(a) Konbanwa.
(b) Shookai shimasu.
(c) Ohayoo gozaimasu.
(d) Yoku furimasu ne.
(e) Yamada desu.
(f) Smith desu Yoroshiku.

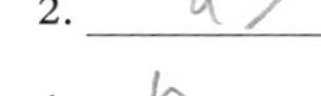

1. ________ 2. ________
3. ________ 4. ________
5. ________ 6. ________

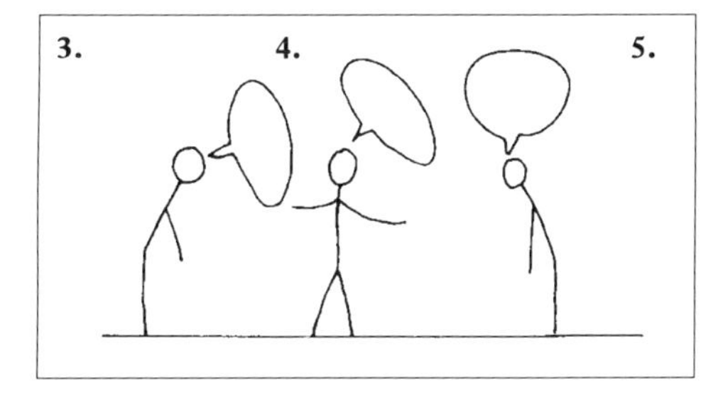

9 Listen to the recording and answer the following questions. You may want to listen several times. (Answers p. 14)

(a) What time of day is this conversation taking place? ________

(b) How is the weather? ________

(c) What is the new friend's name? ________

(d) Is this friend going to go out today? ________

Key words and phrases

Here are the important words and phrases that you have studied in this unit. You should make sure you know them well. Practise saying them aloud.

Konnichiwa.	Hello. (daytime)
________ **to mooshimasu.**	My name is ________.
Watakushi/Boku no namae wa ________ desu.	My name is ________.
Ii o-tenki desu, ne.	It's a nice day, isn't it?
Henna o-tenki desu, ne.	What an awful day!/It's terrible weather, isn't it?
Yoku furimasu, ne?	It rains a lot, doesn't it?
________ **desu.**	It is ________.
Atatakai desu.	It's warm.
Suzushii desu.	It's cool.
Atsui desu.	It's hot.
Samui desu.	It's cold (weather).
Honto desu.	It's true.
ne	tag question ("right?"/"isn't it?")
Chotto shitsurei shimasu.	Excuse me (I have to leave).
sore dewa	well, then
Sayonara.	Goodbye.
Ohayoo gozaimasu.	Good morning.
Soo desu (ka?)	That's right. (Is that right?)
Ee/hai	Yes
Dochira ni o-dekake desu ka?	Where are you going?
O-dekake desu ka?	Are you going out?
Itte irasshai.	Hurry back.
Itte kimasu.	I'll be back.
Konbanwa.	Good evening.
Yuujin o shookai shimasu.	I will introduce my friend.
Yoroshiku onegai shimasu./ Doozo yoroshiku.	Happy to meet you./Please accept my regards.
Hajimemashite.	How do you do?

Grammar

Here are some general rules you should keep in mind:

Sentence order

The verb is always placed at the end of the sentence.

Degrees of politeness

The Japanese will select vocabulary and verb forms according to the degree of politeness required; that is, whether the speaker is talking to a close friend or family member (informal), a stranger or acquaintance (normal polite), or a superior or someone he wants to impress (exalted).

Verb endings usually grow in length with the degree of politeness. For example, the question "Are you going?" can be translated: **Iku no?** (informal), **Ikimasu ka?** (normal polite), **O-dekake desu ka?** (formal/traditional). This course identifies verb forms and certain vocabulary as being specifically informal (*inf.*) or polite (*pol.*).

Nouns, articles, plurals

Japanese nouns are not divided into masculine, feminine and neuter. There are also no articles ("a", "an", "the") in Japanese, and nouns do not change for function or plurality. The word **hon** ("book"), for example, can be translated "a book", "the book", or "books", depending on context.

Pronouns

There is no word for "it" in Japanese, so it is simply omitted in translation. Personal pronouns are often omitted as well.

Grammar markers

These are short words that tell the relationship of a word or phrase to the rest of the sentence. In some cases they are similar to English prepositions ("of", "by", "for", "to", etc.), except that they come after the words they pertain to.

Here is a list of the most important markers for you to learn now. Most of these have been introduced in the dialogues already.

wa topic marker—comes after the topic of the sentence. *Ex.*: **Watakushi wa** = As for me *or* I'm talking about myself.

ga subject marker—replaces **wa** in certain situations.

o direct object marker—follows the direct object of the sentence. *Ex.*: **Yuujin o shookai shimasu.** = I will introduce (my) friend.

no possession marker—comes in the same position as "'s" in English. *Ex.*: **Yoshida-kun no hon** = Yoshida's book; **boku no namae** = my name.

ni/e direction markers—follow the place to or towards which the subject goes, comes, returns, etc. *Ex.*: **kaisha ni** *or* **kaisha e** = to the company.

ka question marker—follows a verb to make a statement into a question. *Ex.*: **Samui desu.** = It's cold. / **Samui desu ka?** = Is it cold?

yo emphasis marker—follows a verb to add emphasis to a sentence.

(Other grammar markers will be explained as they are introduced in later units.)

Verbs

The Japanese verb does not change for person, number or gender of the subject. Also, there are only two basic tenses: present and past. (Future intention is indicated by using the present tense.)

Adjectives

There are two kinds of adjectives:

1. Adjectives that can be inflected to show present or past tense and negative or positive.

Examples:

Samui desu.	It is cold.
Samukatta desu.	It was cold.
Atsui desu.	It is hot.
Atsukatta desu.	It was hot.

2. Adjectival Nouns that do not change, but require that the verb change to show present/past/negative.

Examples:

Hontoo desu.	It is true.
Hontoo deshita.	It was true.
Hen desu.	It is terrible.
Hen deshita.	It was terrible.

These adjectives must be followed by **na** or **no** when placed before a noun; for example, **hen na o-tenki** unpleasant weather; **hontoo no hanashi** true story.

Desu

This is undoubtedly the most commonly used Japanese verb. It is also very different from other verbs, and is usually treated separately. It means "is" or "equals". The past tense of **desu** is **deshita** ("was"/"were"). (Negative and other forms will be introduced in a later unit.) This verb is used to tell what something is or what something is like; for example, **Watakushi no namae wa Smith desu.** = My name is Smith. / **Kyoo wa samui desu.** = Today is cold.

The aim of the Grammar section in each unit of this course is to give the basics of the language, as a foundation to build on. Grammar explanations will be kept as short, simple and pertinent as possible. You will not need your tape recorder when you study this section.

Do not let yourself feel discouraged if you do not understand a grammar principle at first. Language is learned by degrees, and it requires time to become comfortable with it. Remember that making a mistake does not matter, as long as you make yourself understood. The concept of the "Breakthrough" method is that you learn more by listening to the language than by memorizing rules of grammar.

Read and understand

Japanese writing

The Japanese writing system is made up of three kinds of symbols: **Kanji**, **Hiragana** and **Katakana**. For convenience in this course, all material is presented in the Roman alphabet (**Roomaji**). All Japanese students learn *Roomaji* in school, but it is not used for general reading and writing, and many Japanese have a hard time reading and understanding romanized material. All books, newspapers and other printed matter utilize the three kinds of Japanese symbols, as explained below:

Kanji was developed by and borrowed from the Chinese and adapted to fit the Japanese language. **Kanji** characters are pictographs (symbols that represent objects) and ideographs (representing concepts), which function much like the symbols %, $, &, and so on. Each **Kanji** has a certain meaning attached to it, but it may be pronounced any of several different ways, depending on the exact concept, context and function of the word. There are over 1800 **Kanji** in daily use by the Japanese.

The two other sets of symbols are strictly phonetic; that is, each character represents a certain sound or syllable, with no specific meaning. Collectively, they are called **Kana**. Each set represents the same syllables presented on p. ix as the Japanese syllabary. **Katakana** is used primarily for words of foreign origin and to call attention to a word; for this reason, **Katakana** is used extensively in advertising. **Hiragana** is used to write verb endings, grammar markers, and any word for which there is no **Kanji** or the writer does not know the **Kanji**. For comparison, a few words are written below in **Roomaji, Hiragana, Katakana** and **Kanji**.

	Roomaji	**Hiragana**	**Katakana**	**Kanji**
morning	ASA	あさ	アサ	朝
Japan	NIHON	にほん	ニホン	日本
Tokyo	TŌKYŌ	とうきょう	トーキョー	東京

To help you learn to read romanized Japanese, Tanabe-san will pronounce all the basic syllables for you. Listen to the recording and practise saying the syllables in order. Pay close attention to how each syllable is spelled in **Roomaji**.

BASIC SYLLABARY

A	I	U	E	O
KA	KI	KU	KE	KO
GA	GI	GU	GE	GO
SA	SHI	SU	SE	SO
ZA	JI	ZU	ZE	ZO
TA	CHI	TSU	TE	TO
DA	JI	ZU	DE	DO
NA	NI	NU	NE	NO
HA	HI	FU	HE	HO
BA	BI	BU	BE	BO
PA	PI	PU	PE	PO
MA	MI	MU	ME	MO
YA		YU		YO
RA	RI	RU	RE	RO
WA				(w)O
				N

"COMBINATION" SYLLABLES

KYA	KYU	KYO
GYA	GYU	GYO
SHA	SHU	SHO
JA	JU	JO
CHA	CHU	CHO
NYA	NYU	NYO
HYA	HYU	HYO
BYA	BYU	BYO
PYA	PYU	PYO
MYA	MYU	MYO
RYA	RYU	RYO

Did you know?

Bowing

Bowing is one of the oldest customs used in greeting one another and saying goodbye. While it is acceptable for the foreign visitor to observe this custom, it should not be over-used, as there is a certain protocol that is observed by the Japanese. The depth of the bow and how long one holds it depend on the relative status of the people bowing. Many Japanese, especially the younger generation, expect foreigners to shake hands rather than bow. Businessmen also often follow this practice when greeting foreigners.

Japanese people and the English language

Every child in Japan studies English from the age of thirteen. Unfortunately, the knowledge of English and the ability to communicate in English are two different matters. Many people can read English (if it's written very carefully) much better than they can understand it when it is spoken. Carry a small notebook and a pen with you for emergency situations. People will understand HOSPITAL written on a piece of paper much better than being asked, "Can you tell me where the hospital is?" Young people are eager to hear spoken English. You will want to try out your Japanese, but they will want to practise English.

The Japan National Tourist Organization (JNTO)

These quasi-governmental agencies have offices in major cities throughout the world. They provide free maps and brochures and assist in making travel arrangements.

The Japan Travel Bureau (JTB)

Look for JTB signs for quick assistance in Japan.

Answers

Practise what you have learned

Exercise **1**	(1) Nakayama (2) Tanaka (3) Nakagawa (4) Mori
Exercise **2**	Konnichiwa. (*<u>Your name</u>*) to mooshimasu.
Exercise **3**	(a) 2 (b) 1 (c) 3
Exercise **4**	(a) (b) (j) (c) (i) (g)
Exercise **7**	(a) Q (b) Q (c) S (d) S (e) Q (f) Q
Exercise **8**	(a) 6 (b) 4 (c) 1 (d) 2 (e) 3 or 5 (f) 3 or 5
Exercise **9**	(a) day time (b) hot (c) Yamamoto-san (d) He's going out

2

YOURSELF AND OTHERS

You will learn

- to talk about your hometown/country
- to talk about your work
- to talk about your family
- to count from 1–10 and 10–100 by tens
- the days of the week
- about the geography of Japan

Study guide

- **Dialogue 1 + Practise what you have learned**
- **Dialogue 2 + Practise what you have learned**
- **Dialogue 3 + Practise what you have learned**
- **Dialogue 4 + Practise what you have learned**
- **Dialogue 5 + Practise what you have learned**
- **Dialogue 6 + Practise what you have learned**
- **Make sure you know the Key words and phrases**
- **Study: the Grammar section**
- **Read: Did you know?**
- **Listen to all the dialogues once again without the book**

Dialogues

1 *Can you count?*

Adult Namae wa?
Maiko Katō Maiko.
Adult Mai-chan, ikutsu?
Maiko Jussai.
Adult O-tanjoobi wa itsukara?
Maiko Ichigatsu hatsuka.
Adult Nani-yoobi datta?
Maiko Doyoobi.
Adult Ichi kara juu made kazoete kureru?
Maiko Un. Ichi, ni, san, shi, go, roku, shichi, hachi, kyuu, juu.
Adult Kondo ne, juu, ni-juu, tte iu fuu ni kazoete kureru ka na?
Maiko Juu, ni-juu, san-juu, yon-juu, go-juu, roku-juu, shichi-juu, hachi-juu, kyu-juu, hyaku.
Adult Un, arigato.

Katō Japanese surname
Maiko girl's name (*diminutive:* **Mai-chan**)
ikutsu how old? (*eq.* **nan-sai**)
jussai ten years old (See p. 29 for age counters.)
tanjoobi birthday (**o-tanjoobi** = your birthday)
itsu? when?
Ichigatsu January (see p. 216 for names of months.)
hatsuka 20th day of the month (See p. 217)
naniyoobi what day of the week? (*eq.* **nan'yoobi**)
doyoobi Saturday (See p. 29 for days of the week.)
kara from / since
made up to / until
Arigato Thanks. (*inf.*) (*eq.* **Arigatoo gozaimasu.**)

(Note that the tone of this conversation is informal, as the speaker is an adult talking to a child.)

Namae wa (nan desu ka)? (What is) your name? (*inf.*) Simply bringing up a topic is a casual way of asking a question. The question itself is assumed by the listener. Note that the honorific prefix **o-** has been dropped because the speaker is talking to a child. (See p. 12 for more on **desu**.)

Katō Maiko The Japanese surname is given first, followed by the given name. Most Japanese have no middle name.
Mai-chan The **-chan** suffix is a diminutive form of **-san**, used after the name (or, as in this case, an abbreviated form of the name) of a child, a close friend, or a younger sibling.

Ikutsu (desu ka)?...Jussai (desu). How old (are you)?...Ten years old. The suffix **-sai** indicates age. (See p. 29.)

Naniyoobi datta? What day of the week was it? (*inf.*) (*eq.* **Naniyoobi deshita ka?**)

Ichi kara juu made from 1 to 10. See p. 29 for numbers. Note that **kara** and **made** follow the numbers they refer to. (See Grammar section.)

Kazoete kureru? Will you please count (for me)? (*inf.*) The ending **-te kureru** implies that a favour is being asked. (*pol. eq.* **Kazoete kuremasu ka?**) (*dic.* **kazoeru**)

Practise what you have learned

1 Rearrange the numbers in the box so that they will be in sequence from one to ten. You won't need the recording to do this exercise. Check your answers against the dialogue or p. 29.

roku	**hachi**	**ichi**	**juu**	**go**
san	**ni**	**kyuu**	**shi**	**shichi**

(1) ____________ (6) ____________

(2) ____________ (7) ____________

(3) ____________ (8) ____________

(4) ____________ (9) ____________

(5) ____________ (10) ____________

Dialogues

2 *Days of the week*

Adult	Namae wa?
Tsuyoshi	Takarabe Tsuyoshi.
Adult	Nansai?
Tsuyoshi	Nana-sai.
Adult	Getsuyoobi, Kayoobi itte mite kureru?
Tsuyoshi	Getsuyoobi, Kayoobi, Suiyoobi, Mokuyoobi, Kinyoobi, Doyoobi, Nichiyoobi.
Adult	Getsu-yoobi, Ka-yoobi itte mite kureru? Getsu, Ka de ii.
Tsuyoshi	Getsu, Ka, Sui, Moku, Kin, Do, Nichi.

Takarabe Japanese surname
Tsuyoshi boy's given name
Nansai? What age (are you)? (*eq.* **Ikutsu?**) (*pol. eq.* **Nansai desu ka?** or **O-ikutsu desu ka?**)
Nana-sai seven years old (See p. 29 for age counters.)
Getsuyoobi Monday (See p. 29 for days of the week.)
Getsu, Ka Short forms of Monday, Tuesday (etc.)

(Note that the form of this conversation is informal, as the speaker is an adult talking to a child.)

itte mite kureru? Will you try saying...(for me)? (*inf.*) The **-te** form of any verb indicates that another verb follows, either immediately or later in the sentence. (See Grammar section.) This phrase more literally means "Will you say it and see?"

_______ **de ii (desu).** Just _______ is okay.

Practise what you have learned

2 Listen to Dialogue 2, Days of the Week. You will find that knowing the days of the week is very useful when travelling. When you know them well, you can turn off the recording and do the exercise below. The Japanese **Yoobi** are jumbled in this exercise. Write the first two letters of the English word for each day in the box provided. Check your answers against the dialogue or p. 29.

☐	Mokuyoobi	☐	Getsuyoobi
☐	Nichiyoobi	☐	Doyoobi
☐	Kayoobi	☐	Kinyoobi
☐	Suiyoobi		

3 Your turn to speak. Before turning on the recording again, prepare yourself to (a) ask someone how old he is. (b) tell someone your age. (c) ask/say what day of the week it is.

Listen to the recording and follow Aoki-san's prompting.

Dialogues

3 *Where are you from?*

Yoshida O-kuni wa dochira desu ka?
Shōda A, Tochigi-ken desu.
Yoshida Tōkyō e wa kankoo de koraretan desu ka?
Shōda Iie, kankoo ja nain desu. Shigoto de...
Yoshida A, soo desu ka. Sore ja, mata... Sayonara.
Shōda Sayonara.

o-kuni (your) country/home place
dochira where? in what direction? (*pol.*) (*eq.* **doko**)
-ken prefecture (similar to a county)
kankoo sightseeing
koraretan desu (you) came (*pol.*) (*dic.* **korareru**)
ja nain desu is not (*eq.* **dewa arimasen**)
iie no
shigoto work, job
sore ja Well then...
mata See you later. (*lit.* [See you] again.) (*eq.* **Ja mata.**)

Tōkyō e wa to Tokyo. The topic marker **wa** here is almost a token, since there is no grammatical need for it in this case. There are occasions, however, when two particles together are needed for the sense of the sentence.

kankoo de for sightseeing

shigoto de for work/on business (See Grammar section.)

koraretan desu ka? Did you come? The **-rare** portion of this verb form indicates that the subject is someone other than the speaker, who is showing respect for the listener. A simple, casual way of asking the question would be **Kankoo desu ka?**

Practise what you have learned

4

Read the phrases in the two columns below. Supply the most correct response phrases from the numbered column. (Answers p. 32)

(a) O-shigoto desu ka?	______________	**(1)**	Amerika desu.
(b) O-kuni wa?	______________	**(2)**	Ja mata.
(c) Kankoo desu ka?	______________	**(3)**	Honto desu, ne.
(d) Yoku furimasu, ne.	______________	**(4)**	Ee, soo desu.
(e) Sayonara.	______________	**(5)**	Iie, kankoo ja nain desu. Shigoto de...

5

Your turn to speak. Think about what you would say in a casual conversation that includes such things as greetings, weather talk and where you are from. Then turn on the recording and, with Aoki-san's assistance, carry on such a dialogue.

Narita International Airport, near Tokyo

Dialogues

4 *Are you married?*

Yoshida Kekkon wa shite irassharun desu ka?
Shōda E? A! Iie! Mada desu.
Yoshida A! Sore ja, o-sumai wa dochira no hoo...?
Shōda A! Anoo...Nerima no hoo de...Hitori de sunde imasu.
Yoshida A, soo desu ka.

kekkon marriage
E? Huh?
o-sumai your home
Anoo... Uh. .
Nerima a section of Tokyo
hitori de alone, by oneself
sunde imasu living/residing (*dic.* **sumu**)

Kekkon wa shite irassharun desu ka? Are you married? (*pol.*) The **irassharu** portion of this verb form indicates that the subject is someone other than the speaker. This will be explained further at the end of Unit 3.

Mada desu. Not yet. (*lit.* "It is still/yet".) Even though there is no negative word in this phrase, the implication is as if there were.

O-sumai wa dochira no hoo...? Where is your home? (*pol.*) (*Eq.* **O-sumai wa doko desu ka?**)

Nerima no hoo de... It is (in) the area of Nerima. The **de** here is not a grammar marker but the **te-** form of the verb **desu,** giving the impression that the sentence is incomplete. (See the Grammar section.) (*Eq.* **Nerima no hoo desu.**)

Practise what you have learned

6 Read and answer the following questions. You won't need the recording to do this exercise. There are, of course, no set answers.

(1) O-namae wa? ______

(2) O-kuni wa doko desu ka? ______

(3) Kekkon wa shite irassharun desu ka? Hai, ______

Iie, ______

(4) O-sumai wa dochira no hoo desu ka? ______

(5) Kankoo desu ka? Hai, ______

Iie, ______

7 Your turn to speak. Aoki-san will help you strike up a conversation with a Japanese person. First think about how you would say the following. Then turn on the recording.

(1) Say hello and comment on the weather. ______

(2) Say where you are from. ______

(3) Say "Yes, I am on tour", and ask if the other person is there on business. ______

(4) A new phrase is **Suki desu.** "I like it". ______

TABLE OF COUNTRIES	
Australia	**Oosutorarai**
England	**Igirisu**
Britain	**Eikoku**
Scotland	**Sukottorando**
Ireland	**Airurando**
Wales	**Ueeruzu**
Canada	**Kanada**

Dialogues

5 *Family questions*

Mrs. Furukawa O-taku wa o-kosan nannin desu ka?
Mrs. Ogino Sannin orimasu no.
Mrs. Furukawa A, soo desu ka. Uchi wa hitori nan desu yo.
Mrs. Ogino Uchi wa, ano... ichiban ue ga otoko no ko de, mannaka ga onna de, ichiban shita ga otoko desu yo.
Mrs. Furukawa Ja, o-tanoshimi desu ne. O-taku no o-kosan o-ikutsu desu ka?
Mrs. Ogino Juugo-sai to juuni-sai to, ichiban shita ga nana-sai desu.
Mrs. Furukawa A, soo desu ka.

o-taku you/your home, household (*pol.*)
o-kosan your child/children (child = **ko** or **kodomo**)
➧ **nannin** how many (people)?
sannin three people (See below for people counters.)
uchi me/my home, household
hitori one person (See below.)
ichiban ue eldest/uppermost
➧ **otoko** (**no ko**) male (child), boy
mannaka middle
➧ **onna no ko** female (child), girl
ichiban shita youngest/lowest
o-tanoshimi fun, pleasant (*pol.*) (*eq.* **tanoshii**)

O- The frequent use of the honorific prefix is typical of polite conversation between women.

➧ **O-taku wa o-kosan nannin desu ka?** How many children are in your family? There are actually two topics in this sentence—**O-taku** and **o-kosan**—but the second **wa** has been omitted.

O-taku vs. **uchi** These words literally mean "your home" and "my home", but are often used instead of personal pronouns to refer to things/people that belong to you/your family and me/my family. The use of these words emphasizes the feeling of respect for the listener by the speaker.

Sannin orimasu no. The verb **orimasu** requires that the subject be a person other than the speaker. The word **no** at the end is used by women to soften the sentence.

Hitori nan desu yo. The use of **nan** here before desu is to soften the sentence. **Yo** is a grammatical marker that adds a feeling of emphasis to the sentence, similar to an exclamation point but softer.

ga This marker sometimes replaces **wa** to point out the grammatical subject of the verb.

de This is the **te**-form of the verb **desu**. (See the Grammar section.)

O-tanoshimi desu ne. It's fun, isn't it? The implication here is that, with three small children, the home must be a fun, happy place.

Juugo-sai to juuni-sai... 15 years old and 12 years old. (See p. 29 for ages.)

People counters:	**Nan-nin desu ka?**	**Yonin desu.**
	1 person	**hitori**
	2 people	**futari**
	3 people	**sannin**
	4 people	**yonin**
	5 people	**gonin**

Practise what you have learned

8 At restaurants and hotels, you might be asked, **Nannin-sama deshoo ka?** (*pol.*) "How many people are in your party?" When speaking casually, you might just say, **"Nannin desu ka?"** If there are 2 people in the party, the response would be **"Futari desu".** Match numbers with people counters. (Answers p. 32)

(a) sannin ______________ 1 person

(b) hitori ______________ 2 people

(c) yonin ______________ 3 people

(d) futari ______________ 4 people

9 The following exercise also will not require the recording. Read the questions and answer them appropriately. There are, of course, no set answers for this exercise.

(a) There are ____________ people in my family.

(Watashi no) kazoku (family) **wa** ____________ **desu.**

(b) I am ____________ yrs. old.

Boku/Watashi wa ____________ **-sai desu.**

(c) Last year I was ____________ yrs. old.

Kyonen watashi wa ____________ **-sai deshita.**

10 Listen to the recording as two people talk about their families. Jot down what you find out. You will have to infer some of the answers. (Answers p. 32)

(a) The woman is married. Yes ______ No ___✓___

(b) The man is married. Yes ______ No ______

(c) The woman has ______ children. boys ______ girls ______

(d) The man has ______ children. boys ______ girls ______

The phrase **Iie, ie, sonna koto wa arimasen yo** is equivalent to "No, no, it's nothing like that". It is often used as a response to some kind of praise. A phrase like this is used so that people will not think you are boastful.

Dialogues

6 *Where do you work?*

Yoshida Shitsurei desu ga, donna o-shigoto o nasatte irun desu ka?
Shōda A, anoo...hon'yaku jimusho ni tsutomete orimasu.
Yoshida Hon'yaku jimusho tte iu to...nani-go no hon'yaku o nasatte irundesu ka?
Shōda Soo desu nee...Iroiro tori-atsukatte imasu kedo...yappari, ichiban ooi no wa eigo desu, ne.
Yoshida A, soo desu ka. Kaisha wa dochira no hoo ni...?
Shōda Anoo...ichiban chikai eki wa Ōtemachi desu.
Yoshida Ōtemachi desu ka.
Shōda Hai.

➧ **Shitsurei desu.** It is rude./Excuse me.
donna what kind of?
hon'yaku translation
jimusho office
nani-go what language?
iroiro various (kinds)
tori-atsukatte imasu handling, dealing with (*dic.* **tori-atsukau**)
yappari as expected
ooi numerous, prevalent
➧ **eigo** English
➧ **chikai** near
➧ **eki** train or subway station
Ōtemachi a section of Tokyo

➧ **Shitsurei desu ga...** Using this phrase before asking a question or beginning a conversation is a common way of apologizing for the inconvenience or interruption. *Cf.* "Excuse me, but..."

➧ **Donna o-shigoto o nasatte irun desu ka?** What kind of work do you do? The verb choice requires that the subject be someone other than the speaker. A simpler way of saying the same thing would be **Donna o-shigoto desu ka?**

Hon'yaku jimusho ni in a translation office

➧ **tsutomete orimasu** I am working. (*humb.*) **Orimasu** requires that the subject be the speaker. The equivalent **tsutomete imasu** may have either the speaker or someone else as the subject. (*dic.* **tsutomeru**)

________ **tte iu to...** When you say ________ ,...

nani-go no hon'yaku translation of what language(s)?

Iroiro tori-atsukatte imasu kedo... We are dealing with various (languages), but...

ichiban This word literally means "number one", but is used to make a superlative of an adjective that follows it, as in **ichiban ooi no** ("the most common/numerous one") and **ichiban chikai eki** ("the closest station"). (See the Grammar section.)

Practise what you have learned

11

Here is a list of occupations. Before you start reading, CLOSE THE BOOK and listen to the recording. After you listen to the recording for a while, the words will become so familiar that you will be saying them automatically. Listening and saying will help develop better pronunciation than reading words from the book and memorizing them.

(a)	company employee	kaisha-in (or: sararii-man)
(b)	doctor	isha (*pol. eq.*: o-isha-san)
(c)	homemaker/housewife	shufu
(d)	nurse	kangofu
(e)	part-time worker	paato
(f)	retired	mushoku
(g)	sales clerk/shop assistant	ten'in
(h)	secretary/clerk	oo-eru (Eng.) (O-L/office lady)
(i)	student	gakusei
(j)	teacher/instructor	sensei/kyooshi

Follow the instructions on the recording and complete the exercise.

12

If your profession is not listed above, ask someone: **Teacher wa nihongo de nan desu ka?** "How do you say "teacher" in Japanese?"

To talk about occupations, some useful phrases are:

(a)	Donna o-shigoto desu ka?	"What kind of work do you do?"
(b)	(Watashi wa)__________ desu.	"I'm a __________"
(c)	__________ ja nain desu.	"I'm not a __________"
(d)	__________ desu ka?	"(Are you a) __________?"
(e)	O-shigoto wa doko desu ka?	"Where's your work?"

Now listen to the recording, and answer the questions below. (Answers p. 32)

1. What is the woman's profession?
2. What is the man's profession?

13

Your turn to speak. Turn on the recording and Aoki-san will guide you in a conversation about your profession.

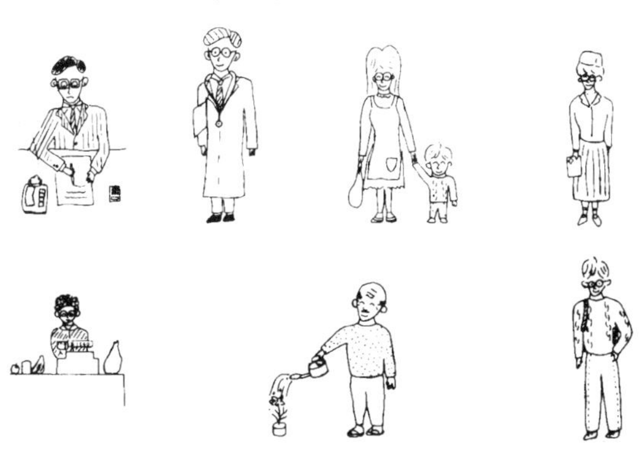

Key words and phrases

(*Question word*) + **desu ka?**	
Ikutsu/Nansai	How old are you?
Itsu	When is it?
Naniyoobi/Nan'yoobi	What day of the week is it?
Dochira/Doko	Where is it?
Nannin	How many people are there?
Nanigo	What language is it?
Donna ____________	What kind of ____________ is it?

People counters	See p. 217
Occupations	See p. 27

kankoo de	for sightseeing
shigoto de	on business
hitori de	alone/by oneself
____________ **ni (sunde imasu)**.	(I am living) in____________
(**ichi**) **kara** (**juu**) **made**	from (one) to (ten)

Arigato.	Thanks. (*eq.* **Arigatoo.**)
Ja mata.	(See you) later.
iie	no

otoko no ko	male child/boy
onna no ko	female child/girl
mannaka	middle
ichiban	most (+ adjective)/number one

The following phrases are short but polite in form because of the honorific **o-** or **go-** used with each noun.

O-namae wa?	Your name?
O-kuni wa?	Your country/hometown?
O-sumai wa?	(Where is) your home?
O-shigoto wa?	Your work?
O-tanjoobi wa?	Your birthday?
Go-kekkon wa?	(Are you) married?

Numbers

0	zero	20	ni-juu
1	ichi	30	san-juu
2	ni	40	yon-juu
3	san	50	go-juu
4	shi/yon	60	roku-juu
5	go	70	nana-juu
6	roku	80	hachi-juu
7	shichi/nana	90	kyuu-juu
8	hachi	100	hyaku
9	kyuu		
10	juu		

100s:		1,000s:		10,000s:	
100	hyaku	1,000	sen	10,000	ichi-man
200	ni-hyaku	2,000	ni-sen	20,000	ni-man
300	san-byaku	3,000	san-zen	30,000	san-man
400	yon-hyaku	4,000	yon-sen	40,000	yon-man
500	go-hyaku	5,000	go-sen	50,000	go-man
600	rop-pyaku	6,000	roku-sen	60,000	roku-man
700	nana-hyaku	7,000	nana-sen	70,000	nana-man
800	hap-pyaku	8,000	has-sen	80,000	hachi-man
900	kyuu-hyaku	9,000	kyuu-sen	90,000	kyuu-man
		11,000	ichi-man-sen		

Age counters

Nansai desu ka? Nijuuyon-sai desu.

1 yr. old	issai	21 yrs. old	nijuuissai
2 yrs. old	ni-sai	22 yrs. old	nijuuni-sai
3 yrs. old	san-sai	23 yrs. old	nijuusan-sai
4 yrs. old	yon-sai	24 yrs. old	nijuuyon-sai
5 yrs. old	go-sai	25 yrs. old	nijuugo-sai
6 yrs. old	roku-sai	26 yrs. old	nijuuroku-sai
7 yrs. old	nana-sai	27 yrs. old	nijuunana-sai
8 yrs. old	hassai	28 yrs. old	nijuuhassai
9 yrs. old	kyuu-sai	29 yrs. old	nijuukyuu-sai
10 yrs. old	jussai	30 yrs. old	sanjussai
20 yrs. old	hatachi/nijussai		

Days of the Week

Nanyoobi desu ka? Getsuyoobi desu.

Monday	Getsuyoobi	Friday	Kinyoobi
Tuesday	Kayoobi	Saturday	Doyoobi
Wednesday	Suiyoobi	Sunday	Nichiyoobi
Thursday	Mokuyoobi		

Map

HOKKAIDO
JAPAN
Niigata
HONSH
Tokyo
Nagoya
Kyoto
Kobe
Osaka
Hiroshima
SHIKOKU
Nagasaki
KYUSHU
Okinawa

Grammar

Grammar markers

Remember that grammar markers follow the words that they refer to. New markers presented in Unit 2 are:

ga This marker sometimes replaces **wa** to point out the subject, to put emphasis on the topic/subject, or when the subject happens to be an interrogative. (question words such as **nani**, **dare**, **dochira**, etc.)

ni follows the location of certain verbs, including **sunde imasu** ("living"/"residing") and some others. *Ex.* **Mori-san wa Tōkyō ni sunde imasu.** = Mr. Mori is living in Tokyo.

de One of the uses for this particle is to indicate purpose, as in **shigoto de** ("on business") and **kankoo de** ("for sightseeing"). When it follows a people counter, it indicates how many people are involved in whatever activity is referred to. *Ex.* **Hitori de sunde imasu.** = I live alone. or **Futari de Kyōto ni ikimashita.** = We (the two of us) went to Kyoto.

kara "from" or "since".

Amerika kara from America
Dooyoobi kara since Saturday

made "up to", "as far as", "until" ("not beyond")

juu made up to ten
Tōkyō made as far as Tokyo
Kin'yoobi made until Friday (through the day, but not beyond)

Ichiban + an adjective

The word **ichiban** literally means "number one", but when it comes before an adjective, it makes that adjective into a superlative. Here are some examples using adjectives you learned in Unit 1:

ichiban samui coldest
ichiban atsui hottest
ichiban atarashii newest

Omission of words

The Japanese often leave out a word or phrase if it may be understood from the context. Particularly in casual conversation, subjects, objects and even verbs are frequently omitted. This is also true in English, though perhaps not to the degree that it is practised by the Japanese. If you just cannot figure out what a person is trying to tell you, be sure to ask questions.

Minimal use of pronouns

Personal pronouns are used sparingly by the Japanese. Instead, they use the person's name (name + **-san** instead of **anata**, his name instead of **kare**, etc.), or they may simply omit the personal pronoun if it is understood who is being addressed or referred to.

You should also be aware that young people sometimes use **kare** and **kanojo** in reference to their boyfriends and girlfriends.

Negative of desu

The negative of **desu** is **dewa arimasen**, meaning "is not", and the negative past is **dewa arimasen deshita**, meaning "was not".

Did you know?

Japan is made up of four principal islands—Hokkaido, Honshu, Kyushu and Shikoku—plus the smaller Ryukyu Island chain, better known as Okinawa. These islands stretch in a north-to-southwesterly direction and are accompanied by thousands of small, scattered islands especially in the Inland Sea, an area between Honshu and Shikoku.

The total land mass of Japan is 1/25 the size of the United States and about 2/3 the size of California. The main island of Honshu is larger than England, Scotland and Wales combined; however, a mountain chain traverses the entire length, leaving only 25% of the land habitable. The population of Japan is approximately one half that of the U.S. and twice that of the U.K.

Japanese countryside seen from the air

Answers

Practise what you have learned

Exercise **4**	(a) 4 (b) 1 (c) 5 (d) 3 (e) 2
Exercise **8**	(a) 3 people (b) 1 person (c) 4 people (d) 2 people
Exercise **10**	(a) No (b) Yes (c) 0 (d) 2, 2, 0
Exercise **12**	(1) kaishain—company employee (2) gakusei—student
Exercise **13**	police officer—keikan

3 **ORDERING DRINKS AND SNACKS**

You will learn

- how to order food
- what kinds of snacks and drinks are available in Japan
- how to take care of the bill at a restaurant

Before you begin

The study pattern for this unit is similar to those you followed in Units 1 and 2. Try to read aloud as much as possible so that you can actually use these phrases in real life situations.

Remember that you do not have to do the whole unit in one sitting; in fact, the best advice for language learners is "little and often"—ten minutes a day is better than an hour once a week. Get into the habit of looking back over what you have learned, and redo exercises until they become easy for you.

Study guide

To help you keep a check on your progress, mark off the various tasks as you complete them.

	Dialogue 1 + Practise what you have learned
	Dialogue 2 + Practise what you have learned
	Dialogue 3 + Practise what you have learned
	Dialogue 4 + Practise what you have learned
	Make sure you know the Key words and phrases
	Study: the Grammar section
	Read: Read and understand
	Read: Did you know?

Dialogues

1 *What shall we have?*

Waiter Irasshaimase. Go-chuumon wa nani ni nasaimasu ka?
Customer Eeto... Soo desu, ne. Ja, nanka tsumetai mono itadakooka? Anata mo aisu koohii de ii? Ja, aisu koohii to...Keeki wa nani ga gozaimasu?
Waiter E...Ichigo no keeki to, e...shooto keeki ga gozaimasu.
Customer Soo shitara...watakushi wa ichigo no keeki ga iin da keredo, anata nani ni nasaru? Shooto keeki no hoo ga ii? Sore ja, shooto keeki. Ja, watakushi wa ichigo no keeki to achira ni shooto keeki. Desu kara, aisu koohi futatsu to sorekara shooto keeki to ichigo no keeki to, onegai shimasu.
Waiter Kashikomarimashita.

Irasshaimase Welcome (to a restaurant or store)
(go)chuumon (your) order (*pol.*)
tsumetai mono something cold
➧ **aisu koohii** iced coffee (*Eng.*)
ichigo no keeki strawberry cake
shooto keeki shortcake (*Eng.*)
soo shitara and in addition
achira ni to that person (*pol.*)
kara so/therefore
futatsu two (things) (See p. 35 for classic counters.)
➧ **sorekara** and then/after that
➧ **Onegai shimasu.** Please (bring us....)
Kashikomarimashita. I understand (your order.)/At your service (*pol.*)

Go-chuumon wa nani ni nasaimasu ka? What would you like to order? (*lit.* As for your order, what will you decide on?) (*pol.*) The expression ____ **ni nasaimasu** means to decide on something. When the customer asks his friend what he will decide on, he uses the same polite verb but in a more casual form: **Anata nani ni nasaru?** The **-masu** ending used by the waiter is more formal. (*eq.* **Nani ni shimasu ka?**)

____ **itadakoo ka?** Shall I have (*lit.* partake of) ____ ? **Itadaku** is a "humble" verb. The ending **-oo ka?** is used to mean "Shall I...?" or "Shall we...?"

Anata mo aisu koohii de ii? Is iced coffee okay for you, too? The marker **mo** means also/too/in addition. See the Grammar section for more.

Aisu koohii to... Iced coffee and...See the Grammar section for more on the marker **to**.

Keeki wa nani ga gozaimasu (ka)? What do you have in the way of cake? (*pol.*) (*eq.* **Keeki wa nani ga arimasu ka?**)

Watakushi wa ichigo no keeki ga iin da keredo... As for me, strawberry cake will be okay, but...(*eq.* **Ichigo no keeki de ii desu**.) The **-n da keredo** ending here is used to soften the sentence.

Shooto keeki no hoo ga ii? Do you prefer shortcake? (*lit.* is shortcake better?) See the Grammar section for comparisons.

Achira ni... For/to that person...(*lit.* "in that direction") **Achira** is a polite way of saying "him/her".

Practise what you have learned

1 The Japanese practice of using special suffixes to count items is similar to the English use of such phrases as "two sheets of paper" or "four cups of tea". You have already learned some of these counters in Unit 2—the age counter **-sai** and the counter **-nin** for people. More on counters will be presented in the Grammar section of this unit; however, below are the "classic counters", which can be used for many things, including food items. Turn on the recording and practise saying these words with Tanabe-san.

Classic counters

	Ikutsu desu ka?		How many are there?		
1	**hitotsu**	5	**itsutsu**	9	**kokonotsu**
2	**futatsu**	6	**muttsu**	10	**too**
3	**mittsu**	7	**nanatsu**		
4	**yottsu**	8	**yattsu**		

For more than ten items, the cardinal numbers (**juu-ichi, juu-ni, juu-san**, etc.) are used.

2 Now go over the food items illustrated below. Then, with Aoki-san's help, place an order for yourself and two of your friends. The order will include a) one pizza and two sandwiches, b) one iced tea, one iced coffee, one regular coffee (**hotto koohii**), and c) three ice creams. *Example:* **koohii futatsu to keeki hitotsu, onegai shimasu.** = "Please (bring) two coffees and one piece of cake". (Answers p. 46)

1. **pitsa** pizza

2. **aisu tii/koocha** iced tea

3. **sandoitchi** sandwich

4. **aisu kuriimu** ice cream

Dialogues

2 *What shall we have for lunch?*

Husband	Kyoo wa takusan aruita kara, tsukareta, ne.
Wife	Soo desu, ne. Moo honto ni sukkari tsukarechaimashita.
Husband	Sorosoro hiru-gohan demo suru ka ne?
Wife	Soo desu, ne. Demo...chotto...moo...tsukareta kara, anmari onaka ga suite nain desu kedo...
Husband	Demo tabeta hoo ga iin ja nai?
Wife	Soo desu, ne
Husband	Yooshoku ni suru? Soretomo, washoku ni shiyoo ka?
Wife	Watakushi wa washoku no hoo ga ii kedo...
Husband	So, ja...nan ni shiyoo ka
Wife	Karui mono wa doo kashira?
Husband	Soo da ne. Ja...o-chazuke demo suru ka na?
Wife	A, sore wa ii desu, ne.

- **takusan** a lot
- **moo** already
- **honto ni** really
- **sukkari** completely, thoroughly
- **sorosoro** soon, right away
- **hiru-gohan** lunch (**hiru-gohan o suru** = have lunch)
- **anmari** hardly (at all)/ particularly (*eq.* **amari**)
- **tabeta** ate, from **taberu/ tabemasu** (to eat)
- **yooshoku** Western cuisine
- **soretomo** or/otherwise
- **washoku** Japanese cuisine
- **karui** light
- **doo** how?
- **o-chazuke** hot tea poured over cold, cooked rice

(The tone of this conversation is informal, since it is between husband and wife.)

Takusan aruita kara... Since (we) walked a lot...The **-ta** at the end of the verb indicates a past tense form. **Kara** is placed at the end of a phrase to show that it is the cause of something that follows in the sentence. (*eq.* **Takusan arukimashita kara...**) See the Grammar section for more on **kara**.

Tsukareta, ne. (We) got tired, didn't we? (*eq.* **Tsukaremashita, ne.**)

Moo honto ni sukkari tsukarechaimashita. I am already really, completely tired out. Changing the verb ending from **-ta** to **-chaimashita** emphasizes the completeness or finality of the action.

Hiru-gohan demo suru ka ne? Maybe we should have lunch or something, huh? **Demo** in this pattern indicates "even if it's only (lunch)" and, along with the marker **ka ne** after the verb, implies that the speaker is open to suggestion.

Anmari onaka ga suite nain desu. I'm not particularly hungry. (*eq.* **Onaka ga suite imasen.** "I'm hungry" = **Onaka ga suite imasu.**)

Demo tabeta hoo ga ii(n), ja nai? But it would be better if we ate, wouldn't it? See the Grammar section for more on **-ta hoo ga ii. Ja nai** is a tag question, similar to **ne**.

Washoku ni shiyoo ka? Shall we make it (decide on) Japanese food? (*inf.*) The **-oo ka** ending means "Shall we...?" (*eq.* **Washoku ni shimashoo ka?**)

Karui mono wa doo kashira? How about something light? Changing the question marker **ka** to **kashira** softens the question and could be translated "I wonder..."

Practise what you have learned

3 To ask someone which of two or more choices he prefers, use the phrase **Dotchi** (**dochira**) **no hoo ga ii desu ka?** If there are only two possible choices, you may mention them first, using the "and" marker **to**. For example: **Pitsa to sandoitchi to, dotchi no hoo ga ii desu ka?** = "Which do you prefer—pizza or a sandwich?" (For more on this form, see the Grammar section.)

The pattern is: **A to B to dotchi no hoo ga ii desu ka?**

Now listen to the recording and practise asking people for their preferences.

The pattern is: **A no hoo ga ii**(**n**) **desu hedo. Ii desu ka?**

Then Aoki-san will prompt you to ask people's preferences for the same items.

(a) aisu-koohii, hotto koohii
(b) washoku, yooshoku
(c) ichigo no keiki, shooto keiki
(d) Getsu-yoobi, Ka-yoobi

4 Listen to the conversation between two friends and answer the following questions. You'll find answers at the end of this unit.

(a) Are they making plans for lunch or an evening meal? ____________

(b) Are they having Western or Japanese cuisine? ____________

(c) What is Miura-san (man) having? ____________

(d) What is Tanabe-san (woman) having? ____________

5 **Your turn to speak.** Listen to the prompts and try your Japanese. After each pause, Tanabe-san will model a phrase that you probably used.

Remember that there is more than one way to get the same idea across.

Dialogues

3 *Talking to a waitress*

Waitress Nani ni nasaimasu ka?
Customer Soo da ne...Ano...o-chazuke ga aru?
Waitress E...ano, gozaimasu.
Customer Donna o-chazuke ga arimasu ka?
Waitress Ume-chazuke toka (ume-chazuke?) shake-chazuke toka....
Customer Ja ne. Ume-chazuke, hitotsu. Sorekara, kanai ni wa, ano...shake-chazuke o hitotsu, onegai shimasu.
Waitress Hai, kashikomarimashita.
Customer Jikan, dono kurai kakaru kashira?
Waitress Ee to, soo desu ne, ano...juugo-roppun de...

ume-chazuke chazuke with pickled plum
shake-chazuke chazuke with salmon
kanai my wife (*m.*)
jikan time
➧ **dono kurai** about how much?
➧ **kakaru** to take/require (as time)
-pun/-fun suffix for minutes

O-chazuke ga aru? Do you have chazuke? (*inf.*) (*eq.* **O-chazuke ga arimasu ka**?) (*lit.* "Is there chazuke?")

____ **to ka** ____ **to ka...** Like ____ or ____, for example...

➧ **Jikan, dono kurai kakaru kashira?** I wonder about how much time it will take. (*lit.* Time, about how much will it take, I wonder.) (*eq.* **Jikan wa dono kurai kakarimasu ka?**)

Juugo-roppun de... In about 15 to 16 minutes... (See p. 217 for minute counters.)

Practise what you have learned

6 Suppose you have just finished a nice meal with your friend. Now you would like to order some dessert (**dezaato**) and coffee. Order for your friend and yourself. Listen to the recording. Aoki-san will give you assistance.

Dialogues

4 *The bill, please.*

Customer Sumimasen. O-kanjoo onegai shimasu.
Cashier Hai. Hassen-yonhyaku-kyuujuu-nana-en de gozaimasu. O-shiharai no hoo, kaado ni nasaimasu ka? Soretomo, kyasshu ni nasaimasu ka?
Customer Kyasshu de, onegai shimasu.
Cashier Hai. Ja, ichiman-en o-azukari itashimasu. Sen-gohyaku-san-en no o-kaeshi de gozaimasu.
Customer Doomo arigatoo. Reshiito itadakemasu ka?
Cashier Hai.

- **Sumimasen.** Excuse me.
- **o-kanjoo** the bill (*pol.*)
- **en** ____ **yen** (Japanese monetary unit)
- **o-shiharai** payment (*pol.*)
- **kaado** credit card (*Eng.*)
- **kyasshu** cash (*Eng.*)
- **o-kaeshi** your change (*pol.*)
- **Doomo arigatoo.** Thank you very much.
- **reshiito** receipt (*Eng.*)

O-shiharai no hoo... As for payment...(*lit.* In the direction of your payment...) (*eq.* **O-shiharai wa...**)

____ **-en de gozaimasu.** It's ____ yen. (*pol.*) (*eq.* ____ **-en desu.**

Kaado ni nasaimasu ka? Soretomo, kyasshu ni nasaimasu ka? Will (the payment) be by credit card or cash? (*pol.*) (*Lit.* Will you decide on credit card? Or will you decide on cash?) When asking "either/or", the Japanese often ask two separate questions. ("Is it this? Or is it that?")

Kyasshu de, onegai shimasu. By cash, please.

Ichiman-en o-azukari itashimasu. Out of 10,000 yen. (pol.) (*Lit.* I accept 10,000 yen.) This phrase is used to acknowledge receipt of payment.

Doomo arigatoo. Doomo is an intensifier, giving the phrase the same approximate meaning as "Thank you very much".

Reshiito itadakemasu ka? Can I get a receipt? (*pol.*) (*eq.* **Reshiito, onegai shimasu.**)

Practise what you have learned

7 In Japan the prices of items are marked as they are listed below in the left-hand column. However, sales clerks will say the figures as listed in the right-hand column. Read both columns and see if you can match the numbers with the Japanese words. (Answers p. 46)

(a) ¥6,500	______________	**(1)**	nanasen-happyaku-en
(b) ¥300	______________	**(2)**	rokusen-gohyaku-en
(c) ¥12,300	______________	**(3)**	sanzen-en
(d) ¥7,800	______________	**(4)**	sanbyaku-en
(e) ¥3,000	______________	**(5)**	ichiman-nisen-sanbyaku-en

After you've finished Exercise 7, turn on the recording to hear how these numbers are pronounced.

8 Listen to two friends talking about their dinner. After listening to the recording, fill in the answers to the questions below. (Answers p. 46)

(a) What did he have for dinner? ______________

(b) What did she have for dinner? ______________

(c) How much was the meal? ______________

(d) Did they charge it or pay cash? ______________

9 In this speaking activity, you are going out to eat with a Japanese friend. Aoki-san will prompt you. Some of the useful phrases are:

Nani ni shimashoo ka?	What shall we have?
Nani ga ii desu ka?	What would you like?
Watashi wa washoku no hoo ga iin desu kedo...	I prefer Japanese cuisine.
______________ **ni shimashoo.**	Let's have
______________ **ni shimasu.**	I'll have

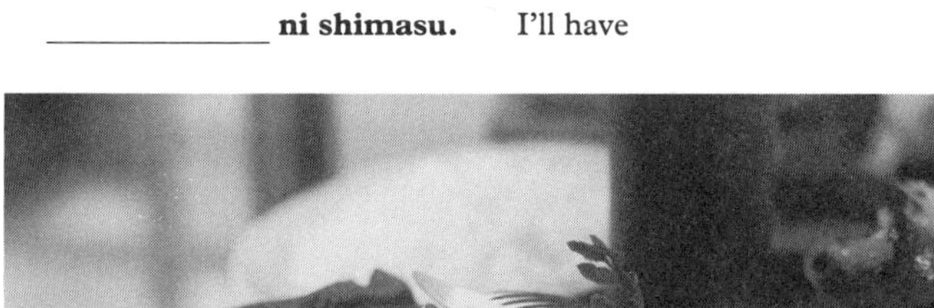

Plastic replica of food in a restaurant

Key words and phrases

Nani ni shimasu ka?	What will you order?
Nani ga arimasu ka?	What do you have?
Donna ____ ga arimasu ka?	What kind of ____ do you have?
____ wa nani ga arimasu ka?	What do you have in the way of ____ ?
Onaka ga suite imasu.	I'm hungry.
Onaka ga suite imasen.	I'm not hungry.
(**O-kanjoo**) **onegai shimasu.**	Please give me (the bill.)
(**Reshiito**) **itadakemasu ka?**	Can I get a (receipt)?
Kaado/kyasshu ni shimasu.	I will make it credit/cash.
Kaado/kyasshu de, onegai shimasu.	By credit card/In cash, please.
____ no hoo ga ii desu.	I prefer ____ . (____ is better.)
Tsukaremashita.	I am tired.
Irasshaimase.	Welcome (to our store).
Onegai shimasu.	Please. (I make a request.)
Doomo arigatoo.	Thank you very much.
Sumimasen.	Excuse me.
Kashikomarimashita.	At your service.
washoku	Japanese cuisine
yooshoku	Western cuisine
o-shiharai	your payment
o-kaeshi	your change
takusan	a lot
anmari/amari	(not) particularly/hardly
jikan	time
en	yen, Japanese monetary unit

Grammar

Degrees of politeness

On p. viii it was mentioned that the Japanese select vocabulary and verb forms according to the degree of politeness required. By the same token, they will choose certain verbs according to who is the subject. These verbs can be divided generally into three categories: exalted verbs, normal-polite verbs and humble verbs.

Exalted verbs require that someone other than the speaker be the subject. For example, the exalted verb **irasshaimasu** means "go" and implies "you go", but it can never be used to mean "I go". It is used to put the other person on a higher level than the speaker.

Normal-polite verbs can be used with either the speaker or someone else as the subject. They are polite and acceptable in most situations. The normal-polite counterpart of **irasshaimasu** is **ikimasu**, which can mean "I go", "you go", "he goes", "we go", etc.

Humble verbs require that the speaker be the subject. When a person uses a humble verb, he puts himself on a lower plane than the other person. The humble counterpart of **irasshaimasu** is **mairimasu**, meaning "I go".

Since the use of exalted and humble verbs—along with other advanced honorific concepts—requires considerable time and experience to master, foreigners are not expected to use them, other than within the context of certain set phrases and patterns such as **Irasshaimase** (*exal.*) and ____ **to mooshimasu** (*humb.*). You will hear them, however, and should try to make yourself aware of how they are used, in preparation for learning to use them yourself as you advance in your Japanese language ability.

Grammar markers

Remember that grammar markers always follow the word or phrase they refer to. New markers presented in Unit 3 are:

mo "also", "too"

Example: **anata mo** you, too
Koohii mo, onegai shimasu. Please (bring me) coffee, also.

to "and" This marker may follow each item in a list of two or more, or the last item in the list may be followed by some other appropriate marker.

Example: **Keeki to aisu koohii to, onegai shimasu.** Please (bring me) cake and iced coffee.

Ichigo no keeki to shooto keeki ga gozaimasu. We have strawberry cake and shortcake.

kara You have learned this previously as "from", as in **ichi kara juu made** ("from one to ten"). It is also used to indicate a cause-and-effect relationship between two parts of a sentence. In English we use a number of words to do this, including "since", "because", "so", "therefore", etc., so the example sentence below could be translated in several ways, as shown.

Example: **Takusan aruita kara, tsukaremashita.**
We got tired, because we walked a lot.
or We walked a lot, so we got tired.
or Since we walked a lot, we got tired.
or We walked a lot; therefore, we got tired.

Notice that in English the cause can come either before or after the result; however, in Japanese the cause always comes first, as in the example given above.

Counters

In English the cardinal numbers—one, two, three, etc.—are used to count anything from people to animals to buildings. In Japanese, however, special words called "counters" are used, and counters differ according to the type of item being counted. For example, the counter for people, as you learned in Unit 2, is **-nin**, while the "classic counters" (**hitotsu**, **futatsu**, etc.) are used to count most food items and things for which there is no special counter.

There are many other counters, some of which will be introduced later in this course. These include a counter for flat objects (**-mai**), a counter for long objects (**-hon**), counters for hours of the clock (**-ji**), etc. If you can't remember the appropriate counter for a particular item, usually the classic counters will suffice.

Comparisons and preferences

The word **hoo** literally means "direction", and you have used this word in the phrase ____ **no hoo ni/e** ("towards/in the direction of ____ "). It is also used to indicate a preference when a choice is given and to make a comparison between two or more things.

Dochira no hoo ga tsumetai desu ka? Which one is colder?
Aisu tii no hoo ga tsumetai desu. The iced tea is colder.

When **ii** ("good") is the adjective used in the comparison, the implication is that there is a preference:

koohii to aisu tii to, dochira no hoo ga ii desu ka?
Which do you prefer—coffee or iced tea?

Koohii no hoo ga ii desu. I prefer coffee. (*lit.* Coffee is better.)

When **hoo ga ii desu** follows a verb that ends in **-ta** (past tense), it indicates that a specified action (the verb) would be better than some alternative.

Example: **Tabeta hoo ga ii desu.** It would be better if we ate.

Read and understand

kyuujitsu
Closed

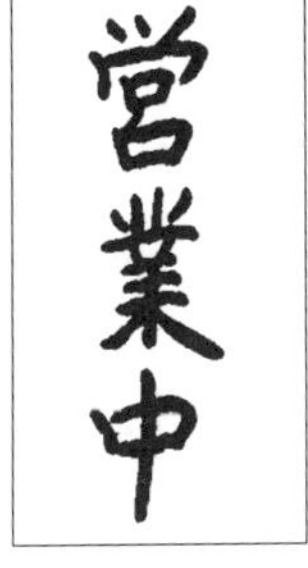

eigyoo-chuu
Open

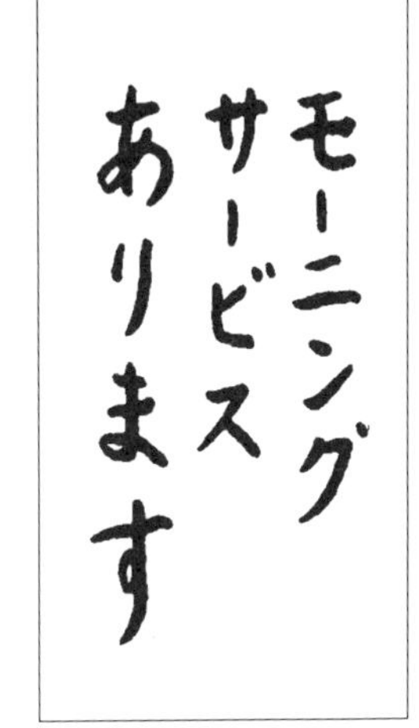

mooningu saabisu arimasu
Breakfast is served

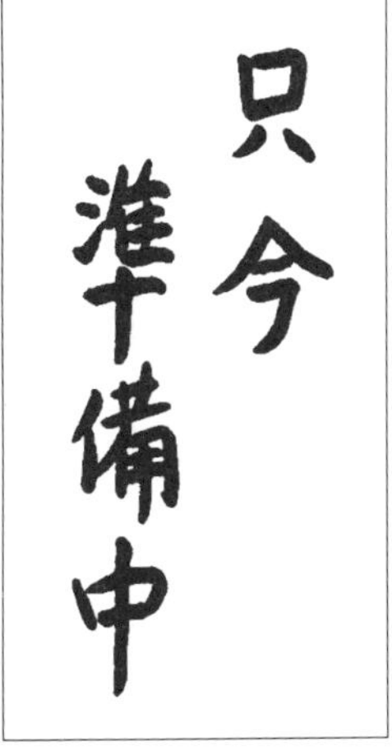

tadaima junbi-chuu
Meals in preparation

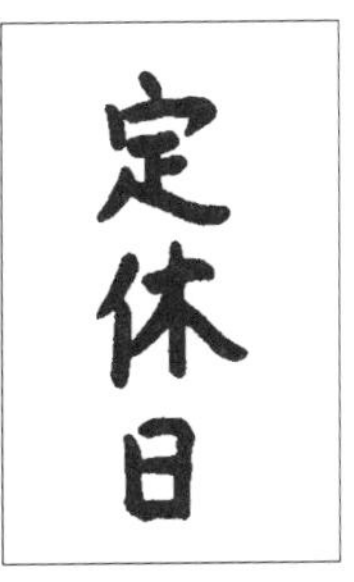

teikyuubi
Regular day off

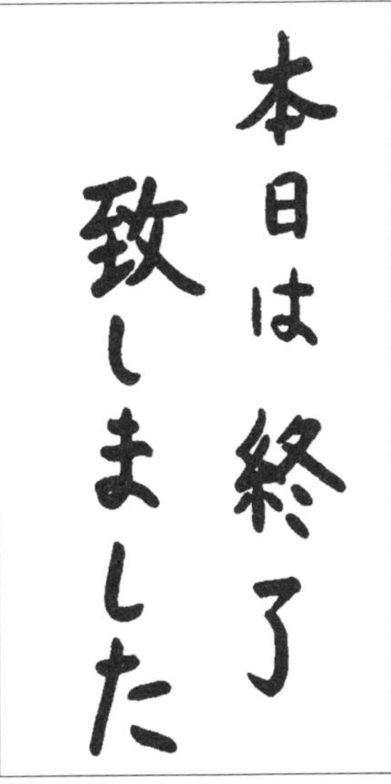

honjitsu wa shuuryoo itashimashita
Closed for the day

Did you know?

If you can be happy with a continental breakfast, take a stroll outside your hotel along any busy street. Inevitably, you will find a small **sunakku** (snack shop) that will have **Mooningu Saabisu** (Morning Service). You can have a piece of buttered toast (extremely thick) with jam, and coffee for a reasonable price. Coffee is generally stronger in Japan than in the U.K.

Orange and grapefruit lovers must also remember that these are very expensive in Japan.

Kissaten (coffee houses) are everywhere in Japan, and a cup of coffee is anywhere from about £1.25 to £3.00. Coffee drinking is very fashionable, and many people are very particular about the blends they drink. The price of a cup of coffee is high, because the customer is paying for atmosphere, space and a place to relax. If you ask for **Amerikan**, the cup is larger, and the brew is not as strong. Sometimes waitresses refer to a cup of hot coffee as **hotto koohii** (hot coffee). You might not have been an iced coffee drinker before, but during a hot and humid summer in Japan, you will find a glass of **aisu koohii** to be very refreshing.

Tipping and Service Charges

The good news is that there is no tipping in Japan. Taxi drivers, waitresses, hotel porters and such are not tipped. Hotels and inns automatically place service charges on bills. In restaurants, when the bill exceeds a certain amount, a service charge is assessed and included in the bill.

Answers

Practise what you have learned

Exercise 2	(a) pitsa hitotsu, sandoitchi futatsu (b) koocha hitotsu, aisu koohii hitotsu, hotto koohii hitotsu (c) aisu kuriimu mittsu
Exercise 4	(a) lunch (b) Western cuisine (c) sandwich (d) spaghetti
Exercise 7	(a) 2 (b) 4 (c) 5 (d) 1 (e) 3
Exercise 8	(a) spaghetti/wine (b) pizza/wine (c) ¥3,600 (d) charge (kaado)

4 GETTING INFORMATION

You will learn

- how to ask for a room
- how to register at a hotel
- how to ask where things are
- more numbers and counters
- about Japanese hotels

Before you begin

Conversations often involve asking for information of one kind or another. With a foreign language it is important to develop the skill of listening for the gist of what someone is saying. All too often people panic because they don't understand every word they are hearing, when in fact, they really do know enough to understand more than they realize.

Study guide

- **Dialogue 1 + Practise what you have learned**
- **Dialogue 2 + Practise what you have learned**
- **Dialogue 3 + Practise what you have learned**
- **Dialogue 4 + Practise what you have learned**
- **Make sure you know the Key words and phrases**
- **Study: the Grammar section**
- **Read: Read and understand**
- **Read: Did you know?**

Dialogues

1 *Sorry, we have no rooms*

Guest A, sumimasen kedo...
Reception Hai.
Guest Anoo...futari nan desu kedo, kyoo o-heya arimasen deshoo ka?
Reception Ee...mooshiwake gozaimasen ga...honjitsu wa zenkan manshitsu ni natte orimasu.
Eeto desu ne, kyoo wa mooshiwake gozaimasen ga... Dantai-sama de subete ippai nan desu, ne.
Guest Komarimashita ne...
Nanka dokoka kyanseru demo arimasen deshoo ka?
Reception Soo desu ne...Kyoo wa chotto o-heya no hoo ga ippai de...oobaa shite imashite...

Listening to this recording, you can sense the traveller's desperate need for a place to stay. Many pauses by both parties show a Japanese way of negotiation where neither side comes to a quick, clear resolution.

(**o-**) **heya** room (*pol.*)
Mooshiwake gozaimasen. I apologize./I am sorry. (*pol.*)
honjitsu today (*pol.*) (*eq.* **kyoo**)
zenkan the entire building
manshitsu fully occupied (rooms)
dantai (**-sama**) group/tour group (*pol.*)
subete all/everything
ippai full
Komarimashita. That's a problem. (*Lit.* I am perplexed.)
dokoka somewhere
kyanseru cancellation (*Eng.*)
oobaa shite overbooked (*Eng.*)

Futari nan desu... There are two of us. (*lit.* It is two people.) ____ **nan** (**desu**) is sometimes added to a verb to soften the sentence. (*eq.* **Futari desu.**)

O-heya arimasen deshoo ka? Do you not have a room? (*pol.*) The use of the negative **arimasen** + **deshoo ka** gives a soft, polite feeling to this question.

Manshitsu ni natte orimasu. [The hotel] is fully occupied. (*humb.*) The speaker uses this humble verb form because he represents the hotel.

Dantai-sama de subete ippai nan desu, ne. [The rooms] are all filled by tour groups.

Komarimashita, ne. That's a real problem, [isn't it?] This phrase is commonly used to express disappointment or to indicate that something is an inconvenience or a more serious problem.

Nanka, dokoka kyanseru demo arimasen deshoo ka? Is there a chance of some kind of cancellation somewhere? Again, the negative **arimasen** + **deshoo ka** softens the question.

Oobaa shite imashite... We are overbooked, and...The use of the **te-**form indicates an incomplete sentence, which softens the statement.

Practise what you have learned

1 Suppose that you and your friend are away from the city and need a room. Read the phrases, and match the appropriate English phrase with the corresponding Japanese phrase. (Answers p. 60)

(a) Futari nan desu.	____	(1) Yes, we have.
(b) Heya arimasu ka?	____	(2) That's a problem!
(c) Hai, gozaimasu.	____	(3) There are two of us.
(d) Sumimasen, manshitsu desu ga...	____	(4) Do you have a room?
(e) Komarimashita, ne...	____	(5) I'm sorry, but we're all booked up.

2 We have not been successful in finding a room. We should try smaller "business hotels" (**bijinesu hoteru**) that do not advertise or cater for foreign tourists. Though rooms are small, they are adequate and the prices are reasonable. First think about how you would say the following phrases; then listen to the recording and give it a try.

(a) Do you have a room with 2 twin beds (**tsuin betto futatsu**)? ________

(b) Well then, in that case, ________________________

(c) Do you have two rooms? ________________________

(d) That's a problem. ________________________

Tourist Information Centre, Tokyo office

Dialogues

2 *Checking in*

Katō Sumimasen, chekku-in shitain desu ga.
Reception A, irasshaimase. Ee, o-namae, kyooshuku de gozaimasu ga…
Katō Katō to mooshimasu.
Reception Katō-sama. Shita no hoo no o-namae wa…?
Katō Hiroki desu.
Reception A, Hiroki-sama, hai, doomo arigatoo gozaimasu.
Katō Yoyaku ga aru to omoimasu ga…
Reception Hai, o-shirabe itashimasu. Hai, doomo Katō-sama, o-matase itashimashita.
Ee to… go-ippaku no o-tomari de yoroshuu gozaimashoo ka?
Katō Soo desu. Ashita dekakemasu.
Reception A, soo de gozaimasu ka…

(Since Hotel Okura is one of the top echelon hotels in Tokyo, the language used by the receptionist is in a very polite form. Did you notice that when the guest mentioned his name, the clerk repeated it with **-sama** added to it ("**Hai, Katō-sama**")?

- **chekku-in** check in (*Eng.*)
- **Kyooshuku de gozaimasu.** I am sorry (to have to ask)…(*pol.*) (*eq.* **Kyooshuku desu.**)
- **shita** bottom, below
- **Hiroki** Japanese given name
- **yoyaku** reservation
- **O-shirabe itashimasu.** I will look it up. (*humb.*)
- **O-matase itashimashita.** I'm sorry to have kept you waiting. (*humb.*)
- **go-ippaku** your one-night stay (*pol.*)
- **o-tomari** stay-over (*pol.*)
- **yoroshuu gozaimashoo ka?** Would it be acceptable? (*pol.*) (*eq.* **ii**)
- **ashita** tomorrow
- **dekakemasu** to leave/depart (*dic.* **dekakeru**)

____ **shitain desu ga…** I want to ____, but… The word **ga** at the end of this phrase is not a grammar marker; this **ga** means "but" or "however" and is used in this case, like **keredomo**, to soften the sentence. See the Grammar section for more on **-tai**(**n desu**).

Shita no (**hoo no**) **o-namae wa…** (What is) your given name (*lit.* "bottom name")? Japanese names, both written and orally, are given family name first, then the given name—opposite to Western order. Since Japanese was originally written vertically, the family name (**ue no namae**) would be on top, followed by the given name (**shita no namae**) beneath. Nowadays it is common to write Japanese either vertically (right to left) or horizontally (left to right).

Yoyaku ga aru to omoimasu. I think I have a reservation. The phrase **to omoimasu** following a verb means "I think (that)…" This is often used not to express any particular doubt, but to soften the sentence, even though the speaker may be quite certain about what he is saying. (*eq.* **Yoyaku shimashita.** = I made a reservation.)

Go-ippaku no o-tomari de yoroshuu gozaimashoo ka? Is a one-night stay acceptable to you? (*pol.*) (*eq.* **Ippaku wa ii deshoo ka?**)

A, soo de gozaimasu ka? Oh, is that so? (*pol.*) (*eq.* **A, soo desu ka?**)

Hotel stay counters	How many nights?	Nan-paku?	three nights	san-paku
	one night	ippaku	four nights	yon-haku
	two nights	ni-haku		

Practise what you have learned

3 A receptionist at a Japanese inn is helping you fill out a registration form. Give the needed information. (There are no answers in the book for this exercise.)

(a) **O-namae wa?**

____

(b) **O-kuni wa?**

____

(c) **Pasupooto nanbaa wa?** (Passport number)

Example: **yon-hachi-ni san-kyuu-ichi yon-nana-go-go** = 482-391-4755

____

(d) **O-tomari wa nan-paku deshoo ka?** (How many nights' stay will it be? (If it's more than four, write the number.)

____

4 It is your turn to check in. The reservation was made in advance. (**Yoyaku ga aru to omoimasu ga...** I think I have a reservation.) Aoki-san will guide you through the exercise.

____

____

Dialogues

3 *What time will you be checking out?*

Reception Asu wa daitai, kyooshuku desu kedo, go-shuppatsu no o-jikan wa nan-ji goro de...

Katō San-ji goro de...

Reception A, san-ji goro ni narimasu ka? (Chekku-in wa nan-ji desu ka?) Ee to...chekku-auto jikan wa juuni-ji de gozaimasu.

Katō A, chekku-auto wa juuni-ji desu ka...

Reception Ha...hai. Moshi, san-ji made go-taizai desu to, ichioo, anoo...tsuika ryookin ga kakatte shimaun desu kedo...Yoroshuu gozaimashoo ka? O-heya dai no sanbun no ichi hodo ni narimasu keredo...

Katō A soo desu ka. Hai.

- **asu** tomorrow (*eq.* **ashita**)
- **daitai** approximately
- **(go-) shuppatsu** your departure (*pol.*)
- **(o-) jikan** time (*pol.*) (*eq.* **jikan**)
- **nanji goro** about what time?
- **chekku-auto** check out (*Eng.*)
- **-ji** counter for time (See below.)
- **moshi** if
- ____ **made** until ____
- **go-taizai** your stay (*pol.*)
- **tsuika ryookin** additional charge
- **o-heya dai** room rate (pol.)
- **sanbun no ichi** ⅓
- **hodo** amount/degree

Go-shuppatsu no o-jikan wa nanji goro de... About what time will your departure be? Note that the politeness level of the receptionist's language is always higher than normal speech.

San-ji goro ni narimasu ka? Will it be (*lit.* become) about 3:00? (*pol.*) (*eq.* **San-ji goro desu ka?**)

Moshi san-ji made go-taizai desu to... If your stay is until 3:00...The marker **to** after a verb means "if..." (See the Grammar section.)

Tsuika ryookin ga kakatte shimaun desu kedo... There will be an additional charge. (*lit.* An additional charge will be required, but...) The verb ending **-tte shimau** indicates that an action is irrevocable or complete. Comparable to "We'll have to (charge an additional amount.)" This ending is sometimes casually shortened to **-chau/-chaimasu.** (Cf. Unit 3 **Tsukarechatta.**)

O-heya dai no sanbun no ichi hodo ni narimasu. It will amount to one third of your room rate. (See the Grammar section for more on fractions.)

Time Counters
What time is it? **Nan-ji desu ka?**

1:00	ichi-ji	5:00	go-ji	9:00	ku-ji
2:00	ni-ji	6:00	roku-ji	10:00	juu-ji
3:00	san-ji	7:00	shichi-ji	11:00	juuichi-ji
4:00	yo-ji	8:00	hachi-ji	12:00	juuni-ji

Practise what you have learned

5 There are five English phrases listed below. Find corresponding Japanese words in the box to fill in the blanks. (Answers p. 60)

(a) reservation ______________

(b) no vacancy ______________

(c) departure ______________

(d) additional charge ______________

(e) How many nights' stay? ______________

(1)	**chekku-in**	(2)	**tsuika ryookin**	(3)	**heya-dai**
(4)	**taizai**	(5)	**manshitsu**	(6)	**shuppatsu**
(7)	**yoyaku**	(8)	**nan-paku**	(9)	**chekku-auto**

6 Listen to the recording as Tanabe-san is checking into the Fujimi Hotel. You already know enough words and phrases to understand what the discussion is about. Listen several times and answer the questions. (Answers p. 60)

(a) What is the Fujimi Hotel's regular check-out time? ______________

(b) What time does Tanabe-san want to check out tomorrow? ________

(c) What time is Tanabe-san leaving the hotel tomorrow? ____________

7 With Tanabe-san's help, ask the hotel clerk when the check out time is. Mention that it is earlier than you had planned to leave, and tell the clerk that that presents a problem. The clerk suggests that the hotel hold your luggage, **o-nimotsu o-azukari shimasu,** and you agree.

(a) When is the check-out time? ______________________________

(b) You wish to leave at one. ______________________________

(c) "Well, that's a problem". ______________________________

(d) The front desk will keep your luggage until ______________ o'clock.

(e) You ask them to take care of it. ______________________________

____

Dialogues

4 *Your room number is 555*

Katō Ee to…ano…kagi wa doko desu ka?

Reception Hai, ee…ja…toriaezu, kochira ni go-tooroku negaimashite… (Hai.) Mooshiwake gozaimasen ga…Hai, doomo arigatoo gozaimashita. Sore ja…honkan no gohyakugojuu-go-ban, go-yooi itashimashita node, ima beru-booi ga go-annai itashimasu node, doozo, go-yukkuri… Arigatoo gozaimasu.

Katō Doomo. Arigatoo gozaimasu.

- **kagi** key
- **toriaezu** first of all/in the meantime
- **kochira** here (*pol.*) (*eq.* **koko**)
- **go-tooroku** register (*pol.*)
- **honkan** main building
- ____ **ban** number ____
- **go-yooi** preparation (*pol.*)
- **beru-booi** bellboy (*Eng.*)/porter
- **ima** now
- **go-annai** guide (*pol.*)
- **Go-yukkuri.** Take your time.

Kochira ni go-tooroku negaimashite… May I ask you to register here? (*pol.*) (*eq.* **Go-tooroku, o-negai shimasu.**)

Doomo arigatoo gozaimashita. Thank you so much (for what you did).

Ja, yoroshiku. Take care of it, please. (*eq.* **Yoroshiku onegai shimasu.**)

Go-yooi itashimashita node. We prepared for you, so… (*pol.*)

Beru-booi ga go-annai itashimasu node… (*pol.*) The porter will show you to the room, so… The humble verb **itashimasu** is used because the bellboy represents the hotel, as does the speaker.

Doozo go-yukkuri. Please take your time. The implication here is "enjoy a leisurely stay".

Ordinal Numbers
What number is it? **Nan-ban desu ka?**

first	**ichi-ban**	sixth	**roku-ban**
second	**ni-ban**	seventh	**nana-ban**
third	**san-ban**	eighth	**hachi-ban**
fourth	**yon-ban**	ninth	**kyuu-ban**
fifth	**go-ban**	tenth	**juu-ban**

Practise what you have learned

Many hotel-related words are of foreign origin, but today they are truly woven into the Japanese language. Following are some words that were originally borrowed from English but are now in common use by the Japanese. Listen and repeat each word as Miura-san and Tanabe-san pronounce it for you. Be sure to close your book and listen to the recording.

(1) air conditioner (cooler)—**kuuraa**
(2) bar—**baa**
(3) cancellation—**kyanseru**
(4) check-out—**chekku-auto**
(5) lift, elevator—**erebeitaa**
(6) arcade—**aakeido**
(7) bellboy—**beru-booi**
(8) check-in—**chekku-in**
(9) dining room—**dainingu ruumu**
(10) Front Desk—**furonto**
(11) gym—**jimu**
(12) radio—**rajio**
(13) sauna—**sauna**
(14) swimming pool—**puuru**
(15) toilet—**toire**
(16) heater—**hiitaa**
(17) room service—**ruumu saabisu**
(18) service charge—**saabisu chaaji**
(19) television—**terebi**
(20) wake-up call—**mooningu kooru**

8

Some commonly used phrases are written below in English. Read the Japanese phrases on the right and find the one that matches each English phrase. You do not need the recording to do this exercise. (Answers p. 60)

(a) Do you have a swimming pool?
(b) Where is the lift?
(c) Don't you have a sauna?
(d) I'd like to have some coffee.
(e) What is the check-out time?

(1) **Sauna nain desu ka?**
(2) **Puuru arimasu ka?**
(3) **Chekku-auto wa nan-ii desu ka?**
(4) **Koohii, onegai shimasu.**
(5) **Erebeitaa wa doko desu ka?**

9

Let's suppose you are travelling with a group. Listen to the recording as the tour guide is assigning rooms. Jot down the room numbers in the spaces given below. (Answers p. 60)

(a) Taylor and Johnson ____________

(b) Bennett and Lyons ____________

(c) Smith and Brown ____________

10

You have just checked into a beautiful Japanese inn with a traditional garden. The staff is showing you to your room through the sprawling structure with several wings and multiple floors. Of course, you took your shoes off and left them at the entry way as you entered the building as is customary in Japan. Listen to the recording. List three specific pieces of information you gathered from the staff's explanations. (Answers p. 60)

(a) ________________________

(b) ________________________

(c) ________________________

Key words and phrases

O-heya arimasen deshoo ka?	Do you not have a room?
Chekku-in shitain desu.	I want to check in.
Chekku-auto shitain desu.	I want to check out.
Yoyaku shimashita.	I made a reservation.
Komarimashita, ne.	That's a problem, isn't it?
O-matase itashimashita.	I'm sorry to have kept you waiting.
Doozo go-yukkuri.	Take your time./Enjoy a leisurely stay.
(o-) **heya dai**	(your) room rate
tsuika ryookin	additional charge
manshitsu/ippai	fully occupied, no vacancy/full
shita no namae	given name
ue no namae	family name
nan-paku	how many nights' stay? (See p. 50 for hotel stay counters.)
____ **ban**	number ____
daitai	approximately
nanji goro	about what time (See p. 52 for o'clock counters.)
tooroku	registration
go-taizai/o-tomari	your stay
go-shuppatsu	your departure
dekakemasu	to leave/depart
toriaezu	first of all/in the meantime
honkan	the main building
zenkan	the entire building
Annai, negaimasu.	Please show me the way.
____ **arimasu ka?**	Do you have ______________ ?
____ **doko desu ka?**	Where is ______________ ?
____ **nain desu ka?**	Don't you have ______________ ?
____ **nan-ji desu ka?**	What time is ______________ ?
____ **nan-ban desu ka?**	What number is ______________ ?

Grammar

"if/when"

There are several verb endings that convey the meaning "if/when". The first one that has been introduced to you is **to**, as in the sentence **sanji made go-taizai desu to, tsuika ryookin ga kakatte shimaun desu** (from Dialogue No. 3), meaning "If your stay is until 3:00, it will cost an additional fee". Study the following examples:

Manshitsu desu to, komarimasu.
If (the hotel) is full, it will be a problem.

Ashita hareru to, kaimono ni ikimasu.
If (the weather) clears up tomorrow, I'll go shopping.

"I want to..."

The Japanese verb ending **-tai(n) desu** means "I want to (do something)". This ending can also be **-tai** (*inf.*), **-tai desu** (*norm.*), or **-tai to omoimasu** ("I think I want to..."). The **-n desu** after **-tai** softens the statement. Here are some examples using words and phrases from this and previous units:

Chekku-in shitain desu. I want to check in.
Kekkon shitain desu. I want to get married.

To make this a question, of course, simply add **ka** after the verb:

Arukitain desu ka? Do you want to walk?

However, if the question "do you want to...?" is intended as an invitation or a suggestion, or simply to soften the question, the Japanese will often use the negative verb ending **-masen ka?** instead of the above form.

Arukimasen ka? Won't you walk?
Nanika tabemasen ka? Won't you eat something?

Fractions

Study the following fractions:
1/3—**san-bun no ichi** one of three parts
2/3—**san-bun no ni** two of three parts
1/4—**yon-bun no ichi** one of four parts
3/4—**yon-bun no san** three of four parts

"One half" is expressed by a special word: **han-bun** half of a part.

Read and understand

Registration at most Western-style hotels can be done smoothly, because they will have a registration form prepared bilingually in Japanese and English. Just remember to write neatly and carefully or, better yet, print each letter carefully, because clerks are not too familiar with Western names or overseas addresses.

Hotel Registration Form (Bilingual Type)

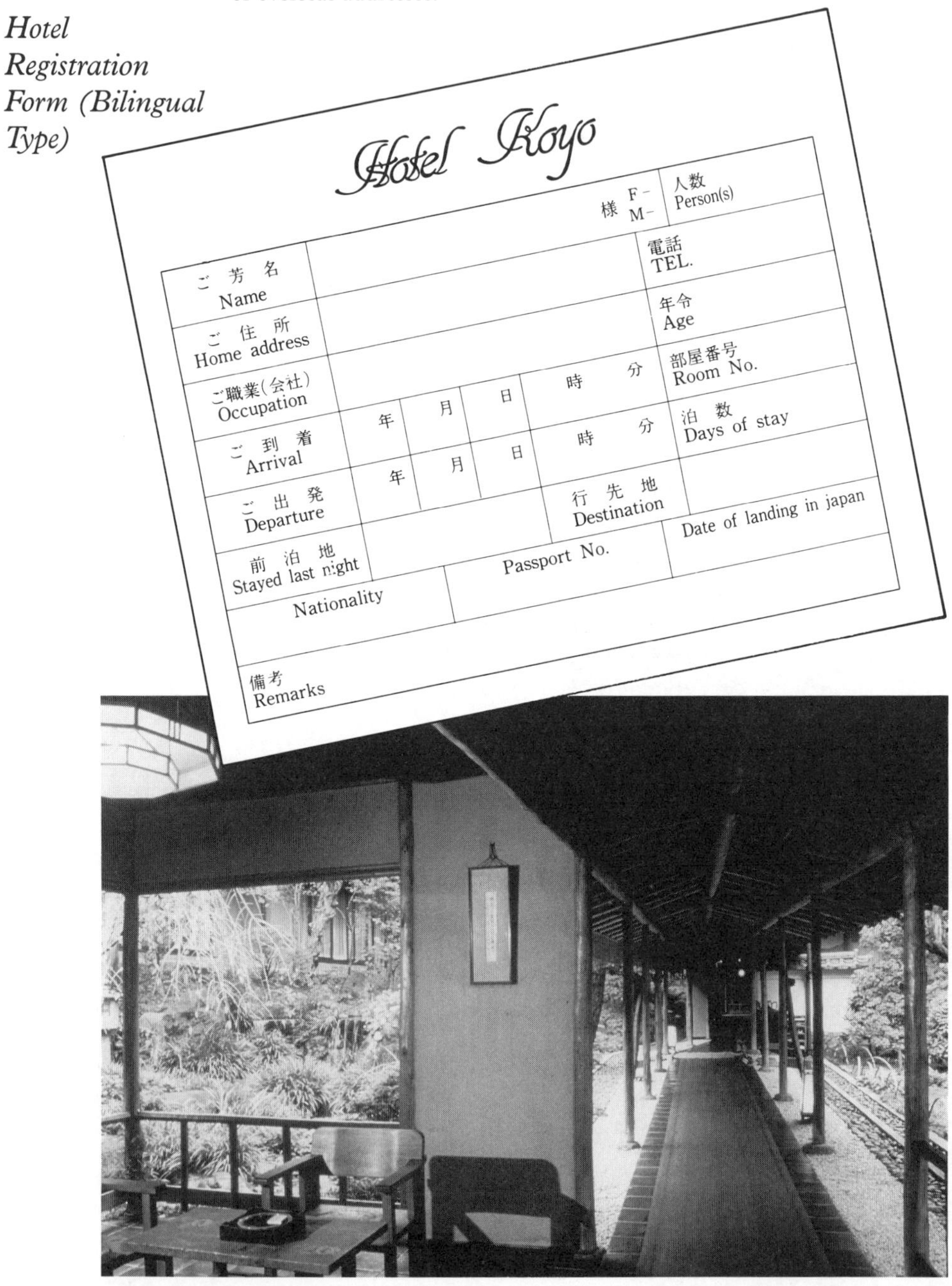

Hotel Koyo

	様 F- M-	人数 Person(s)
ご芳名 Name		電話 TEL.
ご住所 Home address		年令 Age
ご職業(会社) Occupation	時 分	部屋番号 Room No.
ご到着 Arrival	年 月 日 時 分	泊数 Days of stay
ご出発 Departure	年 月 日 行先地 Destination	
前泊地 Stayed last night	Passport No.	Date of landing in japan
Nationality		
備考 Remarks		

Taikanso, a Japanese inn in Atami

Read and understand

1. 受付
desk
uketsuke

2. 案内係
reception
annai-gakari

3. 会計係
cashier
kaikei-gakari

4. 食堂
dining room
shokudoo

5. 浴室風呂
bathroom
yokushitsu-furo

6. 手洗
rest-room/WC
tearai

7. 男子用
gentlemen
danshi-yoo

8. 女子用
ladies
joshi-yoo

9. 使用中
in use
shiyoo-chuu

10. 空き
vacant
aki

Did you know?

You will be surprised to find many types of lodging in Japan.

Top-class hotels

Major cities have top-class, Western-style hotels for international travellers and for Japanese clientele with special events such as weddings and receptions.

Tourist hotels

Both foreigners and Japanese people use this type of Western-style hotel for vacations. These hotels are reasonably priced, and the accommodation is excellent.

Business hotels (Bijinesu Hoteru)

This type of no-frills establishment was developed to meet the Japanese business person's needs. They are clean and comfortable, conveniently located and reasonably priced. These hotels usually have a **Baikingu** ("Viking") buffet-style breakfast—with both Western and Japanese traditional foods—at a reasonable price; however, we recommend for lunch and evening meals that you take a stroll to nearby restaurants to try some interesting, delicious foods.

Ryokan

These Japanese-style inns vary in ranking and style. Unfortunately, only a few traditional **ryokan** are still in operation. They are elegant in decor, and the services are unbelievably good. Each one features its own cuisine and is known for excellence. They are, however, extremely expensive. There are also **onsen** (hot springs) **ryokan**, which are very popular among the Japanese. Since Japan is full of hot springs, you might be able to include an over-night stay at an **onsen ryokan** in almost any sight-seeing tour. **Kankoo-kyaku-yoo** (tourist inns) can be found in numerous locations in a wide price range. If you are interested in trying out Japanese-style accommodation, you should discuss it with a travel agent.

Penshon

This is a small, family-operated boarding house patterned after the European "pension" and is very popular among women travellers and young people. Meals are prepared by the owners and served "family-style".

Minshuku

A popular type of accommodation often found in resort and tourist areas, these are comparable to **penshon** but very Japanese in style. You will find many customs that are quite different from the West, and an adventurous person can enjoy a unique experience.

A word of caution:

Wherever you go and whatever you do, you will feel cramped for space and be surrounded by people. Hotel rooms are small by Western standards and you will be reminded of the lack of space in Japan. If you are able to overcome this feeling, you will fully enjoy the scenery, history and people.

Answers

Practise what you have learned

Exercise **1**	(a) 3 (b) 4 (c) 1 (d) 5 (e) 2
Exercise **5**	(a) 7 (b) 5 (c) 6 (d) 2 (e) 8
Exercise **6**	(a) 11:00 (b) 12:00 (c) 11:00
Exercise **8**	(a) 2 (b) 5 (c) 1 (d) 4 (e) 3
Exercise **9**	(a) Taylor/Johnson 532 Bennett/Lyons 534 Smith/Brown 536
Exercise **10**	(a) swimming pool—yes (b) sauna—no (c) Check-out time is 12:00. Luggage will be held until departure.

5 DIRECTIONS

You will learn

- to ask for directions at the railway station
- to ask for information at the hotel information desk
- to ask for directions inside a building
- to ask for information at a cleaning establishment
- something about the Tokyo railway and subway systems

Before you begin

Asking for directions is relatively easy. It is understanding the answers that proves more of a problem! The best way to prepare for this is to listen over and over again to the directions given in the dialogues, so that you can pick out *key phrases* ("go straight", "turn right/left", "go downstairs", etc.) even when they are obscured by a lot of other words that you do not know. It is usually a good idea to repeat directions when they are given to you, so that you can be corrected if you have misunderstood something.

Study guide

- **Dialogue 1 + Practise what you have learned**
- **Dialogue 2 + Practise what you have learned**
- **Dialogue 3 + Practise what you have learned**
- **Dialogue 4 + Practise what you have learned**
- **Make sure you know the Key words and phrases**
- **Study: the Grammar section**
- **Read: Read and understand**
- **Read: Did you know?**
- **Listen to all the dialogues again without the book**

Dialogues

1 *Where is the Yokosuka-line?*

Student Yokosuka-sen ni noritain desu kedo, dotchi ni ikeba iin desu ka?

Passer-by Yokosuka-sen desu ka? (Hai.) Ja, soko ni kaidan ga aru kara, soko o orite, hidari ni magatte, chikadoo o massugu doko made mo itte kudasai. Soo suru to ne, kaisatsuguchi ga arimasu node...Anata, kippu wa doko made motte irassharu no?

Student Tōkyō eki desu.

Passer-by A, sore ja, ikkai kaisatsu-guchi no soto ni dete...(Hai.) Kippu o kawanai to ikemasen, ne. Sore de mata, Yokosuka-sen no hoomu no hoo ni orite kudasai.

(Yokosuka)-sen (Yokosuka) Line (of a railway or underground)
dotchi which way? (*eq.* **dochira**)
kaidan stairway
hidari ni to the left (**migi ni** to the right)
chikadoo underground street
massugu straight (ahead)
doko made mo as far as possible
kaisatsu-guchi ticket barrier/entry where tickets are punched
kippu ticket
(Tōkyō) eki (Tokyo) station
ikkai once, one time
soto outside
hoomu platform (*Eng.*)

____ **ni noritain desu.** I want to get on ____ .

Dotchi ni ikeba iin desu ka? Which way should I go? (*lit.* In which direction is it good/best to go?)

Soko o orite... Go down (descend) there and... **Soko** (there) refers to the stairway previously mentioned. **Orite** (*dic.* **oriru**) is one of a series of verbs in this sentence. Remember that the **te-** form indicates that at least one other verb will follow, so the word "and" can be included in the translation.

Hidari ni magatte... Turn left and...

Chikadoo o massugu doko made mo itte kudasai. Go straight as far as you can on the underground street. The verb ending **-te kudasai** is a way of making a request or giving instructions. (See the Grammar section.)

Kippu wa doko made motte irassharu no? How far does your ticket take you? (*exal.*) (*lit.* You are holding a ticket up to where?) The marker **no** at the end of the sentence is typical of female speech.

Ikkai kaisatsu-guchi no soto ni dete... Go outside the ticket barrier once, and... The implication here is that the person will have to go to the ticket vending machines, which are located outside the barrier.

Kippu o kawanai to ikemasen. You have to buy a ticket. The ending **-nai to ikemasen** indicates an obligation to do something.

Yokosuka-sen no hoomu no hoo ni orite kudasai. Go down (the stairs) in the direction of the Yokosuka Line platform.

Practise what you have learned

1 Select the appropriate word and fill in the blanks with the appropriate Japanese words. (Answers p. 75)

(a) to the right ______ **(1)** kippu ______

(b) to the left ______ **(2)** massugu ______

(c) go down the stairs ______ **(3)** migi (ni magatte) ______

(d) ticket ______ **(4)** hidari (ni magatte) ______

(e) straight ______ **(5)** kaidan (o) orite ______

2 Let's suppose that you just came back from a **Kamakura** sight-seeing trip. You are still on the **Yokosuka-sen** platform, and you need directions to get to the **Chuo** Line towards **Shinjuku**, where your hotel is. Listen to Miura-san and jot down the essential points of his directions. (Answers p. 75)

(Track 1 = **Ichiban-sen** Track 2 = **Niban-sen**)

(a) ______

(b) ______

(c) ______

3 Listen to the recording. Miura-san will ask you, **Wakarimashita ka?** meaning "Did you understand it?" He wants to know if you understood the directions from the passer-by and now know how to get to the Chuo Line (**Chuuoo-Sen**) platform. You will be asked to describe it in your own words.

______

______

______

______

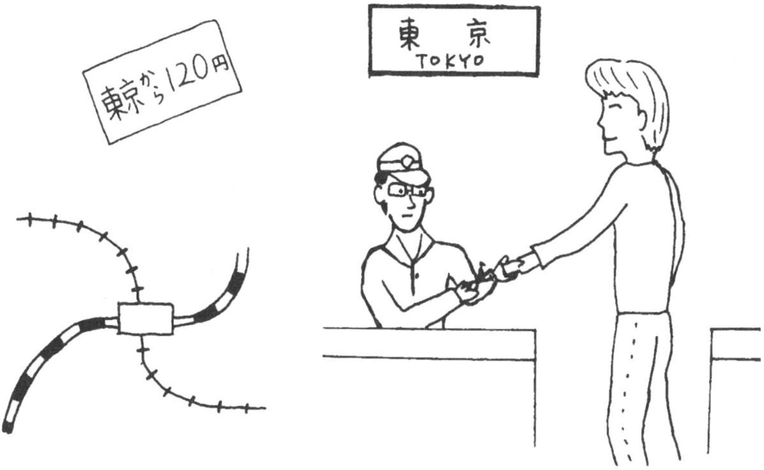

Dialogues

2 *Is there a post office around here?*

Passer-by Kono hen ni yuubinkyoku arimasu ka?

Shop assistant A, arimasu yo. Ee to desu ne, kono mae no rooka o desu ne, anoo...migi e zutto massugu ikimasu. Soo shimasu to, anoo...tsukiatari masu n'de, tsukiatarimashitara, kondo hidari e itte kudasai.
Soo shimasu to, anoo...kaidan ga arimasu node, anoo...kaidan o ano...ikkai made orite kudasai. De, kaidan ikkai orite, ano...migi-gawa e zutto itte kudasai. Soo shimasu to, kono tatemono no soto e demasu node, e...soto e demashitara, ano...deta tokoro, chotto migi ni ikimasu to...oodanhodoo ga arimasu. De, oodanhodoo o, ano...watatte kudasai. E...so suru to...sono migite ni...Chūō Yūbinkyoku tte, okkina yuubinkyoku ga arimasu.

kono hen ni in this area
➧ **yuubinkyoku** post office
kono mae before/in front of this place
➧ **rooka** corridor/hallway
➧ **tsukiatarimasu** to come to a dead end or a T-junction
kondo this time
➧ **ikkai** first (*British*: ground) floor (See p. 65 for floor counters.)
➧ **migi-gawa** right-hand side
zutto all the way
kono tatemono this building
demasu go out/exit (*dic.* **deru**)
deta tokoro where you came out
➧ **oodanhodoo** pedestrian crossing
migite ni on the right hand
okkina big (*inf.*) (*eq.* **ookii**)

Kono mae no rooka o...migi e zutto massugu ikimasu. You go straight as far as you can to the right along the corridor in front of us.

➧ **Tsukiatarimasu n'de...** You will come to a T-junction, so... **n'de** here is a short, casual form of **node.**

Tsukiatarimashitara... When you get to (the T-junction)... The **-tara** ending here indicates "when/if".

Kaidan ikkai made orite, migi-gawa e zutto itte kudasai. Descend the stairway to the first floor (ground floor in Britain), then go to the right all the way (as far as it goes).

Kono tatemono no soto e demasu node... You will exit towards the outside of this building, so...

Oodanhodoo o watatte kudasai. Cross over the pedestrian crossing.

Chūō Yūbinkyoku tte, okkina yuubinkyoku a big post office called "Chūō Post Office". The **tte** here is a casual expression meaning "so-called" or "quote-unquote".

Practise what you have learned

4 Make good sentences by connecting phrases in the two columns below. Write the numbers in the spaces provided. (Answers p. 75)

(a) Kono hen ni	______	(1)	magatte kudasai.
(b) Rooka o massugu	______	(2)	ikkai made orite kudasai.
(c) Oodanhodoo o	______	(3)	yuubinkyoku ga arimasu ka?
(d) Migi ni (turn)	______	(4)	itte kudasai.
(e) Kono kaidan o	______	(5)	watatte kudasai.

5 The counter for the floors of a building is **-kai**.

Floor Counters

What floor is it? **Nan-gai** (or **Nan-kai**)/**desu ka?**

1st (*Brit.*: ground)	**ikkai**	6th (*Brit.*: 5th)	**rokkai**
2nd (*Brit.*: 1st)	**ni-kai**	7th (*Brit.*: 6th)	**nana-kai**
3rd (*Brit.*: 2nd)	**san-gai**	8th (*Brit.*: 7th)	**hakkai**
4th (*Brit.*: 3rd)	**yon-kai**	9th (*Brit.*: 8th)	**kyuu-kai**
5th (*Brit.*: 4th)	**go-kai**	10th (*Brit.*: 9th)	**jukkai**

First, practise with the recording to say the floors in the building. Then listen to Tanabe-san and Miura-san and fill in the blanks in the following sentences. (Answers p. 75)

(a) Katō-san no heya wa ____________ desu.

(b) Tomodachi no kaisha wa ____________ desu.

(c) Yooshoku no resutoran wa ____________ desu.

(d) Kono tatemono wa ____________ desu.

6 Listen to the dialogue again, and draw a diagram showing how to get to the Chuo Post Office according to directions given by the shop assistant. Here's a clue: the clerk is on the second floor (British first floor) of the **Maru-Biru** (Marunouchi Building), a large office complex with many interesting stores) across from the Tokyo station.

Dialogues

3 *How do I get to Meiji Shrine?*

Tourist Sumimasen, Ano...Meiji Jingū e ikitain desu kedo, doo ikeba ii desu ka?

Clerk Hai, kochira kara de gozaimasu to, o-kuruma ka mata wa chikatetsu ni narimasu ga, dochira ga go-kiboo de (irasshaimasu deshoo ka)?

Tourist Soo desu ne...Chikatetsu da to...chikatetsu no eki wa dochira desu ka?

Clerk Chikatetsu no eki wa, Toranomon no eki ga chikoo gozaimashite, e...Ginza-sen ni narimasu. Ginza-sen no Toranomon no eki kara Omote-Sandō made o-de ni narimasu to...sochira hara...

Tourist Ee to, sono chikatetsu no eki made wa, aruku to nanpun gurai kakarimasu ka?

Clerk Honkan no ikkai kara o-aruki itadakimashite, roppun, nanafun gurai de gozaimasu.

Tourist A soo desu ka. Chikai desu, ne.

(**Meiji**) **Jingū** (Meiji) Shrine (of the Shinto religion)
➧ (**o-**) **kuruma** (your) car
mata wa or else/otherwise
➧ **chikatetsu** underground (railway)
go-kiboo your preference (*pol.*)
Toranomon, Ginza, Omote Sandō sections of Tokyo
chikoo gozaimashite is nearby (*pol.*) (*eq.* **chikai desu**)
aruku walk
➧ **nanpun gurai** about how many minutes
(See p. 217 for minute counters.)
kakarimasu to take/require (as time, money)
roppun, nanafun six (or) seven minutes (See p. 217.)

➧ **Doo ikeba ii desu ka?** How do I get there? (*lit.* How is it best if I go?) (*Cf.* **Dotchi ni ikeba...**)

Kochira kara de gozaimasu to... If it is from here/this direction... Note the very polite tone of the clerk. (*eq.* **Koko kara desu to...**)

O-kuruma ka mata wa chikatetsu ni narimasu ga... (You have to go by) car or underground, but... (*lit.* It becomes car or underground.)

Dochira ga go-kiboo de (irasshaimasu deshoo ka)? Which way is your preference? (*pol.*) (*eq.* **Dotchi ga go-kiboo desu ka?**) **irasshaimasu deshoo ka** is implied.

Chikatetsu da to... If it is underground... **da** (*inf.*) = **desu**

Toranomon no eki ga chikoo gozaimashite, Ginza-sen ni narimasu. The Toranomon station is nearby, so that is (becomes) the Ginza Line. (*pol.*)

O-de ni narimasu to... If you exit...(*pol.*) (*eq.* **Demasu to...**)

Honkan no ikkai kara o-aruki itadakimashite... If we have you walk from the ground (*Brit.:* first) floor of this building... (*humb.*)

Practise what you have learned

7 Select words from the box to fill in the blanks in the sentences, according to the translations given. (Answers p. 75)

ka	?	**e**	to (direction)
kara	from	**to**	and
de	by (mode of transportation)	**made**	up to
dono gurai	about how long/much?		

(a) Meiji-Jingū ____________ Ueno Park ____________ ikitain desu ga...(I want to go to Meiji Shrine and Ueno Park.)

(b) Kuruma ____________ ____________ kakarimasu ____________ ? (About how long does it take by car?)

(c) Koko ____________ chikatetsu no eki ____________ chikai desu ka? (From here to the underground station—is it near?)

8 Listen to Katō-san asking how to get to the Meiji Shrine. Answer the questions listed below. (Answers p. 75)

(a) Where will he leave from? ____________

(b) What type of transportation should he use? ____________

(c) How long will it take? ____________

9 If you are in Tokyo during the cherry blossom season, you may enjoy a visit to Ueno Park. First, visit the many museums there, and then wait for dusk. Viewing the cherry blossoms in the evening is a special treat.

Find out how you can get to Ueno Park from your hotel in Shinjuku. Think how you might say the following sentences. Then Tanabe-san will assist you as you listen to the recording.

(a) I want to go to Ueno. ____________

(b) How can I get there? ____________

(c) What line would be good? ____________

(d) Is it far? Approximately how long will it take? ____________

(e) Are there restaurants (**resutoran**) in Ueno? ____________

(f) Thanks. Well then, I'm leaving now. ____________

Dialogues

4 *At the cleaners*

Customer Kono burausu, ano...sentaku onegai shitain da kedo, daitai dono gurai jikan kakarimasu?
Cleaner Daitai isshuu-kan gurai desu, ne.
Customer A so...moo chotto hayaku dekimasen?
Cleaner Soo desu ne...soo suru to, daitai yokka gurai desu, ne.
Customer Yokka. A, so. Sore kara...kotchi no sukaato wa, ne. Shimi-nuki onegai dekimasu?
Cleaner Hai. Ee to. Nan no shimi deshoo ka?
Customer Tabun, tabemono daroo to omoun desu kedo...
Cleaner A soo desu ka. (Un) Sore ja... chotto shirushi o tsukete okimasu ne.
Customer Hai, hai. Yoroshiku onegai shimasu. O-taku wa teikyuubi wa itsu desu ka?
Cleaner Nichiyoobi desu.
Customer A, soo desu ka.

➧ **sentaku** laundry/cleaning (of clothes)
➧ **isshuu-kan gurai** about one week's time
➧ **moo chotto** a little more
➧ **hayaku** quickly/early
➧ **dekimasu/dekimasen** It can/can't be done. (*dic.* **dekiru**)
yokka four days (See p. 87.)
kotchi no this (one) (*eq.* **kono**)
shimi-nuki stain removal
nan no what kind of
shimi stain
➧ **tabun** perhaps/probably
tabemono food
shirushi sign/mark/symbol
➧ **teikyuubi** a store's regular day off

➧ **Daitai dono gurai jikan kakarimasu (ka)?** Approximately how much time will it take?

➧ **Moo chotto hayaku dekimasen (ka)?** Can't you do it a little faster?

Onegai dekimasu (ka)? Can I ask you (to do it)?

____ **daroo to omoun desu kedo...** I think it is probably ____ , but... (*eq.* ____ **deshoo to omoimasu kedo...**)

Shirushi o tsukete okimasu. I will put a mark on it. (*lit.* I'll attach a mark.) The ending **-te okimasu** indicates that the action is being taken for some later purpose—in this case, so that whoever handles the garment later will easily find the stain.

Week Counters

How many weeks? **Nan-shuukan?**

1 week	**isshuukan**	6 weeks	**roku-shuukan**
2 weeks	**ni-shuukan**	7 weeks	**nana-shuukan**
3 weeks	**san-shuukan**	8 weeks	**has-shuukan**
4 weeks	**yon-shuukan**	9 weeks	**kyuu-shuukan**
5 weeks	**go-shuukan**	10 weeks	**jus-shuukan**

Shopping in Tokyo

Practise what you have learned

Close the book and listen to the recording for the pronunciation of Japanese words for various items of clothing. Follow the directions and then practise.

1. **sebiro** business suit

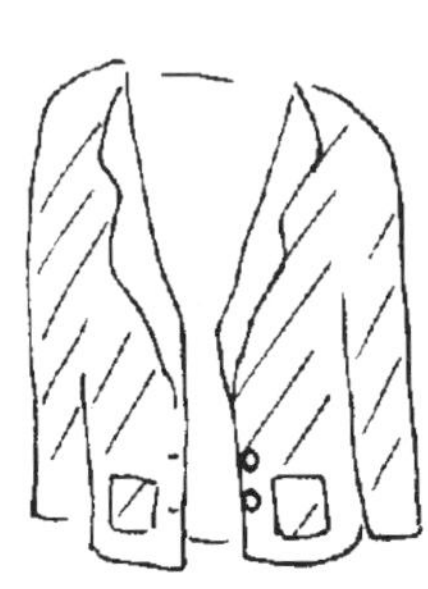

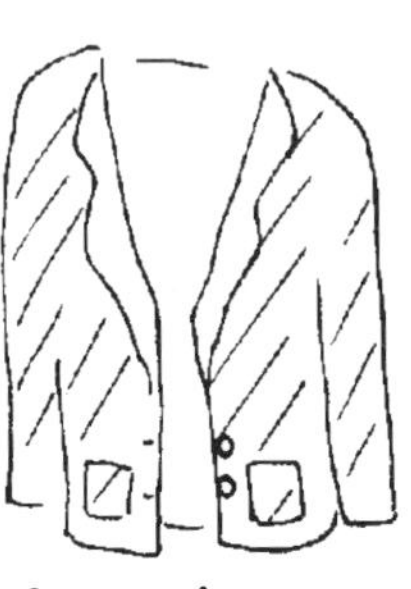

2. **uwagi** coat

3. **zubon** trousers

4. **waishatsu** white shirt (*Eng.*)

5. **seetaa** sweater (*Eng.*)

6. **shitagi** underwear

7. **kutsushita** socks

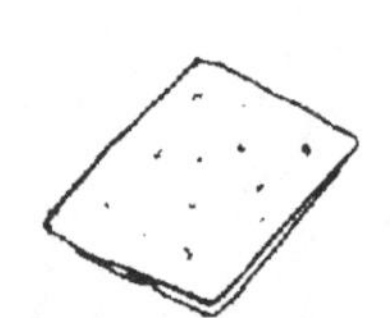

8. **hankachi** handkerchief (*Eng.*)

9. **nekutai** tie (*Eng.*)

10. oobaa overcoat (*Eng.*)

11. suutsu suit (*Eng.*)

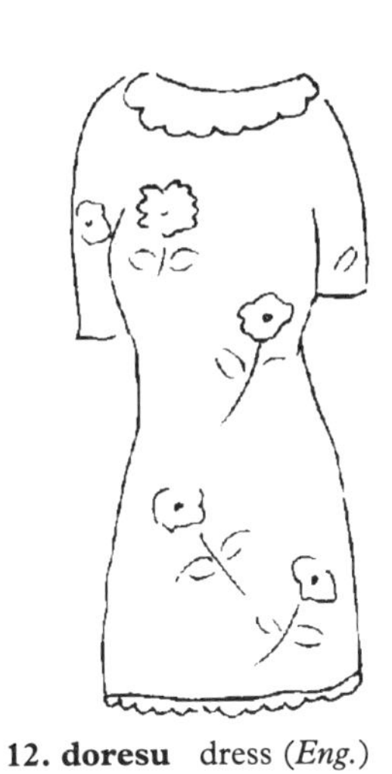

12. doresu dress (*Eng.*)

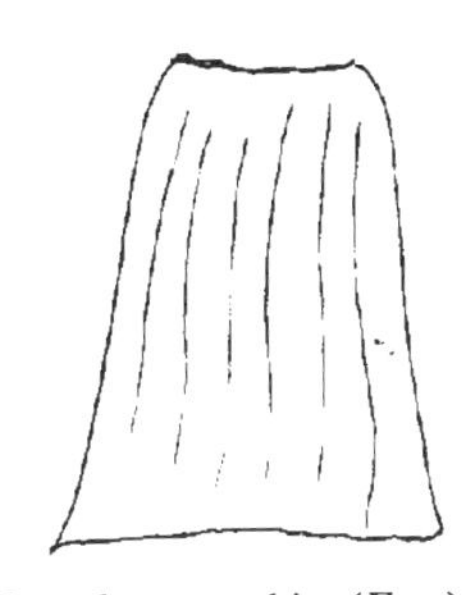

13. sukaato skirt (*Eng.*)

14. burausu blouse (*Eng.*)

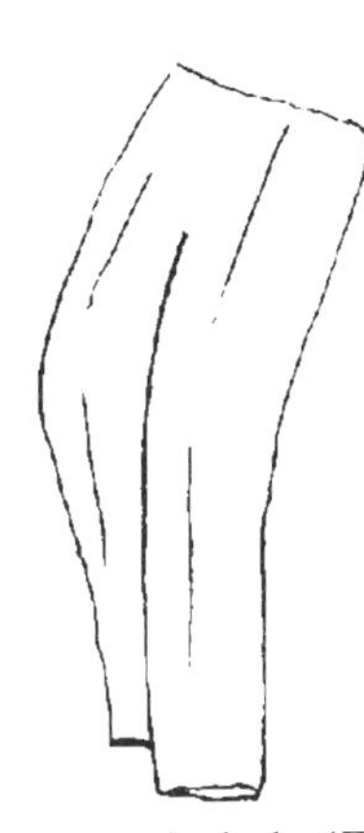

15. pantaron women's slacks (*Eng.*)

16. janpaa windcheater/anorak (*Eng.*)

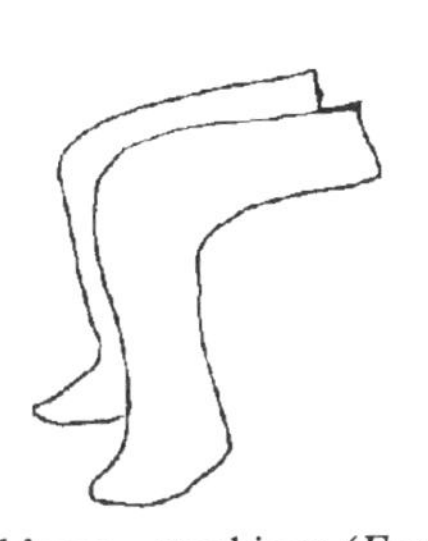

17. sutokkingu stockings (*Eng.*)

10

Complete the following sentences. Review the week counters on p. 69 if you need to. (Answers p. 75)

(a) Kono burausu no sentaku ______________ (one week) kakarimasu ka?
Will it take one week to clean this blouse?

(b) Tōkyō no shigoto wa ______________ (five weeks) desu.
My work in Tokyo will take five weeks.

(c) Nihon no kankoo wa ______________ (three weeks) desu.
My sight-seeing trip in Japan is three weeks.

11

Turn on the recording and listen to the conversation that takes place at the cleaners. Answer the following questions. (Answers p. 75)

(a) What items are to be cleaned? ______________

(b) How many days will it take? ______________

(c) When will it be ready? ______________

(d) On what day is the store closed? ______________

12

It is your turn to take some things to the cleaners. Refer to the illustration on the previous page for some of the Japanese words. You can also refer to items as **kore to kore to kore** ("this and this and this"). Some of the useful phrases are:

(a) Please take care of this and this and this. ______________

(b) How long will it take? ______________

(c) Can't you do it a little faster? ______________

(d) What day is the store closed? ______________

Key words and phrases

____ ni noritain desu.	I want to get on (a vehicle).
Dochira ni/doo ikeba iin desu ka?	Which way should I go?
(Kaidan o) orite kudasai.	Go down (the stairs). (*dic.* **oriru**)
(Hidari ni) magatte kudasai.	Turn (to the left). (*dic.* **magaru**)
(Massugu) itte kudasai.	Go (straight). (*dic.* **iku**)
(Kippu o) katte kudasai.	Buy (a ticket). (*dic.* **kau**)
(Soto ni) dete kudasai.	Exit (towards the outside). (*dic.* **deru**)
(Oodanhodoo o) watatte kudasai.	Cross over (the pedestrian crossing). (*dic.* **wataru**)

(Migi ni) ikimasu to... If you go (to the right)...
(Chikatetsu de) ikimasu to... If you go (by underground)...
Tsukiatarimashitara... When you reach (a T-junction)...
Soto e demashitara... When you exit (towards the outside)...
Dono gurai jikan kakarimasu ka? About how much time will it take?
Nanpun gurai kakarimasu ka? About how many minutes will it take?
Itsu dekimasu ka? When can you do it?
Moo chotto hayaku dekimasen ka? Can't you do it a little faster?
Onegai dekimasu ka? Can I ask you to do it?

doko made mo	as far as possible
mata wa	or else/otherwise
zutto	all the way
tabun	perhaps
-sen	line (of a railway/underground railway)
-kai	(See p. 218 for counters for floors of a building.)
-shuukan	(See p. 69 for counters for weeks.)
burausu	(See pp. 70, 71 for clothing vocabulary.)

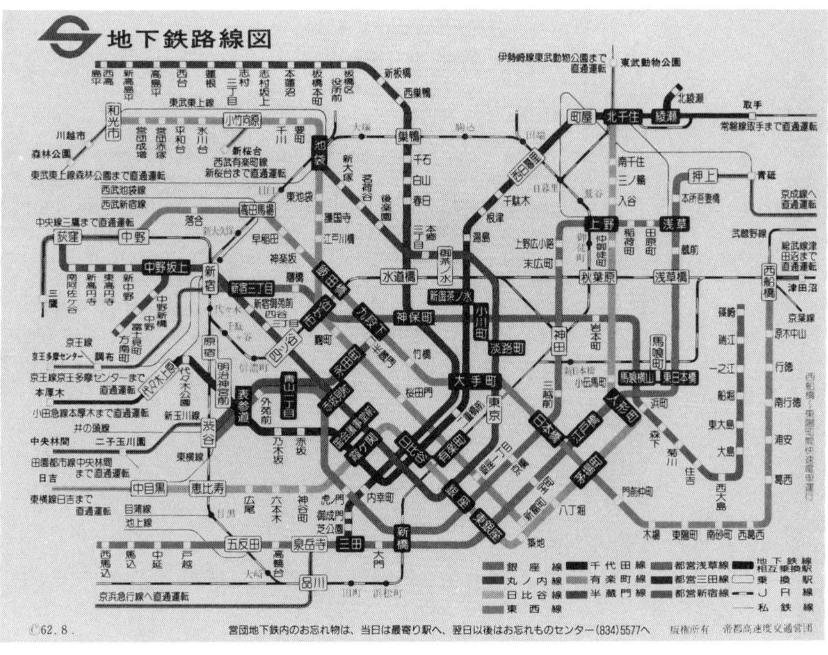

A subway map of Tokyo

Grammar

Polite directives

The verb ending **-te kudasai** is used as a polite way to make a request or give directions.

Juu made kazoete kudasai. Please count to ten.
Yuubinkyoku made aruite kudasai. Please walk up to the post office.
Washoku o tabete kudasai. Please eat Japanese cuisine.

Grammar markers

Remember that the **te-**form always indicates that another verb will follow somewhere in the sentence. In the case of **-te kudasai**, the second verb is **kudasai**, which indicates that a favour is being asked.

Remember that a grammar marker always follows the word or phrase it refers to.

de "by/by means of"

Example: **Kuruma de ikimasu.** I will go by car.
Chikatetsu de ikitain desu. I want to go by subway.
Pen de kaite kudasai. Please write with (by means of) a pen.

"if/when"

Another way to express "if/when" (besides **to**, as presented in Unit 4) is by the ending **-tara**, as in **Tsukiatarimashitara, hidari e itte kudasai** ("When you come to a T-junction, go to the left."—Dialogue 2). Study the following examples:

Tatemono o demashitara, oodanhodoo ga arimasu.
If/when you exit the building, there will be a pedestrian crossing.

Aruitara, juppun gurai kakarimasu.
If/when you walk, it takes about 10 minutes.

Sentence softeners

As you have gone through the first few units of this course, you have noticed the use of certain words and verb endings to "soften" a sentence—that is, to make the sentence less abrupt and more polite or diplomatic. Abruptness, along with frankness, candour, aggressiveness and other characteristics considered positive in Western culture, can be seen as rude or arrogant by the Japanese. It may seem impossible to you at this point to remember all the different ways to soften your Japanese, but one easy way to do so is to end your sentence with **ga** or **keredomo** ("but/however") after the verb, making the sentence sound incomplete, as if you were going to say something else. Other softeners will come to you with time and experience.

Read and understand

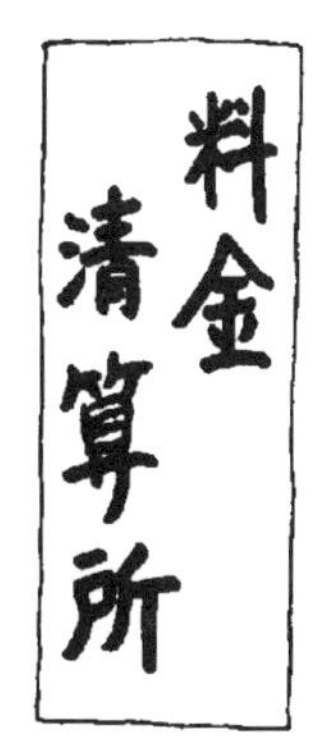

Fare adjustment office

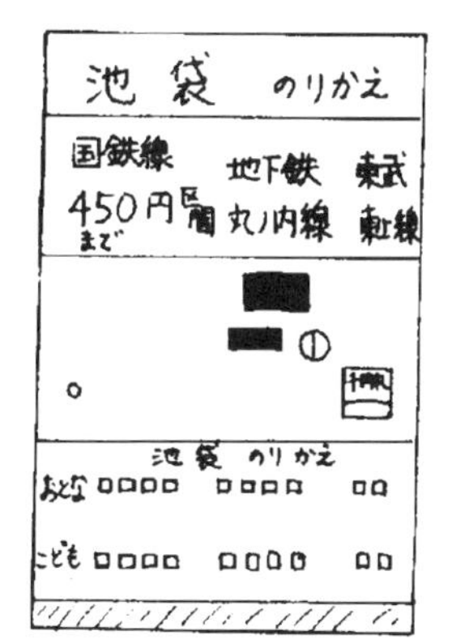

Ticket machine

地下鉄

Underground

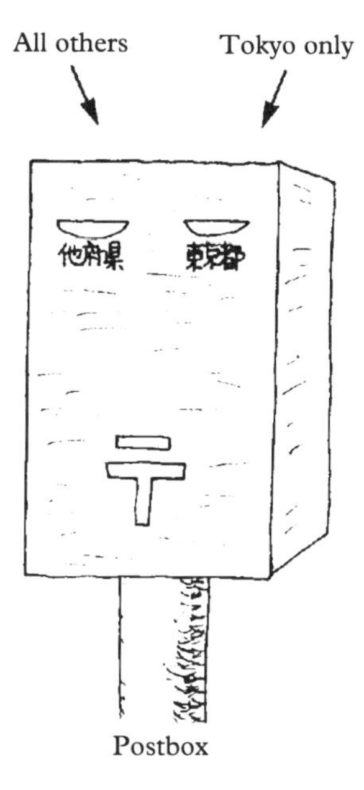

Postbox

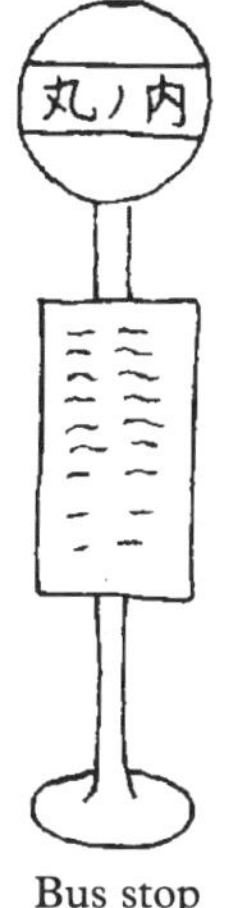

Bus stop

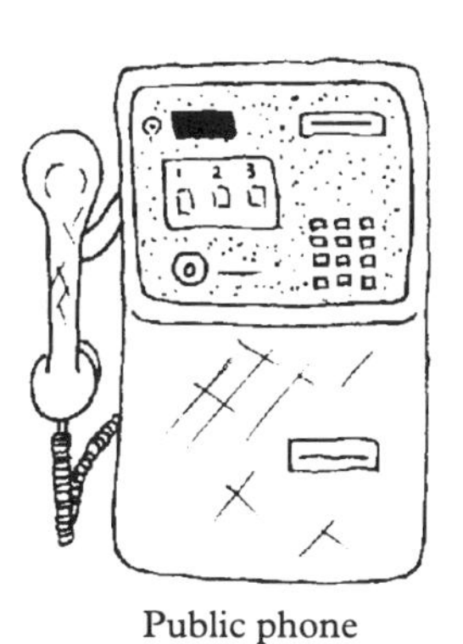
Public phone

Answers

Practise what you have learned

Exercise **1**	(a) 3 (b) 4 (c) 5 (d) 1 (e) 2
Exercise **2**	(1) Go up the stairs (2) Walk through the underground passage—"chikadoo" (3) Chuo Line is Track 1 and Track 2
Exercise **4**	(a) 3 (b) 4 (c) 5 (d) 1 (e) 2
Exercise **5**	(a) 4th floor (b) 17th floor (c) 8th floor (d) 36th floor
Exercise **7**	(a) to, e, (b) de, dono gurai, ka (c) kara, made
Exercise **8**	(a) Shinjuku (b) JR (c) 15 minutes
Exercise **10**	(a) is-shuukan (b) go-shuukan (c) san-shuukan
Exercise **11**	(a) strousers, sweater (b) four days (c) about 11:00 /Thurs (d) Sunday

Did you know?

Public transport

The metropolitan Tokyo area has one of the best—if not the best—public transportation systems in the world. Four underground lines interweave and connect at various points with the main railway lines, and buses also connect and run on frequent schedules. Public transit is clean, fast, safe and very efficient. When in a hurry, local people choose to take the train rather than drive their own cars or go by taxi.

Each station has a large chart on the wall, indicating fares to all points, and tickets are purchased from vending machines. Unfortunately, on most of these charts station names are written only in KANJI, which presents a problem to foreign travellers. When in doubt, we suggest that you buy a ticket for the shortest distance and, when you arrive at your destination, stop at the Fare Adjustment Office (**Seisanjo**) and pay the difference. When you get your receipt, go through the **kaisatsu-guchi.** If you need assistance, go to the green window (**midori no madoguchi**), where a person will be available to help you.

All railway and underground lines require that you turn in your ticket at your destination, when you go through the **kaisatsu-guchi**. If you should lose your ticket, it is nearly impossible to convince anyone that you just got on at the last station, even if that is true.

Once you are on the platform (**hoomu**), you will find signs with the station name in Japanese and **Roomaji** (the Roman alphabet). These signs will also show the names of the previous stop and the station coming up next.

The four underground lines (**Chikatetsu**) in Tokyo are popular among foreign travellers because their colour-coded system is easy to follow, and at each entrance there is a large **Roomaji** chart. By transferring from one line to another, it is possible to cover much of Tokyo by underground.

Some helpful phrases are:

Norikae desu ka?	Do I need to transfer?
Doko de norikae desu ka?	Where do I transfer?
Nani-iro desu ka?	What colour is it?
Nani-sen desu ka?	What line is it?
Shinjuku wa ikutsu-me desu ka?	How many more stops to Shinjuku?

Ask for a wallet-size romanized subway map (**Roomaji no chikatetsu no chizu**) at the station or at any major hotel.

Dry cleaners

Dry cleaning shops (**kuriiningu-ya**) are everywhere in the city, so you won't have any difficulty finding one. Many shops require prepayment when you leave your clothes. Needless to say, the receipt is something you should not misplace!

6 TIME

You will learn

- how to tell time
- the days of the week
- the months of the year
- other useful expressions of time
- about Japanese holidays

Before you begin

Being familiar with the Japanese words for time of day and days of the week can be very important for everyday life. Asking questions like **Itsu?** (When?) and **Nan-ji ni?** (At what time?), etc., is quite simple and will cover many situations. There is little in the way of new grammar in this unit, but there is a good deal of new vocabulary. Revise the days, dates and times carefully, and learn the months of the year. You will find it helpful to practise them aloud. For example, whenever you look at your watch, you could try saying the time in Japanese. Similarly, for dates and days of the week, you should revise/recite them from time to time until you become comfortable with them.

Study guide

- **Dialogue 1 + Practise what you have learned**
- **Dialogue 2 + Practise what you have learned**
- **Dialogue 3 + Practise what you have learned**
- **Dialogue 4 + Practise what you have learned**
- **Make sure you know the Key words and phrases**
- **Study: the Grammar section**
- **Read: Read and understand**
- **Read: Did you know?**

Dialogues

1 *What time is it now?*

Miura Sumimasen, ima nan-ji desu ka?
Kanada Ku-ji nijuu-hap-pun desu.
Miura Aa soo desu ka. Depaato wa nan-ji kara desu ka?
Kanada Ee to...Juu-ji kara desu.
Miura Nan-ji made deshoo ka?
Kanada Saa, yoku wakaranain desu kedo, tabun...hachi-ji goro made to omoimasu yo.
Miura Aa soo desu ka. Doomo.

ku-ji nijuu-happun 9:28 (See below for minute counters.)
depaato department store (*Eng.*)
hachi-ji goro about 8:00
Doomo. Thanks. (*inf.*) (*eq.* **Doomo arigatoo.**)

Depaato wa nanji kara desu ka? What time does the department store open? (*lit.* The department store is from what time?)

Nan-ji made deshoo ka? What time does it close? (*lit.* Until what time is it?)

Yoku wakaranain desu kedo... I don't know for sure. (*lit.* I don't know well, but...) (*eq.* **Yoku wakarimasen.**)

Hachi-ji goro made to omoimasu yo. I think it is (open) until about 8:00. Remember that **to omoimasu** after a verb means "I think...". **Yo** at the end of this sentence adds emphasis, indicating that the speaker is reasonably sure of his answer.

Minute counters

How many minutes? **Nan-pun desu ka?**

1	**ippun**	11	**juu-ippun**	10	**juppun**
2	**ni-fun**	12	**juu-ni-fun**	20	**nijuppun**
3	**san-pun**	13	**juu-san-pun**	30	**sanjuppun**
4	**yon-pun**	14	**juu-yon-pun**	40	**yonjuppun**
5	**go-fun**	15	**juu-go-fun**	50	**gojuppun**
6	**roppun**	16	**juu-roppun**	60	**rokujuppun**
7	**nana-fun**	17	**juu-nana-fun**		
8	**happun**	18	**juu-happun**	4:30 = **yoji han**	
9	**kyuu-fun**	19	**juu-kyuu-fun**	(half past four)	
10	**juppun**	20	**ni-juppun**		

Practise what you have learned

1 Close your book and listen as Tanabe-san reads the minute counters for you. There will be pauses for you to repeat. After going over the section on the recording several times, open the book and look at the "Minute Counters" list again.

2 Fill in the blanks with the Japanese equivalents. (Answers p. 92)

(a) 7:30 ____________ **(b)** about 6:00 ____________

(c) 7:15 ____________ **(d)** from 10:00 ____________

3 With Aoki-san's prompting, ask your Japanese friend some time questions. Basic sentence structures are:

(a) What time does ______ start? ______ **wa nan-ji kara desu ka?**

(b) What time does ______ end? ______ **wa nan-ji made desu ka?**

The kinds of questions you want to ask may be related to:

(a) **gakkoo** (school)
(b) **shigoto** (work)
(c) **kaisha** (your company)
(d) **jimusho** (the office)
(e) **kono mise** (this shop/store)
(f) **paatii** (a party)
(g) **eiga** (a movie)
(h) **kaigi** (a business meeting)

The 11.00 a.m. train has just arrived in the station

Dialogues

2 *Asking for a date*

Miki	Ano sa, kondo dokka ikoo ka.
Shōda	Dokoka tte, doko yo.
Miki	Deito ni...
Shōda	Soo ne...(Un) Watashi...bijutsu-kan nanka ii to omoun da kedo...
Miki	Bijutsu-kan ka...Ja, itsu aite iru?
Shōda	Ee to...ichiban chikai hi wa asatte ka na?
Miki	Ja, asatte no, juu-ichi-ji, Gotanda eki no higashi-guchi de...doo ka na?
Shōda	E, wakatta wa.
Miki	Ja, soo yuu koto de...
Shōda	Hai. Ja ne.
Miki	Ja ne.

kondo next time
dokka somewhere (*inf.*) (*eq.* **dokoka**)
deito ni on a date (*Eng.*)
bijutsu-kan art museum
nanka something (*inf.*) (*eq.* **nanika**)
hi day
asatte day after tomorrow
Gotanda a section of Tokyo
higashi-guchi de at the east entrance

(Note that the tone of this conversation is very casual, since the speakers are a young man and a young woman.)

Ano sa... (*m.*) Comparable to "you know" or "by the way", this phrase is often used at the beginning of a casual conversation as a way of simply bringing up a subject. (*eq.* **Ano.../Ano ne...**)

Dokka ikoo yo. Let's go somewhere. (*m./inf.*) (*eq.* **Dokoka e ikimasen ka?**)

Dokoka tte, doko yo. What do you mean "somewhere"? (*inf.*)

Itsu aite iru? When are you free? (*inf.*) (*eq.* **Itsu aite imasu ka?**)

Ii to omoun da kedo... I think it's okay, but... (*inf.*) (*eq.* **Ii to omoimasu.**)

asatte ka na? maybe the day after tomorrow? The **ka na** marker is similar to **ne** but with more uncertainty. In this and in **Doo ka na?** (How would that be?), the speaker indicates that he is open to suggestion.

Wakatta wa. Understood./Agreed. (*f./inf.*) The marker **wa** after the verb is what makes this phrase typical of feminine speech. (*eq.* **Wakarimashita.**)

Ja, soo yuu koto de... Well, (let's do) that./It's a date. (*lit.* Well, [let's do] that sort of thing...)

Ja ne. Bye. (*inf.*) This phrase is commonly used to signal the end of a conversation, either in person or by phone. It is as if to say, "I am going to leave/hang up now".

Practise what you have learned

4 Read the following phrases and identify each as specifically male (M) or female (F), or if it can be used by either gender (MF). (Answers p. 92)

(a) Dokoka ikimasen ka? ( )
(b) Ashita ikitai no yo. ( )
(c) Wakatta wa. ( )
(d) Ja ne. ( )
(e) Wakarimashita. ( )

5 Miura san and Tanabe-san are making plans for a date. Listen to the recording and answer the questions below. (Answers p. 92)

(a) Where are they going? ______________________

(b) What day of the week are they going? ______________________

(c) What time are they meeting? ______________________

6 You would like to go to Kamakura to see the big statue of Buddha and visit temples and shrines. Make plans to go with your friend. Listen to the recording. Aoki-san will guide you through the conversation.

____

____

____

Open-air museum in Hakone

Dialogues

3 *Let's go shopping*

Junko Ne, Yoshiko, Mokuyoobi ni kaimono ni ikanai?
Yoshiko Gomen ! Mokuyoobi wa o-keiko nano.
Junko Ja, Doyoobi wa?
Yoshiko Doyoobi mo o-keiko nano yo.
Junko Ja, itsu ni suru?
Yoshiko Watashi no aite iru no wa, Getsuyoobi, Kayoobi, Suiyoobi no mikka dake...
Junko Ja, Kayoobi ni shimashoo ka?
Yoshiko Ii wa...

Yoshiko woman's given name
◗ **kaimono** shopping
◗ **Gomen!** Sorry! (*inf.*) (*eq.* **Gomen nasai.**)
o-keiko lesson
mikka three days (See p. 87).
dake only

Ne, Yoshiko... Say, Yoshiko. When speaking to a close friend in a casual setting, it is acceptable to use only the friend's first name.

Mokuyoobi ni kaimono ni ikanai? Won't you go shopping (with me) on Thursday? (*eq.* **...ikimasen ka?**)

O-keiko nano. (I have) a lesson. (*f./inf.*) (*eq.* **O-keiko desu.**)

Itsu ni suru? When shall we make it? (*inf.*) (*lit.* When/what day shall we decide on?) (*eq.* **Itsu ni shimasu ka?**)

Aite iru no wa... As for an open (day)...The word **no** here is not a grammar marker but refers to the thing or topic under discussion. It is comparable to saying "as for an open one..."

mikka dake only three days. See Grammar section for **dake**.

Practise what you have learned

7 Read the dialogue and answer the following questions. (Answers p. 92)

(a) Junko-san wa doko ni ikitain desu ka?
(b) Itsu ikitain desu ka?
(c) Yoshiko-san no aite iru hi (day) wa itsu desu ka?
(d) Futari wa itsu kaimono ni ikimasu ka?

8 Listen to the recording and describe briefly what the two people are talking about. (Answers p. 92)

(a) Where does the young man want to go? ______________________

(b) What day do they decide on? ______________________

(c) How late does the young woman work tomorrow? ______________

(d) What time will they meet? ______________________

(e) Where will they meet? ______________________

9 Tell your friend that you want to go to Roppongi. Ask her/him if tomorrow is okay. Your friend works late tomorrow. Suggest the day after tomorrow, and ask what time you should plan to go. Listen to the recording and work through the conversation with Aoki-san's help.

____

____

____

Department stores in the Nihombashi district of Tokyo

Dialogues

4 *When did you come to Tokyo?*

Furukawa Itsu Tōkyō ni o-mie ni narimashita ka?
Takada Senshuu no Nichi-yoobi ni mairimashita.
Furukawa Tenki ga anmari yokunakute zannen desu, ne.
Takada E...demo, Kayoobi totemo ii o-tenki datta node, shashin o tottari, iroiro na tokoro ni ittari shite, totemo yokattan desu.
Furukawa Itsu Tōkyō o o-tachi ni narimasu?
Takada Raishuu no Doyoobi ni iku tsumori de orimasu.
Furukawa Tenki ga ii to, ii desu, ne.
Takada Ee.

senshuu last week
mairimashita I came. (*humb.*) (*eq.* **kimashita**)
yokunai/yokunakute not good/not good, and...
Zannen desu. It's too bad.
totemo very, extremely
shashin photograph
tokoro place
raishuu next week

(Note that the tone of this conversation is very polite and formal.)

Itsu Tōkyō ni o-mie ni narimashita ka? When did you arrive in Tokyo? (*exal.*) (*eq.* **Itsu Tōkyō ni kimashita ka?**)

Senshuu no Nichiyoobi ni mairimashita. I came on Sunday of last week. (*humb.*) **Mairimashita** can mean either "I came" or "I went".

Tenki ga anmari yokunakute zannen desu, ne. It's too bad the weather isn't very good, isn't it? (*lit.* The weather is not very good, and that's too bad, isn't it?)

Totemo ii o-tenki datta node... Since it was very good weather...(*eq.* **Ii o-tenki deshita node...**)

Shashin o tottari, iroiro na tokoro ni ittari shite,... We took pictures and went to various places, and... See the Grammar section for more on **-tari.**

Yokatta(n) desu. It was good.

Itsu Tōkyō o o-tachi ni narimasu (ka)? When are you leaving Tokyo? (*exal.*) (*eq.* **Itsu go-shuppatsu desu ka?**)

Raishuu no Doyoobi ni iku tsumori de orimasu. I intend to go on Saturday of next week. (*humb.*) A verb followed by **tsumori desu** indicates intention to do something. (*eq.* **...iku tsumori desu.**) See the Grammar section for more on **tsumori desu**.

Practise what you have learned

10 Listen to Dialogue 4 and fill in the blanks below. (Answers p. 92)

(a) Takada-san wa itsu Tōkyō ni kimashita ka? ____________________

(b) Itsu shuppatsu suru tsumori desu ka? ____________________

(c) Kayoobi no tenki wa doo deshita ka? Yokatta desu ka, amari yokunakattan desu ka? ____________________

11 Listen to Dialogue 4 and answer the following questions. (Answers p. 92)

(a) Takada-san wa nanyoobi ni Tōkyō ni kimashita ka? ____________________

(b) Itsu made Tōkyō desu ka? ____________________

(c) Tōkyō no o-tenki wa doo desu ka? ____________________

(d) Takada-san wa Tōkyō de nani o shite imasu ka
(What is Takada-san doing in Tokyo?)

____

The Ginza district of Tokyo

Your turn to speak

12 Suppose you meet a Japanese traveller in your city. Aoki-san is going to help you ask the traveller some questions.

(a) Are you Japanese? (**Nihon no kata desu ka?**)

(b) Where's your hometown/home country? ______________________

(c) When did you come to____________ ?______________________

(d) Did you do some sightseeing? ______________________

(e) How long will you be in Rome? (**itsu made?**) ______________________

____

Key words and phrases

totemo	very, really, extremely
shashin o toru	to take a picture
____ **dake**	only ____
(**Kaimono ni iku**) **tsumori desu.**	I plan to (go shopping).
(**Sore wa**) **yokatta desu, ne.**	(That) is great, isn't it!
Zannen desu.	That's too bad.
Gomen nasai.	I'm sorry.

Time

Following are lists of time-related vocabulary for your reference.

itsu	when?	**senshuu**	last week
ato de	later	**konshuu**	this week
kondo	next time	**raishuu**	next week
kinoo	yesterday	**sengetsu**	last month
kyoo	today	**kongetsu**	this month
ashita/asu	tomorrow	**raigetsu**	next month
asatte	day after tomorrow		

Months

Months of the year: (**nangatsu** what month?)

Ichigatsu	January	**Shichigatsu**	July
Nigatsu	February	**Hachigatsu**	August
Sangatsu	March	**Kugatsu**	September
Shigatsu	April	**Juugatsu**	October
Gogatsu	May	**Juuichigatsu**	November
Rokugatsu	June	**Juunigatsu**	December

Days

Days of the month: (**nannichi** what day of the month?)

tsuitachi	1st	**juuroku-nichi**	16th
futsuka	2nd	**juushichi-nichi**	17th
mikka	3rd	**juuhachi-nichi**	18th
yokka	4th	**juuku-nichi**	19th
itsuka	5th	**hatsuka**	20th
muika	6th	**nijuuichi-nichi**	21st
nanoka	7th	**nijuuni-nichi**	22nd
yooka	8th	**nijuusan-nichi**	23rd
kokonoka	9th	**nijuuyokka**	24th
tooka	10th	**nijuugo-nichi**	25th
juuichi-nichi	11th	**nijuuroku-nichi**	26th
juuni-nichi	12th	**nijuushichi-nichi**	27th
juusan-nichi	13th	**nijuuhachi-nichi**	28th
juuyokka	14th	**nijuuku-nichi**	29th
juugo-nichi	15th	**sanjuu-nichi**	30th
		sanjuuichi-nichi	31st

Note: The words for the days of the month, as shown above, are also used to indicate a period of days (three days, seven days, etc.), with one exception: "one day" is expressed by the word **ichi-nichi**.

Grammar

Hours

Hours of elapsed time: (**nan-jikan** how many hours?)

ichi-jikan	1 hour	**roku-jikan**	6 hours
ni-jikan	2 hours	**shichi-jikan**	7 hours
san-jikan	3 hours	**hachi-jikan**	8 hours
yo-jikan	4 hours	**ku-jikan**	9 hours
go-jikan	5 hours	**juu-jikan**	10 hours

See p. 52 and p. 78 for o'clock counters and p. 29 for days of the week.

Grammar markers

Remember that grammar markers always follow the word/phrase they refer to.

____ **dake** "only"

Example: **Getsuyoobi dake aite irun desu.** Only Monday is open.

Futari dake desu. There are only two of us.

____ **ni** after "specific" time words (hours of the clock, days of the week/month, months, years)

Example: **Ichigatsu ni kimasu.** I will come in January.

Getsuyoobi ni iku tsumori desu. I plan to go on Monday.

Juuji-han ni eki ni ikimasu. I will go to the station at 10:30.

Note: This marker is not used after non-specific time-related words, such as **ima** (now), **ashita** (tomorrow), **konshuu** (this week), etc.

-tari

The verb ending **-tari** is used when there is more than one activity referred to, and not in any particular order. The last verb in a series of two or more in the **-tari** form will usually be followed by some form of **suru** (**shite, shimasu, shimashita**, etc.).

Example: **Shashin o tottari, iroiro na tokoro ni ittari shite...**
We took pictures and went to various places, and...

Depaato ni ittari, iroiro mitari, kattari shimashita.
We went to department stores and looked at and bought various things.

tsumori (desu)

A verb followed by **tsumori desu** indicates intention to do something.

Example: **Ashita iku tsumori desu.** I intend to go tomorrow.

Konban washoku o taberu tsumori desu.
I plan to eat Japanese food tonight.

Read and understand

Signs

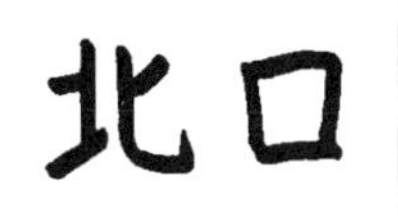

kitaguchi
north entrance

higashiguchi
east entrance

minamiguchi
south entrance

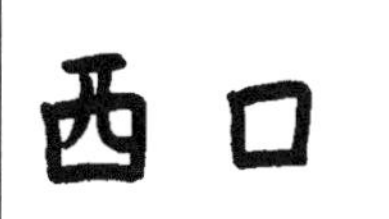

nishiguchi
west entrance

iriguchi
entrance

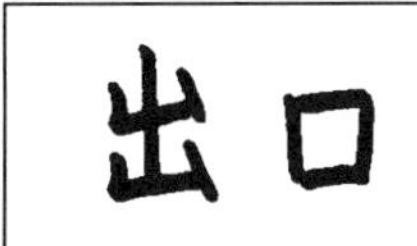

deguchi
exit

norikae
transfer

Kanji 1–10

Did you know?

There are 13 national holidays during the year, which are observed throughout Japan. On these days government and public offices, banks and schools are closed. These national holidays are listed here chronologically.

January 1 New Year's Day (**Ganjitsu**). The beginning of the new year is celebrated as the most important holiday. Most businesses are closed for several days, and Tokyo suddenly becomes a rather quiet place as many people leave to visit their home towns.

January 15 Adults' Day (**Seijin no Hi**). Youths who have reached the age of 20 are honoured and officially accepted as adults.

February 11 National Foundation Day (**Kenkoku Kinenbi**). According to tradition, Jimmu became the first Emperor on this day in about 600 B.C.

March 20 or 21 Vernal Equinox (**Shunbun no Hi**). The first day of spring, when the goodness of nature is celebrated.

April 29 Arbour Day (**Midori no Hi**). The period between April 29 and May 5 is called **Gōruden Wīku** (Golden Week). The three holidays that fall within this period are interconnected in various ways, usually by including weekends to extend the days off. People go on vacations, visit relatives and are generally on the move. Making business appointments and hotel and ticket reservations can be very difficult at this time.

May 3 Constitution Day (**Kenpō Kinenbi**). Anniversary of the post-Second World War Constitution.

May 5 Children's Day (**Kodomo no Hi**).

September 15 Day of Respect for the Elderly (**Keirō no Hi**).

Sept. 23 or 24 Autumnal Equinox (**Shūbun no Hi**). Ancestors are worshipped on this occasion.

October 10 Sports Day (**Tai-iku no Hi**). Sports as a means of maintaining physical and mental health is celebrated.

November 3 Culture Day (**Bunka no Hi**). A day when the government honours those who have made cultural contributions to the country.

November 23 Labour Appreciation Day (**Kinrō Kansha no Hi**). The nation honours its workers.

December 23 The Emperor's Birthday (**Tennō Tanjō no Hi**).

In addition to the national holidays, there are festival days that have special traditional meanings and are widely celebrated.

February 3/4 Bean-throwing ritual (**Setsubun**). Observed at shrines, temples and in the home.

March 3 Doll Festival (**Hinamatsuri**). A celebration for young girls.

April 8 Buddha's birthday (**Hana matsuri**).

May 1 Workers' Day (**Mei Dei**). This day is part of Golden Week, and the unions, Communists and Socialists celebrate the day with marches, picnics and political speeches.

July 7 Festival of Stars (**Tanabata**).

July 15 All Souls' Festival (**Obon**). Everyone returns to their home town to welcome the spirits of their ancestors. Tokyo again becomes virtually empty, and all transportation facilities are extremely crowded during this period. Rural regions celebrate Obon on or about August 15, according to the lunar calendar.

November 15 7-5-3 Festival (**Shichi-go-san**). A special day for 3- and 7-year-old girls and 3- and 5-year old boys to dress up in their best clothes and visit Shinto shrines with their parents to give thanks for good health and receive blessings for the future.

December The last two weeks in December are very busy as the Japanese wind up the old year and prepare for the new. Merchants enjoy a brisk sale season, as many company employees receive their year-end bonuses.

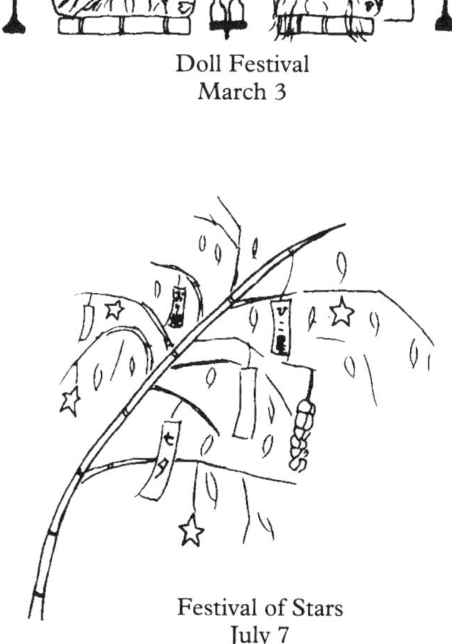

Doll Festival
March 3

Children's Day
May 5

Festival of Stars
July 7

Answers

Practise what you have learned

Exercise **2**	(a) shichi-ji han (b) roku-ji goro (c) shichi-ji juugo-fun (d) juu-ji kara
Exercise **4**	(a) MF (b) M (c) F (d) MF (e) MF
Exercise **5**	(a) Art Museum (b) Saturday (c) 10:30
Exercise **7**	(a) kaimono (b) Mokuyoobi (c) Getsuyoobi, Kayoobi, Suiyoobi (d) Kayoobi
Exercise **8**	(a) to the art museum (b) Wednesday (c) 8:00 (d) 11:00 (e) Shinjuku Nishiguchi (West entrance of Shinjuku station)
Exercise **10**	(a) senshuu no Nichiyoobi (b) raishuu no Doyoobi (c) Totemo yokatta desu.
Exercise **11**	(a) Kayoobi (b) Nichiyoobi (c) Yoku furimasu ne (d) shashin o tottari, iroirona tokoro ni ittari shite imasu.

7 SHOPPING–PART 1

You will learn

- to ask for items in a store
- to purchase medicine
- to get mailing information at the post office
- to say something is too big, too small, too expensive, etc.
- where you can get medical assistance and have prescriptions filled
- about Japanese telephone service

Study guide

Dialogue 1 + Practise what you have learned
Dialogue 2 + Practise what you have learned
Dialogue 3 + Practise what you have learned
Dialogue 4 + Practise what you have learned
Make sure you know the Key words and phrases
Study: the Grammar section
Read: Read and understand
Read: Did you know?

Dialogues

1 *I'll take this and this*

Student Kore to kore kudasai.
Shop assistant Arigato gozaimasu. Kochira no ookii hoo ga yonsen-kyuuhyaku-hachijuu-en. Chiisai hoo ga, sanzen-happyaku-en. Ryoohoo de hassen-nanahyaku-hachijuu-en ni narimasu. Sore ni san-paasento no shoohizei ga tsukimashite, nihyaku-rokujuu-san-en tashimasu. Zenbu de kyuusen-yonjuu-san-en ni narimasu.
Student Ichiman-en de, onegai shimasu.
Shop assistant Hai, wakarimashita.

- **ookii hoo** the big one
- **chiisai hoo** the small one
- **ryoohoo de** both together
- **shoohizei** sales tax
- **tsukimashite** adding (*dic.* **tsuku**)
- **tashimasu** totals (comes to a total of) (*dic.* **tasu**)
- **zenbu de** all together

Kore to kore kudasai. Please give me this and this. The word **kudasai** after a *noun* is used to ask for the thing mentioned. Compare this to the use of **kudasai** after the **te-**form of a *verb* to ask someone to do something.

Ryoohoo de 8,780-en ni narimasu. Both together come to 8,780 yen.

Sore ni 3-paasento no shoohizei ga tsukimashite, 263-en tashimasu. Adding 3% sales tax to that, it totals 263 yen.

Zenbu de 9,043-en ni narimasu. All together, it comes to 9,043 yen.

Ichiman-en de, onegai shimasu. Please take it out of 10,000 yen. (*lit.* Please [take care of it] with 10,000 yen.)

Practise what you have learned

1 Read the dialogue and answer the following questions. (Answers p. 106)

(a) The student purchased two items. How much did the two items cost together?

____

(b) How much did the smaller of the two items cost? ______________

(c) What percentage is the sales tax in Japan? ______________

2 Listen to the recording and find out how many things Miura-san is going to buy at the Rainbow Sandwich shop. Answer in Japanese. (Answers p. 106)

(a) How many things will Miura-san buy altogether? (Use the classic counters—**hitotsu**, **futatsu**, etc.) ______________

(b) What is everyone going to drink? ______________

____

3 Now it's your turn to go to the store and buy. First read this section and then listen to the recording. Someone will assist you by prompting in the background. Listen for the native speaker's response and check your own answer against it.

Traditional Japanese folk-art shop (or Mingei shop) in Aizu-Wakamatsu City

Dialogues

2 *Do you have another one?*

Customer Gorufu no shoohin ni shitain desu ga, kore yori moo hitomawari gurai ookii no arimasu ka?

Shop assistant Mooshiwake gozaimasen. Ima kirashite orimasu kedo, moo, raishuu ni nattara hairimasu.

Customer Kekkoo desu. Onegai shimasu.

Shop assistant Ja, o-namae to denwa bangoo o, doozo.

Customer Hai, Ma-Su-Mo-To desu.
Denwa bangoo wa san-ni-ichi-ichi, ni-go-yon-kyuu desu.

Shop assistant Hai, kashikomarimashita.

gorufu golf (*Eng.*)
shoohin prize
hitomawari one round, one notch, one increment
Kekkoo desu. That's okay/fine.
Doozo. Please./Go ahead.
Masumoto Japanese surname

Gorufu no shoohin ni shitain desu ga... I want to decide on (choose) a golf prize, but...

Kore yori (more) than this (See the Grammar section for more on this expression.)

Moo hitomawari gurai ookii no arimasu ka? Do you have one about one size larger? (*eq.* **Moo chotto ookii no arimasu ka?** = Do you have one a little bit larger?)

Ima kirashite orimasu. We are out of it now. (*humb.*) (*eq.* **Ima kirashite imasu.**)

Raishuu ni nattara, hairimasu. We will have it as of next week. (*lit.* When it becomes next week, it will come in.)

O-namae to denwa bangoo o, doozo. Please (write) your name and telephone number. (*eq.* **O-namae to denwa bangoo o kaite kudasai.**)

San-ni-ichi-ichi, ni-go-yon-kyuu desu. It's 3211-2549. Note that Japanese phone numbers may have 3- or 4-digit prefixes. The marker **no** may be used between the prefix and the rest of the number or after the area code, if one is given: **san-ni-ichi-ichi *no* ni-go-yon-kyuu.**

Practise what you have learned

4 Telephone numbers are given one numeral at a time, the way Mr. Masumoto gave his at the store. Write out the following phone numbers in Japanese. (Answers p. 106)

(a) (381) 475-6835 ________________________________

(b) (815) 204-7731 ________________________________

5 Yamada-san and Tanaka-san will give you their phone numbers. Listen to the recording and write down the numbers in numerals. (Answers p. 106)

Yamada-san no denwa bangoo wa ______________________ desu.

Tanaka-san no denwa bangoo wa ______________________ desu.

6 While sightseeing, you become friends with a Japanese person. You decide to do some sightseeing together the next day. You need to exchange phone numbers so you can make plans later. (Answers for a and b, p. 106)

(a) Hotel Kōyō's phone number is (0467) 45-4141. ______________

____

(b) My room number is 864. ________________________

(c) What is your phone number? ______________________

(d) Please write it down for me. (**Sumimasen ga, kaite kudasai** or **Sumimasen ga, kaite kudasaimasen ka?** *pol.*)

(e) (Write your) name, too, please. **Namae mo, onegai shimasu.**

Craftsperson handpainting wooden dolls

Dialogues

3 *At the pharmacy*

Customer Ano...shigoto de ikkagetsu gurai ryokoo ni detain desu keredo, donna kusuri o motte ittara ii deshoo?

Pharmacist Kazagusuri. Kore wa, chintsuu no imi ni mo narimasu kara...ma, kyootsuu de tsukaimasu. Sore kara, choo no kusuri, ne. Geri-dome. Sore to, ato wa ichoo-yaku; i-no-mukatsuki toka, shooka-furyoo toka, sore kara, nomi-sugi toka ni nomu kusuri to, sono mittsu to, ato wa, kizu-gusuri desu, ne.

Customer A, soo desu ka. Mizu wa doko de nondemo daijoobu desu, ne?

Pharmacist Nihon de wa, daijoobu desu, hai.

Customer Doomo arigatoo gozaimashita. Ja, sore o itadaite ikimasu.

- **ikkagetsu** a period of one month (See p. 102.)
- **ryokoo** travel
- **kusuri** medicine
- **kazagusuri** cold medicine

chintsuu analgesic/pain killer
kyootsuu de for both purposes
choo intestines

- **geri-dome** diarrhoea medicine (*lit.* diarrhoea-stop)

ato wa besides that
ichoo-yaku medicine for the stomach and intestines

- **i-no-mukatsuki** nausea
- **shooka-furyoo** indigestion
- **nomi-sugi** over-drinking
- **kizu-gusuri** antiseptic ointment (*lit.* medicine for wounds)
- **mizu** water
- **Daijoobu desu.** It's okay.

Ryokoo ni detain desu keredo... I want to leave on a trip, but...

Donna kusuri o motte ittara ii deshoo? What kind of medicine should I take? (*lit.* What kind of medicine would it be good if I took with me?)

Kore wa chintsuu no imi ni mo narimasu. This acts as an analgesic also.

Kyootsuu de tsukaimasu. It is used for multiple purposes.

____ **toka** ____ **toka...** (either) ____ or ____ , for example. See the Grammar section.

____ **ni nomu kusuri** medicine that you take for ____ . Putting a verb in front of a noun makes the verb or verb phrase describe the noun. Also note that, while in English we "take" medicine, the Japanese "drink/swallow" (**nomu**) it.

Mizu wa doko de nondemo daijoobu desu. It's okay to drink the water anywhere. (*lit.* As for water, it is okay even if you drink it anywhere.)

Sore o itadaite ikimasu. I will take it. (*humb.*) (*lit.* I will take that and go.)

Practise what you have learned

7 Find the appropriate word from column B for the words in column A. (Answers p. 106)

Column A		Column B
(a) cold medicine	____________	**(1) shooka furyoo**
(b) medicine	____________	**(2) nomi-sugi**
(c) indigestion	____________	**(3) geri-dome**
(d) over-drinking	____________	**(4) kusuri**
(e) diarrhoea relief	____________	**(5) kaza-gusuri**

8 Listen to the recording and learn how to ask the following questions. (Answers p. 106)

(a) Is there a pharmacy in this area? (pharmacy = **kusuriya**)

____

(b) Is the pharmacy far or near? ______________________

(c) Please give me a map. __________________________

(d) How many minutes does it take? ___________________

9 Using the recording, practise with Miura-san how to ask for different types of over-the-counter medicines at the pharmacy.

(a) Let me have some medicine for indigestion.

____

(b) Let me have something for diarrhoea relief.

____

(c) Let me have some medicine for a cold.

____

(d) I'll take that.

____

Dialogues

4 *At the post office*

Customer Ano, gaikoku-muki no kookuubin o dashitain desu keredomo, Yooroppa made tegami wa ikura desu ka?

Postmaster Hai, juu-guramu made hyaku-nijuu-en desu. Ato juu-guramu masu goto ni, hyaku-en zutsu kasan saremasu.

Customer A, soo desu ka. Hyaku-nijuu-en no kitte o gomai kudasai. Sore kara, Kanada wa ikura deshoo ka?

Postmaster Kanada wa juu-guramu made hyaku-en. Ato juu-guramu masu goto ni nanajuu-en zutsu kasan saremasu.

Customer A soo desu ka. Hagaki wa ikura ni narimasu deshoo ka?

Postmaster Nanajuu-en de bankoku kyootsuu desu ga...sentaa-rain oobaa shite kakaremasu to, o-tegami no ryookin ni narimasu kara, go-chuui kudasai.

Customer Doomo arigatoo gozaimashita.

- ➧ **gaikoku-muki** (going) overseas
- ➧ **kookuubin** air mail
- ➧ **Yooroppa** Europe
- ➧ **tegami** letter
- ➧ **ikura** how much?
- **guramu** grams (*Eng.*)
- **masu** a measure
- **-zutsu** each
- **kasan saremasu** is added
- ➧ **kitte** postage stamp
- **Kanada** Canada
- ➧ **hagaki** postcard
- ➧ **bankoku kyootsuu** world-wide standard
- **sentaa-rain** centre line (*Eng.*)
- **oobaa shite** go over (*Eng.*)/go beyond
- **ryookin** fee
- ➧ **Go-chuui kudasai.** Please be careful.

Gaikoku-muki no kookuubin o dashitain desu. I want to send an international airmail letter.

Ato juu-guramu masu goto ni... For every 10-gram measure after that...

Hyaku-en zutsu kasan saremasu. 100-yen is added to each.

Hyaku-nijuu-en no kitte o gomai kudasai. Please give me five 120-yen stamps. The counter for flat objects is **-mai.** (See below.)

Nanajuu-en de bankoku kyootsuu desu. At 70-yen, it is the world-wide standard (rate).

Sentaa-rain oobaa shite kakaremasu to... If/when you write over (beyond) the centre line...(*exal.*) (*eq.* **...kakimasu to...**)

O-tegami no ryookin ni narimasu. It becomes letter-rate.

Counters for flat objects
(paper, postcards, stamps, pictures, clothing, biscuits, etc.)

Nan-mai desu ka? How many (sheets)?

ichi-mai	**roku-mai**
ni-mai	**nana-mai**
san-mai	**hachi-mai**
yon-mai	**kyuu-mai**
go-mai	**juu-mai**

Practise what you have learned

10 Write the appropriate counters for the following items. (Answers p. 106)

(a) four postcards — Hagaki ______ kudasai.

(b) ham (**hamu**) 300 grams — Hamu ______ kudasai.

(c) seven ¥100 stamps — Hyaku-en no kitte ______ kudasai.

(d) ten ¥120 stamps — Hyaku-nijuu-en no kitte ______ kudasai.

11 Miura-san is going to the **yuubinkyoku**. Listen to the recording and fill in the blanks. (Answers p. 106)

(a) **Tegami o nan-mai kakimashita ka?** (How many letters did he write?)

______

(b) **Hagaki mo kakimashita ka?** (Did he write some postcards, too?) **Nan-mai?**

______

(c) **Kitte o nan-mai kaimashita ka?** (How many stamps did he buy?)

______

(d) **Zenbu de ikura deshita ka?** (How much was it altogether?)

______

12 Let's suppose that you wrote 2 letters and 8 postcards. Are you ready to go to the post office for the stamps? Tanabe-san will assist you. Think about the following phrases, and then listen to the recording.

(a) How much is airmail to England?

______

(b) How much is a postcard to Australia? (**Ōsutoraria**)

______

(c) Well then, let me have two ¥120 stamps and ten ¥70 stamps.

______

(d) And give me ten ¥70 stamps.

______

Key words and phrases

Kekkoo desu.	That's okay. That's all right.
Daijoobu desu.	That's okay. That's all right.
Go-chuui kudasai.	Please be careful.
(Sore o) kudasai.	Please give me (that).
(Kore to kore o) kudasai.	Please give me (this and this).
(120)-en no kitte o ____ mai kudasai.	Please give me ____ (120)-yen stamps.
(Tegami) o dashitain desu.	I want to mail (a letter).
Ikura ni narimasu ka?	How much does it come to?
____ -en ni narimasu.	It comes to ____ yen.
____ -en tashimasu.	It adds up to ____ yen.
____ -en de, onegai shimasu.	Take it out of ____ yen.
Moo chotto ookii/chiisai no arimasu ka?	Do you have one a little bit larger/smaller?
ryoohoo de	both together
zenbu de	all together
tegami	letter
hagaki	postcard
kitte	stamp
kookuubin	air mail
-zutsu	each

Elapsed Time Counters: Months

How many months? **Nan-kagetsu desu ka?**

ikkagetsu	1 month	**nanakagetsu**	7 months
nikagetsu	2 months	**hachikagetsu**	8 months
sankagetsu	3 months	**kyuukagetsu**	9 months
yonkagetsu	4 months	**jukkagetsu**	10 months
gokagetsu	5 months	**juuikkagetsu**	11 months
rokkagetsu	6 months	**juunikagetsu**	12 months

Grammar

"It is okay if..."

A verb ending in **-temo** (or **-demo**) means "Even if..." When this is followed by **daijoobu desu** or **ii** (**iin**) **desu**, the sentence takes on the meaning "It is okay if..." or "It is okay to..." Study these examples:

Mizu wa nondemo daijoobu desu ka?
Is it okay to drink the water?

Chikatetsu de ittemo daijoobu desu.
It is okay if you go by underground.

Sanji ni dekaketemo ii desu ka?
Is it okay to leave at 3:00?

Yooroppa de tsukattemo ii desu.
It is okay to use it in Europe.

Comparisons

The word **yori** after a noun means "more than ____ ". What follows it is usually an adjective or adjective phrase that completes the thought. Study these examples:

Kore yori chiisai no arimasu ka?
Do you have one smaller than this?

Kono burausu wa sore yori takai desu, ne.
This blouse is more expensive than that one, isn't it?

Bijutsu-kan wa eiga yori ii to omoun desu.
I think the art museum would be better than a movie.

____ *toka*

The word **toka** following each item in a series of items indicates that other items could also be included in the list, similar to the use of "etc." or "and things like that" in English. Study the following sentences:

Burausu toka, kutsu toka, iroiro kaimashita.
I bought various things—a blouse, shoes, and things like that.

Keiki wa iroiro arimasu—shooto keiki toka, ichigo no keiki toka...
As for cake, we have various kinds—shortcake, strawberry cake, etc.

Read and understand

郵便局 (〒)
yuubinkyoku
Post office

航空便
kookuubin
Airmail

船便
funabin
Seamail

はがき
hagaki
Postcard

切手
kitte
Stamps

書留
kakitome
Registered Mail

速達
sokutatsu
Express

小包
kozutsumi
Parcel Post

Did you know?

Telephone service

Telephone service in Japan is fast, courteous and efficient. Public phones (**kooshuu-denwa**) are colour-coded: Red telephones are for local calls and require ¥10 coins. A local call is ¥10 for 3 minutes. The line will disconnect at the end of 3 minutes, unless you put in more ¥10 coins. For an uninterrupted call longer that 3 minutes, put in as many as 6 coins. Unused coins will be returned.

Blue telephones will accept up to ten ¥10 coins.

Yellow phones accept ¥10 coins and up to nine ¥100 coins, so they are convenient for long distance calls.

Use the green phones or those with golden-olive coloured panels to make international collect calls or international credit calls. Dial 0051 for an international operator. The green phone will accept both coins and magnetic telephone cards (**terehon kaado**), which can be purchased from vending machines or any stores that display the logo. They come in ¥500, ¥1,000 and ¥3,000 denominations.

English-language information numbers

Green phone
Tōkyō: 3502-1461 Kyōto: 371-5649

All others 106
(Say, "COLLECT CALL, T-I-C, please" (a reverse charge call). Remember to speak s-l-o-w-l-y.)

Some things to remember

(a) The cost of having a telephone installed in a home in Japan is about ¥80,900.
(b) Calls originating from Japan are more expensive than incoming calls from overseas. Prearrange to receive calls when you can, or use telegraph or telex.

If you need medical assistance

Medical and dental standards are high in Japan, and excellent care is available throughout the country. Many of the major hotels provide clinics for their guests.

Medical Centres (with English-speaking doctors)

• **Eisei Byōin** (hospital) (Member: International Association for Medical Assistance to Travellers)	Tokyo	3392-6151
• **Sēruka Byōin** (St. Luke's Hosp.)	Tokyo	3541-5151
• **Hibiya Clinic**	Tokyo	3502-2681
• **Tōkyō Medical & Surgical Clinic**	Tokyo	3436-3028
• **The Bluff Hospital**	Yokohama	045-641-6961
• **Japan Baptist Hospital**	Kyoto	075-781-5194
• **Yodogawa Christian Hospital**	Osaka	06-322-2250

Dental care

• **Kutani Dental Clinic**	Tokyo	3265-1111
• **Olympia Ohba Dental Clinic**	Tokyo	3409-7156
• **Japan American Dental Clinic**	Tokyo	3251-7555

Pharmacy

- **American Pharmacy** Tokyo 3271-4033
  In the Hibiya Building near Yurakuchō station.

Postcard regulations

Japanese picture postcards are exceptionally attractive and relatively inexpensive. Japanese postal service regulations pertaining to postcard usage are very strict.

(a) One half of the postcard must be used only for the name of the recipient and the address.

(b) As the dialogue indicated, if the message crosses over the centre line (**sentaa-rain**), it will be charged as a letter.

Answers

Practise what you have learned

Exercise **1**	(a) ¥9,043 (b) ¥3,800 (c) 3%
Exercise **2**	(a) itsutsu (b) aisu-tii, koohii sutoroberi miruku seiki
Exercise **4**	(a) San-hachi-ichi no yon-nana-go no roku-hachi-san-go desu (b) Hachi-ichi-go no ni-zero-yon no nana-nana-san-ichi desu.
Exercise **5**	Yamada-san 3494-5050; Tanaka-san 3698-7704
Exercise **6**	(a) Zero-yon-roku-nana no yon-go no yon-ichi-yon-ichi (b) Hachi-roku-yon (c) Your own phone number
Exercise **7**	(a) 5 (b) 4 (c) 1 (d) 2 (e) 3
Exercise **8**	(a) Kono hen ni kusuriya arimasu ka? (b) Kusuriya wa tooi desu ka, chikai desu ka? (c) Sumimasen, chizu onegai shimasu. (d) Nanpun gurai kakarimasu ka?
Exercise **10**	(a) yon-mai (b) sanbyaku-guramu (c) nana-mai (d) juu-mai
Exercise **11**	(a) ni-mai (b) yon-mai (c) Hyaku-nijuu-en no kitte (o) ni-mai, nanajuu-en no kitte (o) juu-mai (d) kyuuhyaku yonjuu-en (¥940)

8 SHOPPING–PART 2

You will learn

- to buy clothes and specify colour
- to explain your ailments to the pharmacist
- to use credit cards and to have the store deliver your purchase
- to make a grocery list for a picnic
- something about shopping tips
- something about Japanese gift-giving practices

Before you begin

When you are shopping, you need not only to find what you want, but also to know that you are getting the best value for your money. Units 7 and 8 will help you with your shopping and also help you meet some medical needs that might occur.

Review a few of the helpful phrases you learned in previous units.

Kore (**to kore**) **kudasai.**	I would like this (and this).
____________ **arimasu ka?**	Do you have ____________ ?
O-negai shimasu.	Please. (I request that you do that.)
Ikura desu ka?	How much is it?

Study guide

- **Dialogue 1 + Practise what you have learned**
- **Dialogue 2 + Practise what you have learned**
- **Dialogue 3 + Practise what you have learned**
- **Dialogue 4 + Practise what you have learned**
- **Learn the Key words and phrases**
- **Study: the Grammar section**
- **Read: Did you know?**
- **Listen to all the dialogues again**

Dialogues

1 *Can I have it wrapped?*

Shop assistant Irasshaimase.
Customer Kono burausu kirei desu, ne. Musume ni hoshiin desu keredomo, hoka no iro arimasu kashira?
Shop assistant Eeto...kono burausu desu to, hoka no iro wa pinku, kiiro, buruu, guriin de gozaimasu.
Customer A so...Dewa pinku o itadakitain desu keredo...
Shop assistant Hai, wakarimashita.
Customer Tsutsunde itadakemasu ka?
Shop assistant Hai, wakarimashita. Purezento yoo ni o-tsutsumi itashimasu ka?
Customer Hai. Onegai itashimasu.
Shop assistant O-ribon wa nani-iro o-kake shimashoo ka?
Customer Yahari, pinku ni shite kudasai.

kirei pretty/beautiful
musume daughter
iro colour
hoka no iro a different colour
kashira I wonder if...
pinku pink (*Eng.*)
kiiro yellow
buruu blue (*Eng.*)
guriin green (*Eng.*)
Onegai itashimasu. Please (do that). (*humb.*) (*eq.* **Onegai shimasu.**)
nani-iro what colour?
yahari of course/after all (*eq.* **yappari**)

Musume ni hoshii (n) desu. I want it for my daughter. Yet another use for the marker **ni** is to indicate "to" or "for" someone. **Hoshii desu** literally means "is desired".

Hoka no iro wa ____ de gozaimasu. Other colours are ____ . (*pol.*) (*eq.* **Hoka no iro wa ____ desu.**)

Dewa pinku o itadakitain desu... Well, I want to take the pink (one)...(*humb.*) (*eq.* **Pinku ga hoshii desu.**)

Tsutsunde itadakemasu ka? Can I have you wrap it for me? The **te**-form of a verb followed by **itadaku** indicates that the speaker is politely asking something to be done for him. This is a softer way of saying **Tsutsunde kudasai**. The stem change from **itadaki** (as in **itadakitain desu**) to **itadake** alters the meaning to "can (do)". See the Grammar section at the end of this unit for more on this.

Purezento yoo ni As a present. The word **yoo** here indicates manner or purpose of the thing that precedes it.

O-tsutsumi itashimasu ka? Shall I wrap it? (*humb.*) (*eq.* **Tsutsumimashoo ka?**)

O-ribon wa nani-iro o-kake shimashoo ka? What colour ribbon shall I put on it? (*pol.*) The verb **kakeru** means to attach. (*eq.* **Ribon wa nani-iro kakemashoo ka?**)

Practise what you have learned

1 Match the English and Japanese colour words. (Answers p. 120)

(a) blue ______________	**kiiro**
(b) green ______________	**pinku**
(c) yellow ______________	**buruu**
(d) pink ______________	**guriin**

2 Tanabe-san is shopping for someone's birthday present. (**baasudei purezento**) Listen to the recording and answer the questions below. (Answers p. 120)

(a) What colour blouse did she want? ______________________________

(b) What was wrong with the one on display? ______________________

(c) What size did she buy? ______________________________________

(d) Did she find the colour she liked? ___________________________

3 You see a doll you want for a souvenir. Find out how much it is, and see if it meets your budget. You might want a smaller doll. Listen to the recording and complete the transaction with Tanabe-san's help.

____

____

Outdoor market

Dialogues

2 *I have a sore throat*

Customer Sumimasen, ni-san-nichi mae kara, chotto nodo ga itakute, atama mo itain desu keredomo, nanika kazagusuri arimasu ka?

Pharmacist Hai, hai. Ano...soo yuu baai desu to, ano...ma, ima yoku dete imasu no wa Korugen no kaisha, ne. Sore no Korugen no E.T. tte yuu no ga saikin atarashikute, atama no itami desu, ne. Nodo no itami mo toremasu shi...sore kara, ato ma, ippan-teki na hanakaze toka, soo yuu no o-kusuri mo, ma, ichioo soogoo de haitte orimasu. Ichioo genetsu, chintsuu, enshoo to san-shurui kiku yoo ni natte imasu.

Customer A soo desu ka. Sorede wa, sore o itadakimasu.

ni-san-nichi mae kara from 2 or 3 days ago
➧ **nodo** throat
➧ **itai desu** hurts
➧ **atama** head
soo yuu baai a case like that
yoku often (lit. well)
Korugen no kaisha Korugen Company
saikin lately
itami pain
toremasu can take (away)
ippan-teki na common
➧ **hana kaze** head cold (lit. nose cold)
soo yuu no that kind of
soogoo de combined
genetsu fever reducer
enshoo inflammation
san-shurui three types
kiku to be good/effective for...

➧ **Nodo ga itakute, atama mo itai(n) desu.** My throat hurts, and my head also hurts. Although "my" is not stated here, it is assumed the speaker is talking about his own body.

Ima yoku dete imasu no wa... Something that is popular now...(*lit.* One that comes out often now...)

____ **tte yuu no** one called ____ .

Saikin atarashikute, atama no itami desu, ne. It is new these days and is (for) headaches, you see. Similar to the **te**-form of verbs, the **te**-form of an adjective indicates that another adjective or verb follows in the sentence.

Nodo no itami mo toremasu shi... It also can relieve sore throat, as well. **Shi** after a verb indicates an incomplete sequence; in this case, the implication is "in addition to (relieving headaches)".

Soo yuu no o-kusuri mo...soogoo de haitte orimasu. That kind of medication also is combined and included in it. The speaker uses the humble **orimasu** because he is the one recommending the medication.

Genetsu, chintsuu, enshoo to san-shurui kiku yoo ni natte imasu. It is good for fever reduction, pain relief and (reduction of) inflammation—(those) three types.

Practise what you have learned

The simplest way to tell people which part of your body hurts is to point to the spot and say:

Koko ga itain desu.

Then add, "Is there any medicine for it?" **Nanika kusuri arimasu ka?**

eye	**me**	head	**atama**
ear	**mimi**	stomach	**o-naka**
tooth	**ha**	lower back	**koshi**
throat	**nodo**	foot/leg	**ashi**

4

Use the Japanese words shown in the illustration above to complete the following sentences. Listen to the tape and tell the pharmacist:

(a) My head hurts. ____________ ga itain desu.

(b) My tooth hurts. ____________ ga itain desu.

(c) My back hurts. ____________ ga itain desu.

(d) My stomach hurts. ____________ ga itain desu.

5

Listen to the recording and find out how Tanabe-san is feeling. Describe what is ailing her. Was she able to get some help? (Answers p. 120)

(a) What is ailing her? ________________________________

(b) When did the pain start? ____________________________

(c) What was the cause of the pain? ______________________

(d) Did she buy anything other than **nuri-gusuri** (ointment)? __________

____

6

With Aoki-san's help, go to the chemist and get some medicine for your sore throat from the pharmacist.

____

____

Dialogues

3 *Can I use a charge card?*

Customer Kono o-sara o itadakitain desu keredo...
Shop assistant Hai. Kashikomarimashita.
Customer Kokunai de wa haitatsu shite itadakerun desu, ne?
Shop assistant Hai. Kokunai wa Saga-Kyūbin de o-okuri shite orimasu.
Customer Kaado wa tsukaemasu ka?
Shop assistant Hai. Yon-shurui atsukatte orimasu. Dii-Shii, Masuta-kaado, Bisa-kaado, Jei-Shii-Bii de gozaimasu.
Customer Dewa, Jei-Shii-Bii de, onegai itashimasu.
Shop assistant Hai. Kashikomarimashita.
Customer Sorekara, kaigai ni mukete no haitatsu wa onegai dekimasu ka?
Clerk Mooshiwake gozaimasen. Uchi de wa, kaigai wa atsukatte orimasen.

(o-) sara dish/plate
➧ **kokunai** domestic (within the country)
➧ **haitatsu** delivery
➧ **Dii-Shii** Diner's Club ("D.C.")
➧ **Masuta-kaado** Master Card
➧ **Bisa-kaado** Visa Card
➧ **Jei-Shii-Bii** Japan Credit Bureau ("J.C.B.")
➧ **kaigai** overseas
uchi de wa at our place

Kokunai de wa haitatsu shite itadakerun desu, ne? I can have you deliver within the country, can't I? (*eq.* **...itadakemasu, ne?**)

Kokunai wa Saga-Kyūbin de o-okuri shite orimasu. Domestically, we ship via Saga Kyubin. (*humb.*) (*eq.* **Saga-Kyūbin de okurimasu.**)

➧ **Kaado wa tsukaemasu ka?** Can I use a credit card? Again, the change from **tsukaimasu** to **tsukaemasu** indicates "can use" instead of "will use". See the Grammar section.

Yon-shurui atsukatte orimasu. We handle four types. (*humb.*) (*eq.* **...atsukatte imasu.**)

➧ **Jei-Shii-Bii de, onegai itashimasu.** Please (let me pay) with J.C.B. (*humb.*)

➧ **Kaigai ni mukete no haitatsu wa...** As for international delivery...The phrase **kaigai ni mukete** literally means "facing overseas" or "towards overseas".

➧ **Onegai dekimasu ka?** Can I ask you to do that? (See Grammar section for **dekimasu.**)

Uchi de wa, kaigai wa atsukatte orimasen. In this establishment we do not handle overseas (delivery). (*humb.*)

Practise what you have learned

7 What are some of the international credit cards that can be used in this store? (Answers p. 120)

(a) ____________ **(b)** ____________

(c) ____________ **(d)** ____________

8 Listen to the dialogue again and answer these questions. (Answers p. 120)

(a) What is the customer buying? ____________________

(b) Is she going to take it with her or does she want it delivered?

____

(c) Which credit card does she use? ____________________

(d) Does the store deliver overseas? ____________________

9 Suppose you saw a plate that you wanted to buy, but you wouldn't be able to take it with you because you are leaving on a sightseeing tour. Get the point across to the shop assistant that you want to have it sent to room 555 at the Hotel Okura. Make sure that you will have it before leaving for Kyoto on Wednesday, the day after tomorrow. Before you listen to the tape, visualize the situation in your mind. The key to this exercise is how well you can cut down sentences to bare essentials but still use culturally acceptable phrases.

____

____

____

____

Dialogues

4 *Making a grocery list*

Ms. Mushakōji is planning a picnic for a group of people. As she writes her list, she thinks out loud.

Ms. Mushakōji Soo da...ashita no pikunikku no tame no kaimono ni ikanakucha... Mazu wa, sandoitchi. Nani ni shiyoo ka na?
Hamu, yasai, roosuto-biifu, sorekara, tamago mo, ii ka na?
Sorekara...tori-no-kara-age mo ireyoo.
Sooseiji mo, poteto-sarada mo, chiizu mo kawanakucha.
Soo da! Nomimono wa o-cha to koora, sore ni biiru...Kore ja, oosugiru ka na?

- **kaimono ni iku** to go shopping
- **mazu** first of all
- **yasai** vegetable
- **tamago** egg
- **tori-no-kara-age** fried chicken
- **ireru** put in
- **chiizu** cheese (*Eng.*)
- **nomimono** beverage
- **o-cha** tea
- **koora** Cola (*Eng.*)
- **sore ni** on top of that/plus
- **biiru** beer (*Eng.*)
- **oosugiru** be too much

Ashita no pikunikku no tame no kaimono... shopping for tomorrow's picnic. ____ **no tame** means "for ____ " or "on behalf of ____ ". The **no** markers here make each word or phrase describe the next.

Kaimono ni ikanakucha. I have to go shopping. (*inf.*) **Ikanakucha** is an abbreviated form of the verb phrase **Ikanakutewa ikemasen**, meaning "I have to go..."

Tori-no-kara-age mo ireyoo. Let's put in fried chicken, too. (*inf.*) The **-oo** ending (as in **ireyoo**, **shiyoo**, etc.) means "Let's (do something)". The normal-polite equivalent of this ending is **-mashoo** (**iremashoo**, **shimashoo**, etc.)

____ **kawanakucha.** I have to buy ____ . (*inf.*) **Kawanakucha** is an abbreviated form of **Kawanakutewa ikemasen**.

Practise what you have learned

10

What does Ms. Mushakōji include in her shopping list? Write the English word next to each item. Check your answers against the dialogue.

(a) roosuto-biifu ______________ **(d)** nomimono ______________

(b) tori-no-kara-age ______________ **(e)** o-cha ______________

(c) yasai ______________ **(f)** tamago ______________

11

Tanabe-san and Miura san are making a list for the picnic. What are some of the things that they are taking with them? After listening to the recording make a list for them in English. (Answers p. 120)

(a) ______________ **(e)** ______________

(b) ______________ **(f)** ______________

(c) ______________ **(g)** ______________

(d) ______________ **(h)** ______________

12

Listen to the recording and make a shopping list to fill your picnic basket.

(a) sandoitchi: ______________________________

(b) yasai: ______________________________

(c) nomimono: ______________________________

Key words and phrases

Onegai shimasu.	Please do it.
Onegai itashimasu.	Please do it. (*humb.*)
Onegai dekimasu ka?	Can I ask you to do it?
____ ga hoshii desu.	I want ____ .
(Musume) ni hoshii desu.	I want it for (my daughter).
O-tsutsumi itashimasu ka?	Shall I wrap it? (*humb.*)
O-tsutsumi shimashoo ka?	Shall I wrap it? (*pol.*)
(Haitatsu shi)te itadakemasu ka?	Can I have you (deliver it?)
(Haitatsu shi)te kudasai.	Please (deliver it).
(Haitatsu shi)te itadakitain desu.	I'd like to have you (deliver it).
Kaado wa tsukaemasu ka?	Can I use a credit card?
Koko ga itai desu.	It hurts here.
(Nodo ga) itai desu.	(My throat) hurts.
(See p. 111 for other body parts.)	
mae kara	from before
mazu	first of all
yoku	well/frequently
saikin	recently
oosugiru	too much/too many
uchi	I/me, we/us, our house, our establishment
kokunai	domestic (delivery)
kaigai	international/overseas

Grammar

Verbs

There are three types of Japanese verbs:

Irregular—There are only two irregular verbs: **kuru** (to come) and **suru** (to do).

Type 1 Verbs—Most verbs fall into this category.

Type 2 Verbs—Verbs end in **-iru** or **-eru** in the basic dictionary form.

The stem of a verb (the part that is left when you take off the last syllable of the dictionary form) never changes; however, the rest of the verb changes according to what you want to say with the verb. Of course, it changes for past/present tense and for negative and positive mood. It also changes for many other functions; for example, when you need to express "want to", "have to", "should", "can", etc.

In the normal-polite level of speech, a Japanese verb ends in **-masu** to express "(I) do" or "(I) will do". In the case of the ending **-masu**, the last syllable of the dictionary form of a Type 1 verb changes its vowel from **u** to **i**, then **-masu** is added. (**Aruku** becomes **arukimasu**, **tsukau** becomes **tsukaimasu**, etc.) For Type 2 verbs, the last syllable of the dictionary form is simply dropped, and **-masu** is added. (**Taberu** becomes **tabemasu**, **miru** becomes **mimasu**, etc.) The irregular verbs are **kimasu** and **shimasu** in this normal-polite ending.

"can"

To express the idea "(I) can", the last syllable of the dictionary form of a Type 1 verb changes to e instead of **i**, as follows:

aruku—arukemasu ("can walk")
tsukau—tsukaemasu ("can use")
itadaku—itadakemasu ("can partake")
kau—kaemasu ("can buy")

For Type 2 verbs the last syllable of the dictionary form is dropped, and **-raremasu** is added:

taberu—taberaremasu ("can eat")
miru—miraremasu ("can see")
dekakeru—dekakeraremasu ("can go out")
oriru—oriraremasu ("can go down/descend")

The irregular verb **kuru** is similar to Type 2 verbs in this form, but the stem changes to **ko**:

koraremasu ("can come").

The irregular verb **suru** is never used in this form but is replaced by **dekiru** (**dekimasu**), which means "to be able to do". Two-word verbs using **suru** also make this change:

shuppatsu shimasu—shuppatsu dekimasu ("can depart")

onegai shimasu—onegai dekimasu ("can request")
kaimono shimasu—kaimono dekimasu ("can go shopping")

Did you know?

Foreign credit cards and travellers' cheques

Credit cards and travellers' cheques can be used at almost all major hotels and restaurants. Establishments that accept credit cards will display the types of cards that they will accept. Travellers' cheques are not as widely accepted and should be changed to Japanese currency at a bank. (Take your passport with you.) All banks, with the exception of small local banks or savings and loans, will have a designated foreign exchange section. Look for the sign as you enter the bank.

Shopping in arcades and department stores

Major hotel arcades offer shopping of great convenience to foreign travellers. However, for those who wish to see more of everyday life in Japan, a tour through department stores might be more interesting. Japanese department stores are usually smaller in size than U.S. or U.K. department stores, and the top floor of each department store building is full of restaurants where you can try Western or Japanese meals for reasonable prices. If you are interested in folk arts, ask for the **kyoodo zaiku** or **kyoodo miyage** section.

In Kyoto look for the Handicraft Centre, where daily handicraft demonstrations are scheduled. The centre is located near the Heian Shrine (**Heian Jingū**).

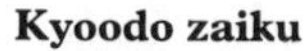

Kyoodo zaiku

Mingei hin
(folk arts)

Handcrafted signs

Gift-giving is an important part of Japanese culture. Traditionally, gifts that are often elaborate and extravagant by Western standards are given on various occasions: births, passing school entrance examinations, graduations, New Year's (for children), weddings and funerals. When a gift is received, the custom is for the receiver to reciprocate with an equally extravagant gift on the next appropriate occasion.

Other major social occasions are:

Chuugen and Seibo

These occasions are shortly before **Obon** in the summer and at the year's end, when subordinates give gifts to their superiors, companies give to their clients, and sometimes stores give to their major customers. The summer gift is called **o-chuugen**, and the winter gift, **o-seibo**.

Senbetsu

A person leaving on an extended trip receives **o-senbetsu**, money from relatives, friends and co-workers. In turn, the person will reciprocate by bringing them **o-miyage** (souvenir gifts).

Miyage

Souvenirs brought back from a trip usually consist of local specialities: foodstuff, folk arts and other gift items. When travelling in Japan, you will see many **miyage** stores in and around the stations.

Tsukaimono

The Japanese almost never visit someone's home without taking a small gift, called **o-tsukaimono**. It can be fruit, sweets, flowers, etc., which are easily purchased at a store near the station of your destination.

By custom, the Japanese do not open gifts in front of the giver. This is gradually changing, and a person might say, "I'll open it—American style", then carefully remove the wrapping without tearing it. But don't be offended if the gift you brought is placed on a table without being opened. It is deeply appreciated.

Answers

Practise what you have learned

Exercise **1**	(a) buruu (b) guriin (c) kiiro (d) pinku
Exercise **2**	(a) blue (b) too small (c) L-size (d) yes
Exercise **5**	(a) koshi/ashi (back and legs) (b) kinoo kara (from yesterday) (c) takusan aruita kara, (because she/he walked a lot) (d) Hai, chintsuu no kusuri, (yes, pain reducing pills.)
Exercise **7**	(a) Visa Card (b) D.C. (Diners Club) (c) Master Card (d) J.C.B.
Exercise **8**	(a) a plate (b) She wants it delivered. (c) J.C.B. (d) No.
Exercise **11**	(a) ham sandwiches (b) roast beef sandwiches (c) tomato (d) lettuce (e) celery (f) oranges (g) Japanese tea (h) beer
Exercise **12**	(a) ham and roast beef (b) potato salad and vegetable salad (c) tea and wine

9 MAKING TRAVEL ARRANGEMENTS

You will learn

- how to make long distance travel arrangements
- how to get to Akihabara using public transportation
- how to buy long distance tickets
- how to make a mini-vacation plan at a travel agency
- about staying at a Japanese-style inn

Before you begin

If you can, make your own travel arrangements, as you will have far more independence and flexibility on your trip. It is also much easier when you have to change your plans because of some unforeseen reason. Travel arrangements involve times and dates, so you may find it helpful to revise Unit 4 before going on with this unit.

Study guide

Dialogue 1 + Practise what you have learned
Dialogue 2 + Practise what you have learned
Dialogue 3 + Practise what you have learned
Dialogue 4 + Practise what you have learned
Learn: the Key words and phrases
Study: the Grammar section
Read: Read and understand
Read: Did you know? and learn the new phrases

Dialogues

1 *I hear you went to Kyoto*

Takada	Kyōto e irashitan desu tte.
Mushakōji	E, sen-shuu.
Takada	Doo deshita, o-tenki wa?
Mushakōji	Ichinichi wa harete itan da kedo, ichinichi ame datta no yo.
Takada	Kono goro Shinkan-sen ga konde irun desu tte, ne.
Mushakōji	Soo na no. Moo o-yasumi-chuu dakara, moo taihen!
Takada	Nan-ji goro no de?
Mushakōji	Ano ne, juuyo-ji-hatsu Tōkyō-eki hatsu no Hikari 234-goo de itta no yo.
Takada	A so. Kippu wa doo yatte, te ni irete...?
Mushakōji	Mae motte Midori no Madoguchi de yoyaku shite, soshite kippu o te ni ireta kara, daijoobu datta.

- **ame** rain
- **kono goro** lately
- **Shinkan-sen** Shinkan Line ("Bullet" train)
- **o-yasumi-chuu** during the holidays
- **taihen** awful/terrible

juuyo-ji-hatsu 2:00 (1400 hours) train (**-hatsu** = departure)
Hikari express trains on the Shinkansen (Line)
234-goo Number 234

- **Midori no Madoguchi** Green Window (Information Service)
- **yoyaku** reservation

soshite and/and so

Kyōto e irashitan desu tte. They said you went to Kyoto. **Irashita** (**n desu**) is a more casual form of the exalted verb **irasshaimashita**, which can mean either "you went" or "you came". **Tte** is a casual way of reporting speech from some other source.

Doo deshita (**ka**)? How was it?

Ichinichi wa harete itan da kedo, ichinichi wa ame datta no yo. One day it was clear; one day it rained. (*inf.*) **No yo** at the end of a sentence is typical of feminine speech.

Kono goro Shinkan-sen ga konde irun desu tte. I hear the Bullet train is crowded lately. (*eq.* **Shinkan-sen ga konde imasu.**)

Soo na no. That's right. (*f./inf.*) (*eq.* **Soo desu.**)

Moo o-yasumi-chuu dakara, moo taihen! Since it's already the middle of the holidays, it's awful! **Moo** is often used as a way of emphasizing a thought, rather than in its usual meaning of "already". **Dakara** (*inf.*) = **desu kara.**

Nan-ji goro no de? About what time (did you leave)? (*lit.* On about what time one/train?)

Juuyo-ji-hatsu no Hikari 234-goo de itta no yo. I went on the 2:00 (1400 hours) Hikari No. 234. (*inf.*) (*eq.* ____ **de ikimashita.**) The Hikari trains on the Shinkan Line are a little faster than some of the other types of train, because they make fewer stops, comparable to the difference between "regular" and "express" trains.

Kippu wa doo yatte, te ni irete... How did you get your ticket? (*lit.* As for the ticket, how did you do it, getting it into your hands, and...?) The use of the **-te** form at the end of a sentence makes it incomplete, a casual way of softening it, allowing the listener to assume whatever may follow.

Midori no Madoguchi de yoyaku shite... I made a reservation at the Information Service window, and...See Grammar section for this use of the marker **de**.

Soshite kippu o te ni ireta kara, daijoobu datta. And since I got the ticket into my hands, it was okay. (*inf.*) (*eq.* **...iremashita kara, daijoobu deshita.**)

Practise what you have learned

1 Match the English words with the Japanese. (Answers p. 134)

(a) Midori no Madoguchi ____	**(1)** "Bullet Train"
(b) yoyaku ____	**(2)** 2:00 (1400 hrs.) departure
(c) Shinkan-sen ____	**(3)** ticket
(d) nihyaku-sanjuu-yon-goo ____	**(4)** Green Window
(e) juuyoji-hatsu ____	**(5)** No. 234
(f) kippu ____	**(6)** reservation

2 Listen to the recording and fill in the blanks below. (Answers on p. 134)

(a) Where is he going? ____________________

(b) When is he leaving? ____________________

(c) **Shuppatsu jikan** (departure time) ____________________

(d) The train name and number are ____________________

(e) **Kippu wa doko de kaimashita ka?** ____________________

3 Suppose you wish to go to Kyoto on Wednesday of next week (**raishuu no Suiyoobi**). Your preferred time of departure is around 10:00, so that you can go sightseeing after you get there. Go to the Midori no Madoguchi and see if you can reserve a seat. Ask how much it is. First think about this scenario, then work through the exercise with Aoki-san's help on the recording.

____

____

____

Dialogues

2 *How do I get to Akihabara?*

Takada Ano ne, chotto...Akihabara made ikitain da kedo, koko kara wa nan de iku no ga ichiban ii kashira?

Mushakōji Soo ne...ima michi ga konde iru kara, takushii wa takusan jikan ga kakatchau wa. Dakara, yappari Jei-Aaru (J.R.) ga hayai deshoo.

Takada Soo. Ja, Jei-Aaru de koko kara Shinjuku ni dete, Chūō-sen?

Mushakōji Yamanote-sen de massugu ikeru wa yo. A, watakushi wa itsumo densha shika tsukawanai wa yo. Takushii wa takai shi, ne... Akihabara de nani o o-kai ni naru no?

Takada Raji-kase kaoo to omotte...iroiro mitain da keredo...

Mushakōji Kono goro wa Shinjuku ya Shibuya ni mo takusan yasu-uri-shoppu ga aru no yo.

Takada Namae shitte iru?

Mushakōji Yodobashi Kamera tte yuun da keredo, denki-seihin mo utte iru no yo.

Takada A, sore Shinjuku deshoo?

Mushakōji Soo yo.

Akihabara, Shinjuku, Shibuya sections of Tokyo
nan de by means of what
michi roads
▶ **Jei-Aaru** J.R. (Japan Railway)
massugu straight/directly
itsumo always
▶ **densha** electric train
shika except for
raji-kase radio-cassette player (*Eng.*)
▶ **yasu-uri-shoppu** discount store (*lit.* cheap-sell-shop)
denki-seihin electrical appliances/equipment
utte iru selling

Nan de iku no ga ichiban ii desu ka? What's the best way to go? (by what kind of transportation?) (*eq.* **Nan de ikeba iin desu ka?**)

Takushii wa takusan jikan ga kakatchau wa. A taxi will take a lot of time. (*f./inf.*) **Kakatchau** is an informal abbreviation of **kakatte shimau**. Adding **shimau** to the **te-** form of a verb is a way of emphasizing the finality or irrevocable nature of the action. **Wa** at the end of the sentence is typical of feminine speech.

J.R. de koko kara Shinjuku ni dete, Chūō-sen (desu ka)? By J.R. from here, getting off at Shinjuku, (is that) the Chuo Line?

Yamanote-sen de massugu ikeru wa yo. You can go directly (there) on the Yamanote Line. (*f./inf.*) (*eq.* **...massugu ikemasu.**)

Watakushi wa itsumo densha shika tsukawanai wa yo. I never use anything but the trains. (*f./inf.*) (*lit.* I always do not use [anything] but the trains.) (*eq.* **...densha shika tsukaimasen.**)

Takushii wa takai shi, ne... Taxis are expensive (etc.), aren't they? **Shi** here implies that there may be other reasons not to take the taxi.

▶ **Akihabara de nani o o-kai ni naru no?** What are you going to buy in Akihabara? (*f.*) (*eq.* **...nani o kaimasu ka?**)

____ **kaoo to omotte...** I'm thinking about buying ____ .

Shinjuku ya Shibuya ni mo... In Shinjuku and Shibuya and places like that...See the Grammar section for more on the marker **ya**.

▶ **Namae shitte iru?** Do you know the name? (*inf.*) (*eq.* **Namae shitte imasu ka?**)

Practise what you have learned

4 The four sentences below all mean "I want to ____ ". Write the number of the corresponding English sentence in the space given after each Japanese sentence. (Answers p. 134)

(a) Kaimono ni ikitain desu. ____ **(1)** I want to drink some water.

(b) Kippu o kaitain desu. ____ **(2)** I want to walk a little.

(c) Chotto arukitain desu. ____ **(3)** I want to go shopping.

(d) Mizu o nomitain desu. ____ **(4)** I want to buy a ticket.

5 Listen to the recording and answer the questions below. (Answers p. 134)

(a) Where did they decide to go? ____________________

(b) What station will they leave from? ____________________

(c) What train line will they take? ____________________

(d) What time will they leave? ____________________

6 Tell your Japanese friend that you want to go to Akihabara. (You heard that Akihabara is the place to shop for sound systems, electronic equipment, cameras, etc.) Before you start working with the recording, think about how you might want to get your point across, then listen to the recording. Of course, Aoki-san will give you assistance.

(a) I want to go to Akihabara. How can I get there?

____

(b) Which is better—cab or underground railway?

____

(c) Is it all right to go alone (**hitori de**)?

____

(d) How long will it take to get there?

____

Dialogues

3 *At the Travel Agency*

Traveller Gomen kudasai.
Agent Irasshaimase.
Traveller Ano, watashi chotto Kyōtō no hoo ni itte mitai to omotte irun desu kedo...Shinkan-sen no kippu wa atsukatte irasshaimasu ka?
Agent E, ano...nan-nichi-ka saki no deshitara, go-yooi dekimasu ga...
Traveller A, soo desu ka. Ano, Kyōtō ni iku toki ni wa, yappari jiyuu-seki ja nai hoo ga ii deshoo ka?
Agent Soo desu ne. Ano, notte, ni-jikan han gurai kakarimasu kara, ee, shitei torareta hoo ga yoroshii to omoimasu.
Tada, Tōkyō-eki ni itte, sanjuppun ijoo narabu kakugo de areba, jiyuu-seki demo, mazu suwareru to omoimasu.
Traveller Hai, doomo.

Gomen kudasai. Hello. Is anyone there? (Used when entering small shops, etc.)
nannichi-ka saki a few days in advance (*eq.* **nannichi-ka mae**)
yooi preparation/arrangement
jiyuu-seki unreserved seating (*lit.* free/open seat)
-han half (an hour)/the half hour
shitei-seki reserved seat
yoroshii good (*eq.* **ii**)
tada only/however
ijoo more than/higher than
kakugo de areba if (you) are willing to

Kyōtō no hoo ni itte mitai to omotte irun desu. I think I would like to go and see the Kyoto area. (*eq.* **...itte mitai to omoimasu.**) See the Grammar section for more on **itte mitai**.

Kyōtō ni iku toki ni wa... When you go to Kyoto... Following a verb with **toki** (a "point in time") or **toki ni** is a way of telling when something happens.

Jiyuu-seki ja nai hoo ga ii deshoo ka? Shouldn't I buy a reserved seat? (*lit.* Isn't it better not to sit in the unreserved seating?)

Notte, ni-jikan han gurai kakarimasu kara... Since it takes about 2½ hours from the time you board... (*lit.* Boarding, it takes about 2½ hours, so...)

Shitei torareta hoo ga yoroshii to omoimasu. I think it is best to have made a reservation. (*pol.*)

Tōkyō eki ni itte, sanjuppun ijoo narabu kakugo de areba... If you are willing/prepared to go to Tokyo station and stand in line for more than 30 minutes...

Jiyuu-seki demo, mazu suwareru to omoimasu. I think you will be able to get a seat even in the unreserved seating section.

Practise what you have learned

7

Find the English phrase to match the Japanese phrases below. (Answers p. 134)

(a) Ni-jikan han kakarimasu.	____	**(1)**	reserved seat
(b) shitei-seki	____	**(2)**	It takes about 2½ hrs.
(c) Suwaremasu ka?	____	**(3)**	unreserved seating
(d) jiyuu-seki	____	**(4)**	10:18 departure time
(e) juu-ji juuhappun hatsu	____	**(5)**	Will I be able to sit down?

8

Listen to the recording and write down the essentials of the conversation. (Answers p. 134)

(a) Where does Kanada-san wish to go? ____________

(b) What days of the week? ____________

(c) About what time? ____________

(d) Is she going on the **Guriin-sha** (1st class?) ____________

(e) Is she going to buy a reserved or unreserved ticket? ____________

9

Some Japanese friends told you that the economical way of travelling is to buy **jiyuu-seki** and ride the **Kin'en-sha** (No-smoking car), which usually has seats available. However, you have to be willing to walk to the end of the platform to get to it. Go to the Midori no Madoguchi and buy tickets to Hiroshima. First go over some of the useful phrases listed below, and then listen to the recording.

(a) I want to go to Hiroshima. ____________

(b) I want to go on Wednesday or Thursday. ____________

____

(c) Well then, I've decided on that. Give me two tickets, please. (Use the counter for flat objects.)

____

(d) How much is it? ____________

Dialogues

4 *I want to go to a hot spring*

Nakagawa Konnichiwa.
Agent Irasshaimase.
Nakagawa Ni-haku-mikka gurai de onsen ni ikitain desu keredomo,...Atami toka Hakone toka...
Agent Ano, heijitsu ni o-tomari desu yo, ne?
Nakagawa Soo desu.
Agent Nimei-sama?
Nakagawa Hai.
Agent Soo desu, ne...Ano...ma, yasui tokoro de, ichiman go-rokusen-en kara, o-takai tokoro desu to, yonman-goman made go-yooi dekiru to omoimasu.
Nakagawa Daitai chuugurai no tokoro de ikahodo gurai deshoo?
Agent Go-yosan-teki ni niman-en kara niman-ni-sanzen-en mite itadaku to go-tehai dekiru to omoun desu ga...
Nakagawa Zuibun takai desu, ne.
Agent A, ano...mochiron, shokuji-tsuki ryookin desu n'de...

ni-haku-mikka two nights and three days
▸ **onsen** hot springs
Atami, Hakone areas famous for their hot springs
▸ **heijitsu** weekday
nimei-sama two people (*pol.*) (*eq.* **o-futari**)
▸ **yasui** cheap/inexpensive
daitai approximately
▸ **chuugurai** about the middle
▸ **ikahodo gurai** about how much? (*pol.*) (*eq.* **ikura gurai**)
go-yosan-teki ni within your budget
go-tehai arrangements (*pol.*)
zuibun quite/very
mochiron of course
▸ **shokuji-tsuki** meals included

▸ **Yasui tokoro de, ichiman go-rokusen-en kara...** At an inexpensive place, (it will be) from 15–16,000 yen...

▸ **O-takai tokoro desu to, yonman-goman made...** If it's an expensive place, up to 40–50,000 (yen)...

Go-yooi dekiru to omoimasu. I believe we can provide (something). (*pol.*) (See the Grammar section.)

Daitai chuugurai no tokoro de ikahodo gurai deshoo? About how much would it be at about a mid-range place? (*pol.*)

Go-yosan-teki ni ____ -en kara ____ -en mite itadaku to... If we have you look at (a place in the range of) from ____ yen to ____ yen, according to your budget...

Mochiron, shokuji-tsuki ryookin desu n'de... Of course, since the fee includes meals... (*eq.* **desu node**)

Practise what you have learned

10 Select the appropriate matching phrases. (Answers p. 134)

(a) yasui tokoro	____	(1)	inexpensive place
(b) shokuji-tsuki	____	(2)	expensive place
(c) chuu-gurai no tokoro	____	(3)	approximately
(d) daitai	____	(4)	budget
(e) yosan	____	(5)	one night, two days
(f) ippaku-futsuka	____	(6)	mid-range place
(g) takai tokoro	____	(7)	meals included

11 Two people are making plans to go to a hot spring. Listen to the recording and provide the information below. (Answers p. 134)

(a) When do they plan to go? ______________________

(b) How long will they be gone? ______________________

(c) About how much do they expect an inn will cost? ______________

12 It is your turn to stop at a travel agency to make arrangements for an overnight trip to a hot spring in Atami. Listen to the recording and have Miura-san help you.

(a) You wish to go to a hot spring in Atami. ______________________

(b) Find out how much it will be. ______________________

(c) Ask if the meals are included. ______________________

(d) Find out when **chekku-in** and **chekku-out** times are. ____________

(e) Make sure that the agency will get you the train ticket, as well.

(____________ **mo onegai dekimasu, ne.**)

Owakudani hot springs in Hakone

Key words and phrases

kono goro	lately
(o-yasumi)-chuu	during (the holidays)
(juuyoji)-hatsu	(2:00) train
(234)-goo	number 234 (train)
soshite	and/and so
Midori no Madoguchi	Green Window (Information Service)
shitei-seki	reserved seating
jiyuu-seki	unreserved seating
shokuji-tsuki	meals included
Mochiron.	Of course.
Gomen kudasai.	Hello. Is anyone there? (when entering a small shop)
Itsumo densha shika tsukaimasen.	I never use anything but trains.
Itsumo densha dake tsukaimasu.	I always use only trains.
(Akihabara) de nani o kaimasu ka?	What will you buy at (Akihabara)?
(Suwareru) to omoimasu.	I think (you'll be able to get a seat).
Go-yooi dekiru to omoimasu.	I think we can make arrangements for you.
Kyōto ni itte mitai to omoimasu.	I think I want to go and see Kyoto.
Nan de (iku no ga) ichiban ii desu ka?	What is the best way (to go)?
Densha ga ichiban hayai deshoo.	By train is probably fastest.
Basu ga ichiban yasui deshoo.	By bus is probably cheapest.

Grammar

shika/dake

You have learned in a previous unit that **dake** after a word means "only ____ ". **Shika** after a word means "except for ____ " *or* "(anything) but ____ ". These two phrases can be used to express the same concept in different ways:

Densha dake tsukaimasu. I use only trains.
Densha shika tsukaimasen. I don't use anything but trains.

Washoku dake tabemashita. I ate only Japanese food.
Washoku shika tabemasen deshita.
I didn't eat anything but Japanese food.

Note that **dake** is followed by a *positive* verb, and **shika** is followed by a *negative* one.

Grammar markers

ya "and/etc." This marker is similar to **to** in that it means "and" when placed after each word in a list. However, **ya** indicates that there may be other things in the list that are not spoken. It compares with "etc." *or* "and things like that". Here are some examples comparing **ya** with **to**:

Burausu to sukaato kaimashita.
I bought a blouse and a skirt (and that's all).

Burausu ya sukaato kaimashita.
I bought a blouse and a skirt (and other things).

Bisa-kaado to Masuta-kaado wa atsukatte orimasu.
We handle Visa and Master Card (only).

Bisa-kaado ya Masuta-kaado wa atsukatte orimasu.
We handle (cards like) Visa and Master Card.

de "at"/"in" Another use for this marker is to indicate where an action takes place, as in **Midori no Madoguchi de yoyaku shimashita** ("I made a reservation at the Green Window"). Compare this with **ni**, which indicates where something is (**imasu/arimasu**), stays (**tomarimasu**) or is living (**sunde imasu**). Study the following examples:

Resutoran de tabemashita. I ate at the restaurant.
Resutoran ni imashita. I was in the restaurant.
Akihabara de kaimono shimashita. I shopped in Akihabara.
Akihabara ni sunde imashita. I was living in Akihabara.

-te miru

The **te-**form of a verb indicates that another verb follows somewhere in the sentence. In a series of verbs, "and" can be included in the translation.

If the verb **miru** (to see) follows the **-te** form, it can simply mean "and see" (as in **Itte mimasu**, "I will go and see") or it can indicate a "try-and-see" attitude. Study the following example sentences.

Washoku o tabete mimashita.
I tried Japanese food. (I "ate and saw" how I liked it.)

O-cha o nonde mitain desu.
I want to try Japanese tea. (I want to "drink it and see" what it tastes like.)

to omou

This verb ending means "I think (that)..." Study the following examples:

Ashita Kyōto ni itte miru to omoimasu.
Tomorrow I think he will go and see Kyoto.

Takada-san wa sengetsu kitan da to omoimasu.
I think Mr. Takada came last month.

Kyasshu ni shitai to omoun desu. I think I'd like to make it cash.

You should be aware that the use of **to omou** by the Japanese does not necessarily indicate uncertainty about something, but is often used to make the sentence less abrupt.

Read and understand

1. 各駅停車
   Stop every station
2. 特急
   Super Express
3. 急行
   Express
4. 準急
   Limited Express
5. 回送
   Out of Service
6. 運賃
   Fares
7. 往復
   Round trip
8. 片道
   One way
9. 両替機
   Change machine
10. タクシー乗り場
    Taxi stand
11. 夜間割増料金
    Off hour extra charge
12. 空車
    For hire

Did you know?

Japanese Inns–Ryokan

Staying at a Japanese inn (**ryokan**) for a couple of nights is a unique experience that you will enjoy. **Ryokan** are still constructed in the traditional architectural style, and the service will always be superb. Most **ryokan** in tourist areas are expensive, and each one has its speciality: a scenic view, hot springs, special cuisine, special decor, etc. Here are some pointers that might help minimize the surprises you will probably encounter in the traditional lodging style.

Shoes are removed as you enter the **ryokan**, just as in private homes. There will be slippers for you at the entrance. Slippers are worn on any wood or tile floor. Be sure to leave them at the doorway before entering any **tatami** (straw-mat) room.

After you are settled in your room, the maid will bring tea and a bag for any valuables you wish to keep in the vault. If your room has a mini-safe, that's the best place to store your valuables.

Bath (**o-furo**) facilities are "common bath" or "family style". The maid will inform you of bath hours: **O-furo no jikan wa ____ ji kara ____ ji made ni natte orimasu**. If you need to ask, then say: **O-furo wa nan-ji kara nan-ji made desu ka?**

Elaborate Japanese-style breakfasts and evening meals are usually served in your room. The maid will ask, **"O-shokuji** (meal) **wa nan-ji ni itashimashoo ka?"** To which you can reply: **"Asa** (morning) **wa ____ -ji ni, onegai shimasu**. **Ban** (evening) **wa ____ ji ni, onegai shimasu".** Meal hours are usually about 6:30 to 9:00 a.m. for breakfast and 6:00 to 7:00 p.m. for dinner. Alcoholic drinks and beverages (**nomimono**) other than tea are not included in the room charge, so you should give your preference to the maid in advance. You can also buy what you need from your room refrigerator or from the vending machines in the building. Remember to stay with Japanese brands if possible, rather than buying imported brands, as import duties are exorbitant.

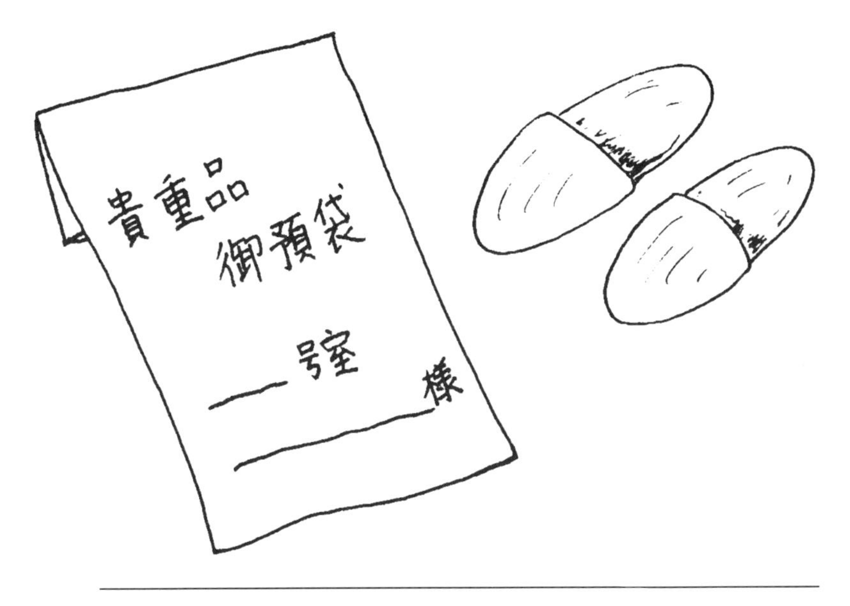

In your room there may be a small alcove (**tokonoma**)—an area that is slightly raised and has a hanging scroll and flower arrangement. A seat directly in front of the **tokonoma** is the best seat in the room. If you are having guests, save the choice seats for them. If you should want to examine the scroll closely, remember not to step onto the **tokonoma.** Also, you *must not sit* on the **tokonoma,** even to stretch your legs.

The **ryokan** provides: 1) a cotton kimono (**yukata**) and sash (**obi**) to relax in or to sleep in. When wearing a **yukata,** be discreet and keep the front from flapping open. Fold in the right side first and then the left. (The reverse is done for the dead only.) If you should want a **yukata** for a souvenir, you can buy one at a nearby shopping area. 2) toothpaste/ toothbrush, and soap. 3) a face towel (**tenugui**), which may double as a bath towel. (You need to wring out the excess water repeatedly as you dry yourself with it.) At the bath, you will find lotions, creams, hairspray and other toiletries, as well as a hair dryer for your use.

Father and daughter in yukatas provided by a ryokan

Answers

Practise what you have learned

Exercise 1	(a) 4 (b) 6 (c) 1 (d) 5 (e) 2 (f) 3
Exercise 2	(a) Kyōto (b) the day after tomorrow (c) 13:05 (d) Hikari 250 (e) Midori no Madoguchi
Exercise 4	(a) 3 (b) 4 (c) 2 (d) 1
Exercise 5	(a) to Nikkō (b) Ueno station (c) Jōban Line (d) 9:30
Exercise 7	(a) 2 (b) 1 (c) 5 (d) 3 (e) 4
Exercise 8	(a) Atami (b) Thursday–Saturday (c) about 10:00 (d) no (e) unreserved ticket
Exercise 10	(a) 1 (b) 7 (c) 6 (d) 3 (e) 4 (f) 5 (g) 2
Exercise 11	(a) May (b) 2 days—Tuesday and Wednesday (c) ¥30,000

10 FOOD AND DRINK

You will learn

- phrases used when offering and accepting food
- how to place an order by phone
- how to choose a dish from a restaurant food display
- about Japanese restaurants
- some tips on Japanese table manners

Before you begin

Revise Unit 3 for restaurant phrases.

Study guide

Dialogue 1 + Practise what you have learned
Dialogue 2 + Practise what you have learned
Dialogue 3 + Practise what you have learned
Dialogue 4 + Practise what you have learned
Study: the Key words and phrases
Study: the Grammar section
Read: Did you know?

Dialogues

1 *At a friend's house*

Uchida O-koocha, doozo.
Takarabe A, doomo...
Uchida O-satoo to miruku o-ire ni naru?
Takarabe Ja, miruku dake itadaku wa.
Uchida Keiki mo arun da kedo...
Takarabe Moo o-kamai naku. Sonna ni shinpai nasaranaide...

- **koocha** black tea
- **satoo** sugar
- **miruku** milk (*Eng.*)
- **O-kamai naku.** Don't trouble yourself.
- **shinpai** worry

O-satoo to miruku o-ire ni naru? Do you take sugar and milk? (*pol.*) (*lit.* Do you put in sugar and milk?) It is common among women to combine informal verb forms with more polite structures. In this sentence the exalted form **o-** ____ **ni narimasu** is combined with the informal use of the dictionary form (**naru**).

Miruku dake itadaku wa. I'll have just milk. (*f./inf.*) (*eq.* **Miruku dake itadakimasu.**) The use of **wa** at the end of a sentence and the frequent use of the honorific prefix **o-** (as in **o-satoo** and **o-koocha**) are typical of feminine speech. **Itadakimasu** is a standard expression used before eating a meal and literally means "I will partake".

Moo o-kamai naku. Please don't trouble yourself further. This is a standard phrase used to decline more food offered by a host.

Sonna ni shinpai nasaranaide (kudasai). Please don't worry so much. (*f./pol.*) This is also a standard phrase. (*eq.* **Shinpai shinaide kudasai.**)

Practise what you have learned

1 Listen to the dialogue until you can say it along with the recording confidently. Then study the notes, paying particular attention to the "standard" phrases presented. Select appropriate phrases to be used on different occasions as follows. (Answers p. 148)

(a) What do you say before you partake of food offered to you?

____

(b) What do you say to decline the host's offer to replenish your plate?

____

(c) How do you tell the host not to worry so much?

____

2 Next on the recording is a dialogue consisting mostly of set phrases such as those you will hear when invited to a meal. A good host coaxes a great deal and sometimes makes standard comments like, "Perhaps this sort of food doesn't suit your taste". Listen to these phrases on the recording. There will be opportunity for you to practise, as well.

Hostess **Sa, doozo. Nani mo arimasen ga...** Go right ahead. It's nothing, but...
Guest **A, oishi-soo desu, ne!** It looks delicious! (A phrase used before starting the meal. Wait for the second nudging by the hostess.)
Hostess **Sa, doozo. Enryo shinaide!** Please, go ahead. Don't hesitate.
Guest **Ja, itadakimasu.** *Lit.*, I will partake. This is a standard phrase spoken before eating a meal.
Totemo oishii desu. It's very good.
Hostess **Sa, motto, doozo, doozo ikaga desu ka?** Have some more, please!
Guest **Iie, moo kekkoo desu.** No, I have had enough.
Go-chisoo-sama deshita. Thank you for the meal. (A standard phrase to indicate that the meal is finished.)
Hontoo ni oishikatta desu. It was really delicious.
Hostess **Soo desu ka? Nanimo nakute...** Really? It wasn't anything...

3 Instead of inviting someone home for dinner, the Japanese often prefer to entertain guests at a restaurant. Polite mealtime phrases are the same as the ones used at someone's home. Tanabe-san will help you be a gracious guest. Listen to the recording and follow Aoki-san's direction.

Dialogues

2 *Calling room service*

Room service	Ruumu-saabisu de gozaimasu.
Hotel guest	Moshi moshi, ruumu-saabisu onegai shitain desu ga...
Room service	Hai, doozo.
Guest	Ee to desu ne, koohii o sannin-bun,...
Room service	Koohii o sannin-mae.
Guest	Sore kara, ano, fingaa sandoitchi ka nanika arimasu ka?
Room service	Osore irimasu ga, sandoitchi no hoo wa, juuichi-ji han kara to natte orimashite...
Guest	A, soo desu ka.
Room service	Tadaima, chooshoku-nomi no menyuu ni natte orimasu.
Guest	Hahaa...nanika karui tabemono wa gozaimasen ka?
Room service	Karui tabemono to iimasu to, toosuto desu toka...
Guest	Jaa ne, ano...koohii dake, onegai shimasu.

Moshi moshi Hello. (on the telephone)
sannin-bun portions for three people (*eq.* **sannin-mae**)
Osore irimasu ga,... I'm sorrry, but...
tadaima just now/at this moment (*eq.* **ima**)
chooshoku breakfast
-nomi only (*pol.*) (*eq.* **dake**)
karui tabemono light food

koohii o sannin-bun/sannin-mae coffee for three people. The use of **-bun** is a little less formal than **-mae**.

(**fingaa sandoitchi**) **ka nanika** (finger sandwiches) or something like that.

11:30 kara to natte orimasu. It is from 11:30. (*pol.*) (*eq.* **11:30 kara desu.**)

chooshoku-nomi no menyuu menu for breakfast only (*pol.*)

Hahaa... (*m.*) Mmm... (a sound made while pondering)

Nanika karui tabemono to iimasu to... If you're talking about some kind of light food...

Practise what you have learned

4 Complete the following sentences, using the words listed on the right. (Answers p. 148)

(a)	Koohii o ____________ onegai shimasu.	**(1)**	sannin-bun
(b)	Ee to, sore kara ____________ futari-mae.	**(2)**	nan desu
(c)	Chooshoku no menyuu wa ____________ ka?	**(3)**	toosuto

5 Listen to the recording and find out what Tanabe-san is ordering. (Answers p. 148) New additional words you will hear are:

kudamono	fruit
meron	melon (*Eng.*)
tomato juusu	tomato juice (*Eng.*)
hamu-eggu	ham and eggs (*Eng.*)
beekon	bacon (*Eng.*)

(a) **nomimono** ________________________________

(b) **chooshoku** ________________________________

(c) **kudamono/juusu** ____________________________

6 With Miura-san's help, call Room Service. Your room number is 555. Order three finger sandwiches, coffee for two and tea for one. Ask how long it will take. Close your order with, **Ja, onegai shimasu.**

____

____

____

Suginoi Hotel in Beppu

Dialogues

3 *Let's have something to eat*

Miki Ne, onaka suita, ne. (Soo ne.) Nanika tabeyoo ka?
Shōda Un. Moo, ichi-ji da mono, ne.
Miki Soo da ne. Ja, nani-ryoori ga ii ka na?
Shōda Un, watashi...kyoo wa, washoku ga tabetai, na.
Miki Washoku ka. Kono mise ka na?
Shōda Soo ne. Kono mise oishi-soo ja nai? (Un.) Nani ni suru?
Miki Soo da ne. Ja, boku wa hidari kara ni-ban-me no tsukimi soba ni suru.
Shōda A, ii wa ne. Ja, watashi wa asoko no tanuki-udon ni shiyoo.

- **nani-ryoori** what kind of cooking?
  mise store/shop
- **oishi-soo** looks delicious
  ni-ban-me the second one
- **soba** buckwheat noodles
  asoko over there
  tsukimi soba soba with raw egg
  tanuki udon udon in a particular style
- **udon** noodles

O-naka suita. I'm hungry. (*inf.*) (*eq.* **O-naka ga sukimashita.**)

Nanika tabeyoo ka? Shall we eat something? (*inf.*) (*eq.* **Nanika tabemashoo ka?**)

Un. Yeah./U-huh. (*inf.*) (*eq.* **Hai./Ee.**)

Moo ichi-ji da mono... It's already 1:00. (*inf.*) **Da mono** is a casual way of emphasizing a statement. (*eq.* **desu**)

Washoku ka. Japanese food, huh? (*inf.*) (*eq.* **Washoku desu ka?**)

Kono mise (**wa**) **oishi-soo ja nai?** This shop looks good (delicious), doesn't it?

Hidari kara ni-ban-me no tsukimi soba ni suru. I'll have the "tsukimi" noodles, second from the left. (*inf.*) (*eq.* **...ni shimasu.**)

Practise what you have learned

7 Match the phrases on the left with the corresponding casual phrases on the right. (Answers p. 148)

(a)	Kono mise doo desu ka?	____	**(1)**	Nani-ryoori ga ii ka na?
(b)	So desu, ne.	____	**(2)**	Oishi soo ja nai?
(c)	Nani-ryoori ga ii desu ka?	____	**(3)**	Soo da ne.
(d)	Onaka ga sukimashita, ne.	____	**(4)**	Kono mise doo ka na?
(e)	Oishi-soo desu, ne.	____	**(5)**	Onaka ga suita, ne.

8 You are standing in front of a restaurant where plastic food models are displayed. Each dish is identified in Japanese. Listen to the recording and follow Aoki-san's directions.

UE (top)

HIDARI (left) ← **MANNAKA** (centre) → **MIGI** (right)

SHITA (bottom)

(1) **supagetti** spaghetti

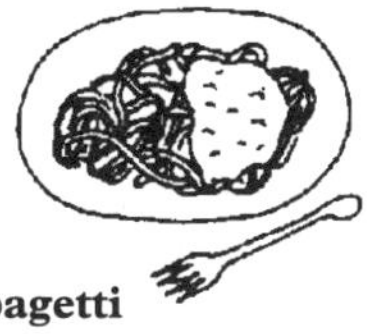

(2) **mikkusu sando** mixed sandwiches

(3) **piza** pizza

(4) **tonkatsu** pork cutlet

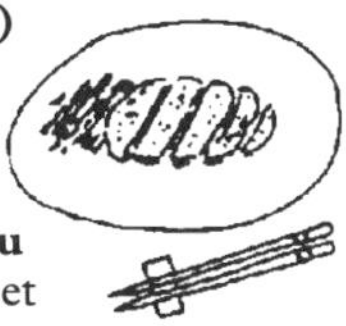

(5) **karee raisu** curried rice

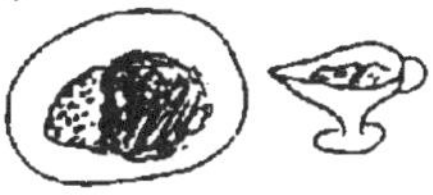

(6) **chashuumen** pork with noodles

(7) **remoneido** lemonade

(8) **aisu kuriimu** ice cream

(9) **koora** Cola

(10) **koocha** black tea

(11) **koohii** coffee

9 Work out how to ask a passer-by for the name of a bowl of noodles on the second shelf, on the right. Remember to start with a polite phrase, such as **Sumimasen**, and don't forget to express thanks afterward. Tanabe-san will assist you with this exercise. ____________________

Dialogues

4 *How about going to dinner?*

Yoshida Kon'ya shokuji demo ikimasen ka?
Miki Soo desu ne.
Yoshida Chuuka-ryoori nanka doo desu ka?
Miki Chuuka-ryoori wa kinoo tabechattan desu yo.
Yoshida Sore ja, nani-ryoori ni shimashoo ka?
Miki Un, Itaria-ryoori nanka doo desu ka?
Yoshida Soo desu ne. Ii mise shitte imasu ka?
Miki Ee, chotto...shitte irun desu.
Yoshida Koko kara chikai desu ka? Dekireba, chikai tokoro no hoo ga iin desu keredo...
Miki Chikai tokoro wa amari shiranain desu.
Yoshida A soo desu ka. Sore jaa, boku no shitte iru Supein-ryoori no mise, ikimashoo ka.

kon'ya this evening (*eq.* **konban**)
▸ **shokuji** dinner
▸ **Chuuka-ryoori** Chinese food
▸ **Itaria-ryoori** Italian food
amari hardly/(not) particularly (*eq.* **anmari**)
▸ **Supein-ryoori** Spanish food

▸ **Shokuji demo ikimasen ka?** Would you like to go to dinner? (*lit.* Won't you go to dinner?) The use of **demo** here implies "(dinner) or something", softening the invitation and leaving it open to suggestion.

Kinoo tabechattan desu yo. I ate (Chinese food) yesterday. **Yo** adds emphasis. The ending **-chattan desu** implies finality or irrevocability.

Ii mise shitte imasu ka? Do you know a good shop? The use of **mise** implies a casual meal at a small shop, as opposed to a larger restaurant (**resutoran**).

▸ **Koko kara chikai desu ka?** Is it near here? (*lit.* Is it near from here?)

▸ **Dekireba...** If it's possible.../ If we can...

Chikai tokoro amari shiranain desu. I don't really know (any) nearby places. (*eq.* **...amari shirimasen.**)

Boku no shitte iru Supein-ryoori no mise... A Spanish-cuisine shop that I know...The verb phrase **Boku no shitte iru** describes the noun phrase that follows it, **Supein-ryoori no mise**.

Practise what you have learned

10 Match the English and Japanese words. (Answers p. 148)

(a) washoku	____	**(1)**	Italian cuisine
(b) Supein-ryoori	____	**(2)**	Chinese cuisine
(c) yooshoku	____	**(3)**	Japanese cuisine
(d) Furansu-ryoori	____	**(4)**	Spanish cuisine
(e) Itaria-ryoori	____	**(5)**	French cuisine
(f) Chuuka ryoori	____	**(6)**	Western cuisine

11 Listen to the recording and find out what Miura-san and Tanabe-san decided to do. (Answers p. 148)

(a) When are they going? ______

(b) What time are they meeting? ______

(c) Where are they meeting? ______

(d) What kind of food will they have? ______

12 Listen to the recording and invite a Japanese friend to go out to dinner with you tomorrow night.

(a) How about dinner tomorrow night?______

(b) Chinese? I had that yesterday. ______

(c) How about Mexican or Italian cuisine?______

(d) Okay, let's make it Italian cuisine. ______

(e) What time and where shall we go? ______

New vocabulary: Mexico **Mekishiko**
Italy **Itaria**

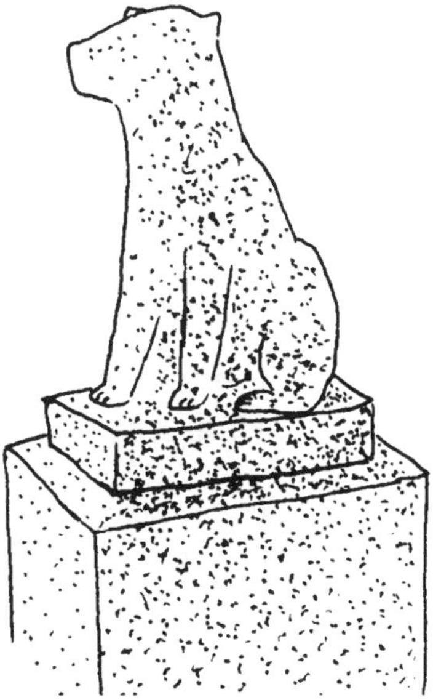

Hachikō, the famous stone dog at Shibuya Station

Key words and phrases

O-kamai naku.	Please don't trouble yourself.
Shinpai shinaide kudasai.	Please don't worry.
Itadakimasu.	I will partake. (spoken before a meal)
Go-chisoo-sama deshita.	Thank you for the food. (after a meal)
Oishi-soo desu.	It looks delicious.
Moshi moshi.	Hello. (on the telephone)
Osore irimasu ga...	I'm sorry, but...
O-naka suita./O-naka ga sukimashita.	I'm hungry.
Shokuji demo ikimasen ka?	Would you like to have dinner?
(**Chuuka-ryoori**) **nanka doo desu ka?**	How about (Chinese food) or something?
(**Fingaa sandoitchi**) **ka nanika doo desu ka?**	How about (finger sandwiches) or something?
(**Ii mise**) **shitte imasu ka?**	Do you know (a good shop)?
(**Supein-ryoori no mise**) **shitte imasu.**	I know (a Spanish cuisine place).
(**Chikai tokoro**) **amari shiranain desu.**	I don't really know (a place nearby).
(**Yasui tokoro**) **shirimasen ka?**	Do you know a cheap place?
(____ **nin**) **-bun/-mae**	portions (for ____ people)
(**ni**)**-ban-me**	the (second) one
chooshoku	breakfast
shokuji	dinner
tadaima	just now/at the moment
nani-ryoori	what kind of cooking/cuisine?
washoku	Japanese cuisine
yooshoku	Western cuisine
(**Chuuka-**)**ryoori**	(Chinese) cuisine

Grammar

Adjectives

In the Grammar section of Unit 1, it was explained that there are two kinds of adjectives—those that can be inflected and those that cannot.

Adjectives that can be inflected always end in the syllable **-i** (not just the sound /i/) in the dictionary form: **atarashii, samui, ookii, yasui,** etc.

Besides past/present and negative/positive inflections, these adjectives can take on other changes to express certain concepts. In this unit the phrase **Oishi-soo desu** ("It looks delicious".) was presented. Any inflectable adjective can be changed in this way to mean "It looks ____ " by dropping the final syllable (**-i**) of the dictionary form and adding **-soo** (**desu**).

Examples: **Samu-soo desu, ne?** It looks cold (outside), doesn't it?
Sono koohii wa tsumeta-soo desu. That coffee looks cold (to the touch).
Sono burausu wa taka-soo desu. That blouse looks expensive.
Ano kuruma wa atarashi-soo desu. That car looks new.

One exception to this rule is the adjective **ii** ("good"), which becomes **yosa-soo desu** ("It looks good").

desu/masu

The normal polite level of speech is sometimes called the **Desu/masu** form, because most verbs at this level end in some form of **desu** or **masu**.

The ending **-masu** indicates present tense, but it is also used to show future intention, as in **Ashita ikimasu** (I will go tomorrow). To show past tense, **-masu** is changed to **-mashita**. Negative and negative past endings are **-masen** and **-masen deshita**. The ending **-mashoo** means "Let's..." These endings are collectively called the **Masu** form.

ikimasu	"(I) go/will go".
ikimashita	"(I) went".
ikimasen	"(I) do not/will not go".
ikimasen deshita	"(I) did not go".
ikimashoo	"Let's go".

The corresponding endings for the verb **desu** are similar, with some interesting differences:

desu	"is"
deshita	"was"
dewa/ja arimasen	"is not"
dewa/ja arimasen deshita	"was not"
deshoo	"probably/possibly is"

Future intention is not normally expressed by **desu**; instead, the verb **naru** (**narimasu**) is usually used. Also, **deshoo** would never be used to mean "Let's be..."; again, **narimashoo** would take its place.

Did you know?

Noren

Noren is a traditional, half-size curtain that hangs in the entry way of shops that specialize in traditional goods and specific Japanese foods such as **sushi, soba, unagi,** etc.

The noren is usually split into two or three sections, making it easy to push one section aside with the back of the hand, rather than bending down to walk under it. Tall foreigners should be especially careful, as a noren may hide the actual height of the doorway, creating the danger of bumping one's head on the door frame.

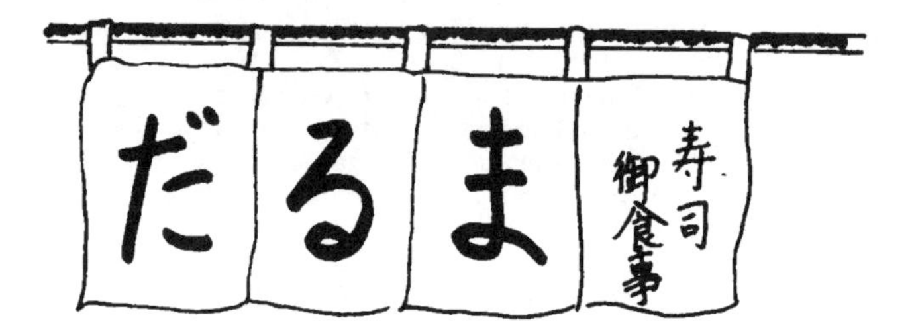

Restaurant procedure

With the exception of hotels and large restaurants, it is up to the customer to find his own table. During busy hours you may have to share a table with strangers. This system is called **aiseki**. If you should have to sit at an occupied table, simply say, **Shitsurei shimasu**, and sit down wherever there is an empty chair. You are not expected to strike up a conversation with strangers.

Drinking etiquette

When drinking with friends, Japanese etiquette requires that you do not pour your own drink but allow a friend to pour for you. If you are in the middle of eating, quickly put your fork or chopsticks down and lift your glass or cup, saying, **A, doomo**. Then you quickly fill your friend's glass. When you are drinking **sake** (often called **Nihon-shu**—Japanese wine), a tiny cup (**o-choko**) is used, and this pouring back and forth becomes almost an art.

As soon as you take a sip of your drink, your glass will be filled again. To signal that you have had enough, simply don't drink any more. If you have already emptied your **o-choko**, turn it up-side down to show you have reached your limit.

Table manners

Chopsticks (**o-hashi**) are the preferred eating utensil in Japan, especially when eating Japanese food. There are certain things that you should be careful not to do when using chopsticks:

- Never play with your chopsticks. Using them to drum on the table, gesturing or pointing with them is considered ill-mannered.
- Never leave your chopsticks sticking upright in your rice or other food. This is part of a funeral ritual and should not be done at the dinner table.
- Never pass food from your chopsticks to someone else's or vice-versa.
- Never use your own chopsticks to take food from a common bowl. Use the serving chopsticks that are provided. In some cases it may be acceptable to turn your own chopsticks around and use the clean ends to serve, but only as a last resort.
- Disposable wooden chopsticks (**waribashi**) that break apart are often used, particularly at less expensive eating places. People sometimes rub the two sticks together after breaking them apart, to remove any splinters. This is considered discourteous. Also questionable form is the practice of dipping the chopsticks into your water glass before eating with them, so that food doesn't stick to them. See illustrations for other "no nos".

You might notice that the Japanese use soy sauce (**shooyu**) more sparingly than foreigners tend to do. Using too much soy sauce tends to obscure the flavour of the food, rather than enhancing it as intended.

Also, the small dish of pickled vegetables (**tsukemono**) that you get with your food should be eaten towards the end of the meal.

Picking something else up

Gesturing...

Jabbing food

Pushing a dish

Sticking chopsticks in food

Examples of bad table manners

Answers

Practise what you have learned

Exercise **1**	(a) Itadakimasu. (b) Moo, o-kamai naku... (c) Shinpai shinaide kudasai.
Exercise **4**	(a) 1 (b) 3 (c) 2
Exercise **5**	(a) coffee/hot tea (b) ham and eggs, bacon and eggs, toast (c) tomato juice
Exercise **7**	(a) 4 (b) 3 (c) 1 (d) 5 (e) 2
Exercise **10**	(a) 3 (b) 4 (c) 6 (d) 5 (e) 1 (f) 2
Exercise **11**	(a) Saturday (b) 7:00 (c) front of the statue of Hachikoo (Shibuya) (d) Spanish cuisine

11 LIKES AND DISLIKES

You will learn

- to express likes and dislikes
- to describe a region/town/area
- to say what you enjoy doing
- the names of shrines, temples, universities you might want to visit in Kyōto
- something about religion as you get ready to visit Kyōto.

Study guide

Dialogue 1 + Practise what you have learned
Dialogue 2 + Practise what you have learned
Dialogue 3 + Practise what you have learned
Dialogue 4 + Practise what you have learned
Learn: the Key words and phrases
Study: the Grammar section
Read: Did you know?

Dialogues

1 *I love to travel*

Miki Ano...ryokoo ga shumi da tte kiitan desu kedomo...
Yoshida Soo desu, ne. Ryokoo wa suki desu.
Miki Doo iu yoo na kuni e ikaremashita ka?
Yoshida Toku ni Higashi Yōroppa ga suki nan de, Pōrando ya Hangarii ya Chekosurobakiya atari e itte kimashita.
Miki Dono kuni ga ichiban omoshirokatta desu ka?
Yoshida Soo desu, ne. Chekosurobakiya atari ga, machinami mo kirei de, tottemo ii desu ne. Toku ni, chikaku ni Puraha-joo to iu o-shiro ga atte, totemo soko wa kirei deshita.

shumi hobby, special interest
Suki desu. I like it.
Doo iu yoo na what kind of?
kuni country
toku ni especially
Higashi Yōroppa Eastern Europe
atari area/environs
omoshiroi interesting (**omoshirokatta** = was interesting)
machinami ambience of a town (as its "quaint appearance")
tottemo very (*eq.* **totemo**)
chikaku ni nearby (*eq.* **chikai**)
Puraha-joo Prague Castle
o-shiro castle

Ryokoo ga shumi da tte kiitan desu. I heard that travel is your hobby. (*eq.* **Ryokoo ga shumi da to kikimashita.**) The Japanese word **shumi** is a more casual concept than the English word "hobby", which indicates a more or less organized activity. Although the Japanese usually use "hobby" as a translation of **shumi**, a more accurate translation is "special interest".

Ryokoo wa (ga) suki desu. I like travelling. (*lit.* Travelling is liked.)

Doo iu yoo na kuni e ikaremashita ka? What kinds of countries have you travelled to? (*exal.*) (*eq.* **Donna kuni e ikimashita ka?**)

Toku ni ____ ga suki nan de(su). I especially like ____ . **de**, as used in this sentence in the dialogue, is the **te**-form of **desu**.

____ **ya** ____ **ya** ____ **atari** the area of ____ and ____ and ____ , etc.

____ **e itte kimashita.** *Lit.* I went to ____ and came (back). This form is used to indicate that it was a short trip, as opposed to a long-range stay.

Puraha-joo to iu o-shiro ga atte... There was a castle called Prague Castle, and...

Kirei deshita. It was pretty. Although the adjective **kirei** ends in the syllable **-i**, it is not an inflectable adjective, so the past tense must be indicated by the verb (**deshita**).

Practise what you have learned

1 Match the Japanese place names with their English counterparts. (Answers p. 162)

(a) Higashi Yōroppa	____	**(1)**	Hungary
(b) Hangarii	____	**(2)**	Czechoslovakia
(c) Pōrando	____	**(3)**	Eastern Europe
(d) Chekosurobakiya	____	**(4)**	Poland

2 Listen to the dialogue again and answer the following questions. (Answers p. 162)

(a) What does Yoshida-san like to do? ____________________

(b) How many countries did he visit? ____________________

(c) Which country did he like the best? ____________________

SALE

1. **kaimono** shopping
2. **shigoto** work 
3. **shashin** photos 
4. **ryokoo** travel 
5. **supootsu** sports 
6. **ryoori** cooking 
7. **hon** books 
8. **ongaku** music 

3 To tell someone what you like, use the pattern ____________ **ga suki desu**. To say what you don't like, use ____________ **ga kirai desu**.

Listen to the recording and familiarize yourself with these phrases. Then practise with Miura-san.

(I) like __________ .	__________ **ga suki desu.**
(I) like __________ very much. (I love it.)	__________ **ga dai-suki desu.**
I don't like __________ very much.	__________ **ga amari suki ja nain desu.**
(I) like __________ the most.	__________ **ga ichiban suki desu.**
(I) dislike __________ the most.	__________ **ga ichiban kirai desu.**
(I) dislike __________ .	__________ **ga kirai desu.**
(I) dislike __________ very much.	__________ **ga dai-kirai desu.**

Dialogues

2 *I hear it's a nice place!*

Miki Kondo shigoto de Kyōto ni iku koto ni nattan desu.
Yoshida A, soo desu ka. Boku no ryooshin wa Kyōto ni sunde irun desu yo.
Miki Kyōto wa ii machi rashii desu, ne.
Yoshida Soo desu ne. Chuugakusei toka kookoosei ga yoku kankoo ni ikimasu, ne. Kondo wa nannichi kan gurai Kyōto ni irassharu no desu ka?
Miki Ee to...Mikka gurai ni naru to omoimasu.
Yoshida A, soo desu ka. Sore deshitara, zehi boku no ie ni yotte kudasai.
Miki E? Iin desu ka?
Yoshida Juusho to denwa bangoo o watashimasu kara...
Mikiki Chizu o kaite kudasaimasen ka?
Yoshida Wakarimashita.

ryooshin (both) parents
machi town
rashii desu looks like/appears to be
chuugakusei middle school student (junior high)
kookoosei high school student
kankoo ni iku go sightseeing
zehi certainly/for certain
ie house/home
juusho address
watashimasu give/present (to someone)
chizu map

Kyōto ni iku koto ni nattan desu. I'm going to Kyoto. The phrase **koto ni nattan desu** after a verb indicates that something "has come to pass". This is a way of indicating that the action was not necessarily planned by the speaker. It is comparable to "It has been decided that I will go to Kyoto". (*eq.* **...iku koto ni narimashita.**)

Ii machi rashii desu, ne. It looks like a good/nice town, doesn't it? (*Cf.* **yosasoo desu.**)

yoku kankoo ni ikimasu. ...go sightseeing (there) a lot.

Nannichi kan gurai Kyōto ni irassharu no desu ka? About how many days will you be in Kyoto? (*exal.*) (*eq.* **...Kyōto ni imasu ka?**)

Mikka gurai ni naru to omoimasu. I think it will be about three days. (*lit.* I think it will become...)

Sore deshitara... If that's the case...

Zehi boku no ie ni yotte kudasai. Please visit my house without fail.

Chizu o kaite kudasaimasen ka? Won't you draw a map for me? (*pol.*) (*eq.* **Chizu o kaite kudasai.**)

Practise what you have learned

4 The formula (*noun*) **wa** (*adjective*) **rashii desu** indicates the noun "seems to be (*adjective*)". Translate the following sentences into English. (Answers p. 162)

(a) Eki wa chikai rashii desu, ne. ____________________

(b) Ashita wa samui rashii desu yo. ____________________

(c) Kono mise wa oishii rashii desu. ____________________

5 Tanabe-san and Miura-san are talking about the places where their parents live. Listen to the recording and answer the questions. (Answers p. 162)

(a) Where do Miura-san's parents live? ____________________

(b) How far is their city from Nagoya? ____________________

(c) Does Tanabe-san like her hometown? ____________________

(d) What does Miura-san ask Tanabe-san to do? ____________________

6 Listen to the recording. With Miura san's help, practise how you can exchange your address and phone number with a Japanese friend.

____

____

____

Narita International Airport

Dialogues

3 *The place is convenient but noisy*

Furukawa Ima wa doko ni tomatte irasshaimasu?
Takada Ano, Shibuya no eki no wariai to chikai tokoro no hoteru o mitsukete, soko ni tomatte orimasu.
Furukawa Totemo benri-soo de, ii desu ne.
Takada E, demo ne...yahari, chotto, machi no oto ga kikoete urusain desu yo.
Furukawa A, soo desu ka.
Takada Demo, ano...hooboo aruite shashin o tottari, o-mise ni ittari dekiru kara, Shibuya mo waruku arimasen, ne.
Furukawa Hoka ni dokka ni ikaremashita?
Takada Ee, ano, Tōkyō Tawā ni mo nobottari, kitto ii shashin ga toreta to omotte, tanoshimi ni shite orimasu.
Furukawa Sore wa yokatta desu, ne.

wariai to somewhat
mitsukeru find
▸ **benri-soo** looks convenient
▸ **oto** sound
kikoete be audible, can hear (and...) (*dic.* **kikoeru**)
▸ **urusai** noisy/bothersome
hooboo everywhere/in all directions
▸ **warui** bad (**waruku arimasen** = not bad)
hoka ni otherwise/other (places)
Tōkyō Tawā Tokyo Tower
kitto certainly
Tanoshimi ni shite orimasu. I'm looking forward to it. (*humb.*)
Yokatta desu. It turned out well. (*lit.* It was good)

Tōkyō Tawā

Doko ni tomatte irasshaimasu ka? Where are you staying? (*exal.*) Compare the response given: **Soko ni tomatte orimasu.** (*humb.*) (*norm. eq.* **...tomatte imasu.**)

wariai to chikai tokoro no hoteru a hotel that is fairly close

Benri-soo de, ii desu, ne. It looks good and convenient, doesn't it? (*lit.* It looks convenient and [therefore] is good, isn't it?)

Machi no oto ga kikoete urusai(n) desu yo. You can hear the sounds of the town, and (so) it is bothersome.

Hooboo aruite... Walking around everywhere... (*dic.* **aruku**)

Shashin o tottari, o-mise ni ittari dekiru kara... Because you can take pictures and go to the shops... (*dic.* **shashin o toru, o-mise ni iku**) The **-tari** ending is used when several actions are listed in a sentence, but not in chronological sequence.

Shibuya mo waruku arimasen, ne. Shibuya isn't so bad, is it? See the Grammar section.

Hoka ni dokka ni ikaremashita (ka)? Did you go any place else? (*exal.*) (*eq.* **...dokoka ni ikimashita ka?**)

Tōkyō Tawā ni mo nobottari,... I climbed Tokyo Tower and... The implication is that there were other things the speaker did that are not mentioned. (*dic.* **noboru**)

ii shashin ga toreta to omotte... I think I took some good pictures and (so)...

Practise what you have learned

7

Match the English phrase with the Japanese. (Answers p. 162)

(a) Where are you staying? (lit. Where is your hotel?) ____

(b) It's in Shibuya. ____

(c) How is the hotel? ____

(d) (*lit.*) It's a bit noisy, but it's convenient. ____

(1) Hoteru wa doo desu ka?

(2) Chotto urusain desu kedo benri desu.

(3) Shibuya desu.

(4) Hoteru wa doko desu ka?

8

To make an inflectable adjective negative, drop the final **-i** and add **-ku arimasen** or **-ku nain desu.** (*inf.*)

Listen to the recording and practise changing the following adjectives to a negative form.

chikai	______________	**tooi**	______________
atsui	______________	**samui**	______________
amai	______________	**oishii**	______________
takai	______________	**urusai**	______________
ureshii	______________	**yasui**	______________

9

Tell your Japanese friend that you are staying at a small hotel near a railway station. It is very convenient but a little noisy. It is a business hotel, so it is not too expensive.

____

____

____

____

____

Listen to the recording and work through the dialogue.

Dialogues

4 *What's your hobby?*

Female 1 O-keiko shite irasshaimasu?
Female 2 Ee...anoo...e o shite orimasu no yo.
Female 1 Ara soo? Doo iu e nan desu ka?
Female 2 Ano, abura-e desu.
Female 1 Abura-e? (E...) Anoo...fuukei toka...soo desu ne...? Doo iu mono o kaite irassharun desu ka?
Female 2 Ichiban ooi no wa rafu nan desu kedo...
Female 1 Rafu tte...watakushi wakaranain desu kedo...
Female 2 Nuudo nan desu.
Female 1 E? Nuudo? A... so...
Female 2 Sono hoka, seibutsu toka, fuukei toka o kaite orimasu keredo...
Female 1 A, soo desu ka. Soo...omoshiroi deshoo, nee.
Female 2 Soo desu ne. Ano...ironna o-keiko-goto shimashita kedo, ichiban, ano...watashi, daisuki desu. Nanika go-shumi wa?

o-keiko(-goto) lessons (arts and crafts)
e painting (art)
abura-e oil painting
fuukei scenery
ooi many
Wakaranain desu. I don't understand. (*eq.* **Wakarimasen.**)
rafu nude art (specifically female)
nuudo nude (*Eng.*)
sono hoka other than that
seibutsu still life
ironna various (*eq.* **iroiro na**)
go-shumi your hobby/special interest

E o shite orimasu no yo. I am taking an art class. (*humb.*) (*lit.* I am doing pictures [drawings and paintings].) **No yo** at the end is typical of feminine speech.

Doo iu e nan desu ka? What kind of pictures (are they)? (*eq.* **Doo iu e desu ka?**) **Nan** in this case is short for **na no** and really has no grammatical value but is a way of softening the sentence.

Doo iu mono o kaite irassharun desu ka? What kind of things do you draw/paint? (*exal.*) (*eq.* **Doo iu mono o kaite imasu ka?**)

Ichiban ooi no wa rafu nan desu kedo... Most are nudes...

Rafu tte...wakaranain desu. I don't understand (what you mean by) "Rafu". **Tte** is a short, colloquial way of say "quote-unquote".

Ironna o-keiko-goto shimashita kedo, (kore wa) ichiban daisuki desu. I have taken various classes, but (this) is my favourite. The use of **ichiban** with **daisuki** is redundant but fairly common at the informal level, particularly among women.

Nanika go-shumi wa (arimasu ka)? (Do you have) some kind of hobby?

Practise what you have learned

10 Changing **desu ne** to **deshoo ne** adds emphasis to a statement. **Omoshiroi desu, ne.** It is interesting, isn't it? **Omoshiroi deshoo, ne.** It must be interesting!

Complete the following sentences with **deshoo, ne.** (Answers p. 162)

(a) The weather **will be good** tomorrow (for certain.)

Ashita no o-tenki wa ______________________

(b) This **must be expensive!** Kore wa ______________________

(c) The J.R. **is faster.** J.R. no hoo ga ______________________

11 Listen to the recording and find out what Tanabe-san and Miura-san are talking about. Answer the questions below. (Answers p. 162)

(a) What is the topic of conversation?______________________

(b) What does Tanabe-san like?______________________

(c) What is it that Miura-san doesn't like?______________________

12 Listen to the recording and hear how a man talks about his hobby. He is going to ask you about your hobby.

(a) I like travelling. ______________________

(b) Europe is very interesting. ______________________

(c) I went to Hawaii in December with a friend. ______________________

____

(d) It was very warm. ______________________

Learning the tea ceremony

Key words and phrases

____ ga suki desu.	I like ____ .
____ ga kirai desu.	I dislike ____ .
____ ga omoshirokatta desu.	____ was interesting.
____ ga ookatta desu.	____ was plentiful/numerous.
____ ga urusakatta desu.	____ was noisy/bothersome.
____ ga warukatta desu.	____ was bad.
____ ga kirei deshita.	____ was pretty. (not inflectable)
____ e itte kimashita.	I went to ____ (for a short stay).
Tōkyō ni sunde imasu.	I live in (Tokyo).
(Hoteru) ni tomatte imasu.	I am staying at (a hotel).
Nani o shite imasu ka?	What are you doing?
(E o kai)te imasu.	I am (draw)ing (a picture).
(Chizu o kai)te kudasai/ kudasaimasen ka?	Please/Won't you please (draw me a map)?
Tanoshimi ni shite imasu.	I'm looking forward to it.
Doo iu (yoo na) ____ ?	What kind of ____ ?
shumi	special interest/hobby
machi	town
ryooshin	(both) parents
chuugakusei	middle school student
kookoosei	high school student
zehi	certainly/for certain
kitto	certainly
sono hoka	other than that

Grammar

Standard request vs. polite request

Up to now in this course, the standard form used for making a request or giving instructions has been the **-te** form of the verb, followed by **kudasai**. To make the request more polite, change **kudasai** to **kudasaimasen ka?**, as in the following example sentences:

Kuji ni kite kudasai. Please come at 9:00.
Kuji ni kite kudasaimasen ka? Won't you please come at 9:00?

Shashin o totte kudasai. Please take a picture.
Shashin o totte kudasaimasen ka? Won't you please take a picture?

Hoteru o yoyaku shite kudasai. Please make a reservation at the hotel. (*lit.* Reserve the hotel.)

Hoteru o yoyaku shite kudasaimasen ka?
Won't you please make a reservation at the hotel?

Arakawa train line in Tokyo

Past and negative of adjectives

You learned in Unit 1 that the past tense of inflectable adjectives is created by dropping the final syllable (**-i**) of the dictionary form and adding **-katta** (**desu**). A negative adjective is created by changing the ending to **-ku arimasen** or **-kunai** (**desu**).

Waruku arimasen. It is not bad.
Warukunai desu. It is not bad.
Warukunai. It is not bad. (*inf.*)

The endings **-ku arimasen** and **-kunai desu** are both within the range of normal-polite speech, **-ku arimasen** sounding a little more formal than **-kunai desu**. Leaving off **desu**, however, makes the ending informal and typical of casual speech. The same is true of the negative past endings:

Samuku arimasen deshita. It was not cold.
Samukunakatta desu. It was not cold.
Samukunakatta. It was not cold. (*inf.*)

Here are more examples of inflected adjectives:

Takai (**desu**). It is expensive.
Takakatta (**desu**). It was expensive.
Takaku arimasen. It is not expensive.
Takakunai (**desu**). It is not expensive.
Takaku arimasen deshita. It was not expensive.
Takakunakatta (**desu**). It was not expensive.

Oishii (**desu**). It is delicious.
Oishikatta (**desu**). It was delicious.
Oishiku arimasen. It is not delicious.
Oishikunai (**desu**). It is not delicious.
Oishiku arimasen deshita. It was not delicious.
Oishikunakatta (**desu**). It was not delicious.

The adjective **ii** is inflected as follows:

Ii (**desu**). It is good.
Yokatta (**desu**). It was good.
Yoku arimasen. It is not good.
Yokunai (**desu**). It is not good.
Yoku arimasen deshita. It was not good.
Yokunakatta (**desu**). It was not good.

Adjectival Nouns do not change, but require that the verb change to show present/past/negative:

Kirei desu. It is pretty.
Kirei deshita. It was pretty.
Kirei dewa arimasen. It is not pretty.
Kirei dewa arimasen deshita. It was not pretty.

Did you know?

Kyoto

From the year 794 A.D. to 1868, Kyoto was the capital city of Japan. Today visitors can go from Tokyo to Kyoto in two hours and 43 minutes by Shinkan-sen. There are over 1500 Buddhist temples and 200 Shinto shrines in Kyoto. It is the centre of Buddhism, with headquarters for some thirty sects located in the city. Among the "must see" spots are: the **Gion** area, with the Gion corner offering traditional arts and performances; **Kinkakuji** (the Golden Pavilion), **Ryōanji** rock and sand garden; the old **Kyōto Gosho** (Imperial Palace); the **Nijo Shōgun Palace**; **Kyōto Daigaku** (the University of Kyoto) and **Dōshisha** University; **Daitoku-ji** (Daitoku Temple); **Kiyomizu dera** (Kiyomizu Temple); **Sanjūsan-gen-dō**; **Koke Dera** (the Moss Temple); **Ginkakuji** (the Silver Pavilion); and the **Arashiyama** area. Both **Katsura Rikyū** (Katsura Detached Palace) and **Shūgakuin** are also not to-be-missed places. Since the Katsura Rikyu is still used by the Imperial Household, you will have to arrange for an entry pass beforehand.

Religions in Japan

The spiritual life of the Japanese is derived from the various beliefs and faiths held by the people. **Shinto** is the native religion, but Taoism and Confucian teachings from China and Buddhism from India have solid roots in the Japanese way of thinking.

Shintō (Shinto), *lit.* "the way of the gods" is the indigenous religion stemming from nature worship. Shrines can be recognized by their **torii**, a large open gateway. Originally a form of animism, **Shintō** teaches that certain mountains, trees, lakes, the sun, the sky and natural things are endowed with the spirit of **kami**, supernatural gods. Revered places and objects are marked off with **shimenawa**, a sacred rope and special white papers.

Bukkyō (Buddhism) originated in India and reached Japan in the sixth century via China and Korea. There have been many periods in Japanese history when Buddhism was actually considered the official national religion. It has greatly influenced Japanese cultural life and social order, adding much to the arts, government, education, literature, language and behaviour of the people.

Kirisutokyō (Christianity), associated with Western culture and spirituality, was first introduced in the Nagasaki area in 1549 by Francis Xavier, a Spanish Basque Jesuit. Like Buddhism, Christianity was first welcomed, but for nearly three hundred years Catholicism was officially banned, and the practice of Christianity was punishable by death until the Meiji Restoration (1876). Christianity was then re-introduced to Japan, making contributions especially in the areas of education, hospital work and social services. The Constitution drawn in 1947, following the second World War, guarantees religious freedom in Japan. Christians have remained relatively small in number (approx. 2% of the population), although the political and educational influence of Christianity has been much greater than that number would indicate.

In Japan it is no longer possible to separate pure Shintoism from pure Buddhism, or the Taoist and Confucian ways of thinking from the Japanese way of life. When asked, many Japanese respond that they are not members of a specific religious institution, yet most are actively involved in programmes fostered by shrines, temples and churches. It is not unusual for a child to make his first visit to a Shintō shrine and later actively participate in Buddhist temple festivities, attend the 7-5-3 Festival at a shrine, learn foreign languages at a Christian Church, get married in Christian or Shintō tradition, and be buried according to Buddhist rites.

How to find religious services

In large cities most religions, including Judaism and Islam, have services available for foreign visitors. English language newspapers usually include a list of religious services.

Answers

Practise what you have learned

Exercise **1**	(a) 3 (b) 1 (c) 4 (d) 2
Exercise **2**	(a) travel (b) at least 3 (c) Czechoslovakia
Exercise **4**	(a) There seems to be a station nearby (b) It seems tomorrow will be cold (c) This store (restaurant) seems delicious (...seems to have good food)
Exercise **5**	(a) Toyoda City of Aichi Prefecture (b) about 2 hours (c) yes (d) visit her parents
Exercise **7**	(a) 4 (b) 3 (c) 1 (d) 2
Exercise **10**	(a) ii deshoo ne (b) takai deshoo ne (c) hayai deshoo ne
Exercise **11**	(a) music (b) rock/American jazz (c) heavy metal

12 THE WEATHER

You will learn

- to ask about the weather
- to describe weather conditions in your country
- what a radio weather forecast is like
- about the climate in Japan

Before you begin

Temperatures are read on the Celsius scale in Japan. The conversion to Fahrenheit, though not complicated, can be cumbersome. You simply divide by 5, multiply by 9 and add 32. Here are a few converted values:

F	*C*
98.4	36.9 (body temperature)
86	30
77	25
59	15
50	10
32	0
14	-10
5	-15
-13	-25

Since "weather-talk" is an important part of daily casual greetings and conversation, revise Unit 1 before continuing.

Study guide

- **Dialogue 1 + Practise what you have learned**
- **Dialogue 2 + Practise what you have learned**
- **Dialogue 3 + Practise what you have learned**
- **Dialogue 4 + Practise what you have learned**
- **Study: the Key words and phrases**
- **Study: the Grammar section**
- **Read: Did you know?**

Dialogues

1 *It rains a lot, doesn't it!*

Yoshida Saikin ame ga yoku furimasu nee...
Miki Soo desu ne.
Yoshida Tsuyu da kara, shiyoo ga nai no kamo shiremasen keredo...Demo iya desu, ne.
Miki Soto ni derarenakute, uzu-uzu shimasu yo.
Yoshida A, saikin, tenki-yohoo wa doo nan desu ka?
Miki Ashita mo kekkoo furu rashii desu yo.
Yoshida Aaaa...Boku wa konshuu-matsu, gorufu demo ikoo to omottan desu kedo, moo, kore jaa, dame desu ne.

saikin lately
tsuyu rainy season
Shiyoo ga nai. It cannot be helped.
iya unpleasant/disgusting
Uzu-uzu shimasu. It frustrates (me).
tenki yohoo weather forecast
konshuu-matsu this weekend (**shuu-matsu** = weekend)
dame hopeless/bad, unacceptable

Shiyoo ga nai ka mo shiremasen. Perhaps it can't be helped. The expression **ka mo shiremasen** always follows the word or phrase it refers to and literally indicates "It cannot be known". (*Cf.* "for all we know")

Soto ni derarenakute... (One) can't go outside, and...

Doo nan desu ka? How is it? (*eq.* **Doo desu ka?**)

Ashita mo (ame ga) kekkoo furu rashii desu. It looks like it will rain quite a bit again tomorrow. There is no Japanese verb meaning "to rain"; instead the phrase **ame ga furu** (**furimasu**) is used, meaning literally "the rain falls". **Kekkoo** in this sentence indicates "quite a bit", and **rashii desu** means "it looks like..." (See the Grammar section.)

Gorufu demo ikoo to omottan desu. I had thought about going golfing or something. The ending **-oo to omoimasu** means "I think I might..." or "I'm thinking about (doing)..."

Moo, kore jaa...dame desu, ne. Well, with things as they are...it's impossible, isn't it? The phrase **Moo, kore jaa** is a casual expression referring to the current situation and usually indicates a negative feeling. **Dame desu** literally means "it's bad", but is used to express a range of feeling from "Don't do that" to "It's no use".

Practise what you have learned

1

Select the equivalent Japanese phrases from the box. (Answers p. 174)

(a) the rainy season	____	**(1)**	Yoku furimasu, ne.
(b) the weather forecast	____	**(2)**	Iya desu, ne.
(c) It rains a lot, doesn't it?	____	**(3)**	tenki yohoo
(d) It is hopeless.	____	**(4)**	tsuyu
(e) I'm not pleased about it. ("It's unpleasant".)	____	**(5)**	Dame desu, ne.

2

Listen to Miura-san and Tanabe-san talk about the weather, and answer the questions below. (Answers p. 174)

(a) What sort of weather are they having? ______________

(b) What season is it? ______________

(c) What is the forecast for the weekend? ______________

3

Miura-san will ask you about the weather in your country. Read the following phrases and think about them before you listen to the recording. Of course,there are no answers in the book for this exercise.

(a) Watashi no kuni wa ______________ .

(b) Ima ______________ ni sunde imasu.

(c) (Place) no ichiban ii toki wa ____ gatsu to ____ gatsu desu.

(d) Ichiban samui toki wa ____ gatsu kara ____ gatsu made desu.

(e) Ame ga ooi toki (when it rains the most) wa ____ gatsu desu.

(f) __________ ga suki desu. Or _________ ga amari suki ja nain desu.

Dialogues

2 *When will you come back?*

Ogino Kondo wa itsu irassharun desu ka?
Takada Nigatsu goro ni kitai to omotte irun desu kedo, Nigatsu no o-tenki wa doo deshoo?
Ogino Samuin ja nain deshoo ka?
Takada Nigatsu wa, yahari, ichiban samui koro deshoo ka?
Ogino Soo desu ne. Shigatsu goro ga yoroshiin ja nain desu ka?
Takada Shigatsu ni wa, sakura no hana ga saite iru deshoo ka?
Ogino Soo desu ne. Ichiban, anoo, kisetsu to shite wa ii toki desu yo ne.
Takada Soo desu ne. Rokugatsu ni haitte shimau to, mata ne, tsuyu ni narimasu kara... Sore jaa, tabun, mata, Shigatsu goro ni dete mairimasu kara, sono toki ni wa anoo, o-me ni kakarimashoo.
Ogino Soo desu ne. Tanoshimi ni shite orimasu wa.
Takada Hai. Jaa, gomen kudasai.
Ogino Gomen kudasai.

koro approximate time
sakura cherry tree
hana flower, blossom
saite iru is blooming
kisetsu season (of the year)
toki point in time
tabun most likely
O-me ni kakarimashoo. Let's meet. (*pol.*)
Gomen kudasai. Goodbye. (*pol.*)

Nigatsu goro ni kitai to omotte irun desu. I am thinking I would like to come about February. (*eq.* **...kitai to omotte imasu.**)

Samui(n) ja nai(n) deshoo ka? Won't it be cold? The speaker is using a long and redundant phrase as a tag question. (*eq.* **Samui, deshoo?**)

Shigatsu goro ga yoroshii(n) ja nai(n) desu ka? About April would be all right, wouldn't it? Again the speaker uses **ja nain desu ka?** as a tag question where a simple **ja nai** or **deshoo** would have sufficed. Often the Japanese will lengthen an expression to add to the feeling of politeness.

Kisetsu to shite wa... as a season.../as far as seasons go...

Rokugatsu ni haitte shimau to... When we get into June...

Shigatsu goro ni dete mairimasu. I'll come back in about April. (*humb.*) (*eq.* **...dete kimasu.**) (*lit.* I'll go out and come.)

Tanoshimi ni shite orimasu wa. I'm looking forward to it. (*f./humb.*) (*eq.* **Tanoshimi ni shite imasu.**)

Practise what you have learned

4 Complete the following sentences by inserting an appropriate month from the box. (Answers p. 174)

Rokugatsu	**Nigatsu**	**Shigatsu goro**

(a) Tōkyō no ichiban samui kisetsu wa ____________ desu.

(b) Tōkyō de ____________ sakura no hana ga sakimasu.

(c) Tōkyō no tsuyu wa ____________ desu.

5 Listen to the recording and get the gist of what is being said. (Answers p. 174)

(a) Where is the young fellow from? ____________________

(b) What is the weather like in the winter? ____________________

(c) What months does he like? ____________________

(d) Does he know when he is coming back to Japan? ____________________

6 Before listening to the recording, prepare yourself to ask a Japanese friend some questions. Ask when he/she is planning to visit Canada, where you live. You may use, for example, **Kanada ni itsu *irassharun desu ka?*** or **Kanada ni itsu *kimasu ka?*** Choose the verb form that suits you best, depending on your age, the situation, and to whom you are speaking.

(a) When are you coming to Canada? ____________________

(b) I see. So it's in July? ____________________

(c) July is a good season. (**ii kisetsu**) ____________________

(d) Well, telephone me, all right? ____________________

(e) I'm looking forward to it, you know. ____________________

Listen to the recording and follow Aoki-san's prompts.

Bullet Train passing Mount Fuji

Dialogues

3 *Weather Forecast*

Announcer Kantō Chihō no kyoo wa antei shita natsu-zora ga tsuzuku mikomi desu.
Kono tame, kakuchi de wa 30-do o koeru manatsu-bi to naru deshoo.
Asu no sora moyoo desu.
Oomune hare no mikomi desu ga, engan-bu de wa kumo ga de-yasuku, gogo ni wa ichiji ame no tokoro ga arisoo desu. Nitchuu mo kyoo dooyoo, atsusa ga kibishii deshoo.

Kantō-Chihō Kanto area
antei shita settled/stable
natsu-zora summer sky (summer weather)
tsuzuku to continue
mikomi prediction
kakuchi all areas
30-do thirty degrees
koeru to exceed
manatsu-bi mid-summer day (weather)
➧ **sora moyoo** the weather (*lit.* condition of the sky.)
oomune mostly
➧ **hare** clear
engan-bu coast-line area
➧ **kumo** cloud
deyasui easily appear
➧ **gogo** p.m./afternoon
ichiji for a while
➧ **nitchuu** during the day time
kyoo dooyoo same as today
atsusa heat
kibishii severe/intense

—**ga tsuuku mikomi desu.** It is expected ______________ to continue.

—**to naru deshoo.** It will probably become ______________ .

ame no tokoro ga arisoo desu. There may be rain in places. (*lit.* It looks like there will be places of rain.)

天気予報
tenki yohoo
weather forecast

晴
hare
clear

雨
ame
rain

曇
kumori
cloudy

雪
yuki
snow

きょうの天気
kyoo no tenki
today's weather

今夜の天気
konya no tenki
tonight's weather

あすの天気
asu no tenki
tomorrow's weather

Practise what you have learned

7 Here are some standard weather terms.

Hare	**Kumori**	**Ame**	**Yuki**
________	________	________	________
(1) clear	**(2)** cloudy	**(3)** rain	**(4)** snow

(a) hare nochi ame	(clear followed by rain)
(b) ame nochi kumori	(rain followed by cloudy skies)
(c) Ame no moyoo desu.	([it is] rainy conditions.)
(d) Hare no mikomi desu.	(Clear weather is predicted.)
(e) tokoro ni yotte ame	(rain in some areas)

After learning these expressions, describe today's weather.

8 Match the English and Japanese phrases. (Answers p. 174)

(a) It is expected to clear up.	____	**(1)**	Ame moyoo desu.
(b) It will be rainy.	____	**(2)**	ame nochi kumori
(c) rain followed by cloudy skies	____	**(3)**	hare nochi ame
(d) clear but turning to rain	____	**(4)**	Hareru mikomi desu.

9 Dialogue 3 is the only recording of real Japanese broadcasting that you will hear while studying this book. The announcer's presentation is crisp, clear and fast.

Weather terminology will become very familiar to you if you watch Japanese TV. Japan being an island country, the weather may change suddenly, especially during the typhoon (**taifuu**) season. Weathermen always use many visual aids, so it is easy to grasp the important information.

週間天気
shuukan tenki
weekly forecast

注意報
chuuihoo
warnings

霧
kiri
fog

波浪
haroo
high waves

波の高さ
nami no takasa
wave height

気圧
kiatsu
pressures

kookiatsu
high pressure

teikiatsu
low pressure

Dialogues

4 *When is the best time to visit Japan?*

Customer Gaikoku kara yuujin ga kitai tte itte irun desu keredomo, Rokugatsu nanka ikaga deshoo ka?
Travel Agent Rokugatsu wa tsuyu desu kara, amari kankoo-kyaku ni wa mukanai jiki desu ne.
Customer Soo suru to...itsu ga ii deshoo?
Agent Natsu wa...Nihon no natsu wa atsu-sugimasu shi...Yahari, aki no Juugatsu, Juuichigatsu, akibare desu shi...momiji ga kirei na kisetsu desu, ne.
Customer Soo shimasu to...yappari, haru ka aki...
Agent Soo desu ne. Shigatsu no sakura ga saku koro wa, gaikoku kara irassharu o-kyaku-sama ni wa ichiban ii toki kamo shiremasen, ne.
Customer Aa soo desu ka. Doomo arigatoo gozaimashita.

yuujin friend
Ikaga deshoo ka? How would it be? (*pol.*) (*eq.* **Doo deshoo ka?**)
kankoo-kyaku tourists
mukanai unsuitable
jiki season
➧ **natsu** summer
➧ **Atsu-sugimasu.** It's too hot.
➧ **aki** autumn
akibare clear skies (typical of autumn)
➧ **haru** spring
momiji coloured leaves (of autumn)
o-kyaku-sama guest

Yuujin ga kitai tte itte irun desu. A friend is saying that he wants to come. **Tte** refers to reported speech. (*eq.* **Yuujin ga kitai to itte imasu.**)

Amari kankoo-kyaku ni wa mukanai jiki desu. It's a period (season) that isn't particularly suitable for tourists.

Nihon no natsu wa atsu-sugimasu shi... Japanese summers are too hot, and... **shi** indicates that there may be other reasons unstated.

haru ka aki... spring or autumn...

Shigatsu no sakura ga saku koro (at about the time) when cherry trees blossom in April

Gaikoku kara irassharu o-kyaku-sama ni wa... To/for guests who come from foreign countries...(*exal.*)

Ichiban ii toki ka mo shiremasen. It may be the best time, for all we know.

Practise what you have learned

10 To say something is in excess, drop the final -i from the adjective and add sugimasu.

Atsu-sugimasu.	It's too hot.
Samu-sugimasu.	It's too cold.
Taka-sugimasu.	It's too expensive.

Convert the following adjectives into this form. (Answers p. 174)

(a) It's too heavy (**omoi**) ____________

(b) It's too sweet (**amai**) ____________

(c) It's too far (**tooi**) ____________

11 Go back to the recording and listen again to the dialogues in the unit to see how people describe different times of the year in Japanese. Then select an appropriate phrase from the box that matches the sentences.
(Answers p. 174)

New words are, **taifuu ga kuru** (a typhoon comes) and **Hachigatsu no owari kara Kugatsu goro made** (from the end of August to September).

(a) Tōkyō no ichiban samui toki. ____________________

(b) Tōkyō no ichiban atsui toki. ____________________

(c) Otenki ga ichiban ii toki. ____________________

(d) Tōkyō no ichiban ame ga ooi toki. ____________________

(e) Taifuu no ichiban kuru koro. ____________________

(1) Juugatsu to Juuichigatsu
(2) Hachigatsu no owari kara Kugatsu made
(3) Rokugatsu
(4) Shichi-gatsu to Hachigatsu
(5) Nigatsu

12 Invite a Japanese friend to your home country. With Miura-san's help, tell your friend when the best time for sightseeing is and when it is the best time for you. Listen to the recording after thinking about how you would say the following.

(a) Won't you come to ____________ ?

(b) How about (June or July)?

(c) Sorry, (August) is no good.

(d) Winter is too cold.

(e) (date) to (date) is okay for me.

Key words and phrases

Shiyoo ga nai.	It can't be helped.
____ ka mo shiremasen.	It may be that ____ .
Tanoshimi ni shite imasu.	I'm looking forward to it.
Gomen kudasai.	Goodbye. (*pol.*)
Dame desu.	It's no good./It's no use.
Uzu-uzu shimasu.	It's frustrating.
Ikaga deshoo ka?	How would that be?
Yoroshii desu ka?	Is it okay? (*eq.* **Ii desu ka?**)
(**Ame ga furu**) **rashii desu.**	It appears that (it will rain).
(**Ikoo**) **to omoimasu.**	I think (I will go).
(**Kitai**) **to omoimasu.**	I think (I want to come).
Nihon no natsu wa atsu-sugimasu.	Japanese summers are too hot.
tsuyu	rainy season
shuu-matsu	weekend
iya	unpleasant/disgusting
saikin	recently
toki	point in time
koro/goro	period of time
kisetsu	season of the year
haru	spring
natsu	summer
aki	autumn
fuyu	winter
yuujin	friend
o-kyaku-sama	guest/customer/patron
kankoo-kyaku	tourist (*lit.* sightseeing guest)

A ryokan surrounded by summer foliage

Grammar

Adjective + sugimasu

As you have seen in the text, the concept "too (hot, cold, etc.)" is expressed in Japanese by dropping the final **-i** of an adjective and adding **sugimasu**. Study the following examples:

(**Takai**) **Takasugimasu.** It's too expensive.
(**Samui**) **Samusugimasu.** It's too cold.
(**Muzukashii**) **Muzukashisugimasu.** It's too difficult.

Adjectives such as **kirei** and **benri** can be followed by **sugimasu** with no change to the adjective.

Kirei sugimasu. It's too pretty.
Benri sugimasu. It's too convenient.

______ *rashii desu*

This expression means "It appears to be ____ " or "It appears that ____ " and can follow a noun/noun phrase, a verb/verb phrase, or an adjective. Look at the following example sentences:

Ii machi rashii desu. It appears to be a good town. (noun phrase)
Ame ga furu rashii desu. It looks as if it will rain. (verb phrase)
Totemo benri rashii desu. It looks very convenient. (adjective)

Verbs that describe nouns

In the sentence "The person who comes every day", the phrase "who comes every day" describes or identifies "the person". The descriptive phrase contains both a subject ("who") and a verb ("comes"). In Japanese such descriptive phrases are placed before the nouns they describe. "The person who comes every day" would be **mainichi kuru hito.** Following are some examples from the dialogues in this unit:

Sakura ga saku koro about the time when the cherry trees blossom
Gaikoku kara irassharu o-kyaku-sama
Guests who come from foreign countries

Cherry blossoms

Did you know?

The four seasons

Although three of Japan's four main islands lie in the Temperate Zone, there are significant differences in climate as the chain of islands stretches in a bow shape from the northwest to the southeast. The northern-most area experiences long winters and bitter cold, while palm trees and pineapples grow in subtropical southern Kyushu and Okinawa. (See the map on page 30.)

With the exception of Hokkaido, **Tsuyu** (mid-June to mid-July) brings high humidity and rainfall to Japan. In normal years there are continuously cloudy skies and off-and-on drizzles throughout this period. Farmers plant rice just before the **Tsuyu** season. When it is over, the very humid, hot summer season begins. School children start their summer vacation from about July 21, and the trains are crowded with families heading for tourist spots or cooler resort areas.

From late August to September is the typhoon season. Everyone closely follows the development of a **taifuu** (typhoon), its strength and its route, fearful of the possible harm and damage it can cause to human lives, homes, the rice harvest, etc.

October and November bring a celebration of clear blue skies, mild temperatures, low humidity and beautiful changing colours (**momiji**) on the mountainsides. Since 75% of the Japanese land mass is mountainous or hilly terrain, the views are magnificent. Two especially noted areas for autumn colours are Arashiyama in Kyoto, and along the Oirase River in Aomori Prefecture.

The winter climate (December to February) in the Temperate Zone is dry, and the days are clear. People lament the harshness of winter days, when the temperature may be in the low 30s (°F), each other with **Samui desu nee**. Most private homes do not have central heating, so they can be quite chilly. Of course, hotels, **ryokan** and other modern structures have excellent heating systems. February is considered to be the coldest month in most areas, but plum blossoms will begin blooming by the end of the month, announcing the coming of spring.

On or around March 20 is the last day of school. Leaving and other school ceremonies are held. After a short spring break (**haru-yasumi**) the new school year begins around April 1, when cherry blossoms are just about in full bloom.

Answers

Practise what you have learned

Exercise **1**	(a) 4 (b) 3 (c) 1 (d) 5 (e) 2
Exercise **2**	(a) It rains every day (b) the rainy season (c) rain
Exercise **4**	(a) Nigatsu (b) Shigatsu goro (c) Rokugatsu
Exercise **5**	(a) Montreal, Canada (b) very cold (c) April/October (d) not sure
Exercise **8**	(a) 4 (b) 1 (c) 2 (d) 3
Exercise **10**	(a) omosugimasu (b) amasugimasu (c) toosugimasu
Exercise **11**	(a) 5 (b) 4 (c) 1 (d) 3 (e) 2

13 MORE ABOUT YOURSELF

You will learn

- to talk about daily routines
- to discuss sports
- to describe where you live
- to find a place to live in Japan
- about Japanese gestures and body language

Study guide

Dialogue 1 + Practise what you have learned
Dialogue 2 + Practise what you have learned
Dialogue 3 + Practise what you have learned
Dialogue 4 + Practise what you have learned
Study: the Key words and phrases
Study: the Grammar section
Read: Read and understand
Read: Did you know?

Skiing in Hakuba

Dialogues

1 *My daily routine*

Takada Mai-asa nanji goro okimasu ka?
Shiraishi Watashi desu ka? Roku-ji desu.
Takada E? Roku-ji? Hayai desu ne.
Shiraishi Ja, Takada-san wa nan-ji ni okirun desu ka?
Takada Watashi wa shigoto ga juu-ji kara desu. Dakara asa wa yukkuri desu.
Shiraishi Ii desu nee. Sore ja, asa terebi-nyuusu o mitari, shinbun o yondari dekimasu ne.
Takada Nyuusu wa mimasu kedo, shinbun wa densha no naka de yonde i masu. Shiraishi-san wa itsu shinbun o yomun desu ka?
Shiraishi Shigoto de yondari, uchi de yondari kimatte inain desu. Watashi no shigoto wa yo-ji made desu kara, tokidoki eiga e ittari, tomodachi ni attari...
Takada Sore wa ii desu ne. Urayamashii desu ne.

mai-asa every morning
➧ **okimasu** wake up
okirun desu wake up (casual)
yukkuri leisurely (time spent)
➧ **nyuusu** newscast
➧ **shinbun** news bulletin
yondari read and (*dic.* **yomu**)
➧ **densha** train
naka inside
Shiraishi last name
kimatte inai not decided
➧ **tokidoki** once in a while
➧ **eiga** movies
ittari go and (*dic.* **iku**)
attari meet and (*dic.* **au**)
urayamashii envious

Ja Takada-san wa nan-ji ni okirun desu ka? Then what time do you get up? Proper names are used wherever possible instead of 'you' as it is considered more polite.

Nyuusu o mitari shinbun o yondari dekimasu ne. You can watch news and read papers, etc., can't you?

densha no naka de... in the train (*lit.* inside the train)

kimatte inain desu. It's flexible. (*lit.* It hasn't been decided.)

Practise what you have learned

1 Read the dialogue again and circle the appropriate responses below. (Answers p. 188)

(a) Takada-san wakes up early every morning. Y N

(b) Shiraishi-san always reads her paper in the morning. Y N

(c) Takada-san's work begins early. Y N

(d) Takada-san reads her morning paper at the office. Y N

(e) Shiraishi-san goes to movies sometimes. Y N

2 Listen to the recording for this exercise. Did you hear some of the comments Miura-san made as he listened to Tanabe-san talk? What would be your comments when someone tells you: (Answers p. 188)

(a) Mai-asa go-ji ni okirun desu.

____

(b) Mainichi nihongo o sanjup-pun benkyoo shite imasu.

____

(c) Erai desu, ne!

____

3 Listen to the recording. Aoki-san will assist you in completing this exercise.

____

____

____

Dialogues

2 *Do you like sports?*

Miki	Nanika supootsu wa shimasu ka?
Yoshida	Soo desu ne, boku wa gorufu ga suki nan de, gorufu o yatte imasu kedo...
Miki	Gorufu desu ka. Dono gurai joozu nan desu ka?
Yoshida	Iyaa...naka-naka umaku naranakute, soko-soko desu.
Miki	Soo desu ka. Boku wa tenisu o yoku shimasu kedo...
Yoshida	Tenisu desu ka. Tenisu wa kaiin-sei no kurabu ka nanka ni haitte irarerun desu ka?
Miki	Hai, haitte imasu.
Yoshida	Haa. Boku mo gorufu o kaiin-sei no tokoro de yatte imasu.
Miki	Aa soo desu ka.

Golf and tennis are popular sports; however, they are status sports and very costly. Visitors to Japan find the fees prohibitively expensive.

➧ **supootsu** sports (*Eng.*)
yatte imasu doing (*eq.* **shite imasu**)
➧ **dono gurai** to what degree?/how much?
iya... no.../ well...
naka-naka (not) easily, (not) readily
➧ **joozu** good/skilful
➧ **soko-soko** so-so
kaiin-sei no kurabu membership club (*Eng.*)

➧ **Nanika supootsu wa shimasu ka?** Do you play any sports? (*lit.* Do you do some kind of sports?) The Japanese do not use the word "play" to refer to sports as in English. Instead, they "do" sports.

Dono gurai joozu nan desu ka? About how good are you?

Naka-naka umaku naranakute... I just don't seem to improve...The word **naka-naka** is comparable to "no matter what I do..." **Umaku** is from **umai**, meaning "skilful" (*eq.* **joozu**); **umakunarimasu** is "to become skilful". (See Grammar section.) Literally, this phrase means "Not becoming skilful no matter what I do,..."

Tenisu o yoku shimasu. I play tennis often. Although **yoku** literally translates as "well", **joozu ni** ("skilfully") is used more often to indicate quality of performance.

Kurabu ka nanka ni haitte irarerun desu ka? Are you in a club or something? (*exal.*) (*eq.* **Kurabu ni haitte imasu ka?**)

➧ **Gorufu o (kaiin-sei no tokoro de) yatte imasu.** I play golf (at a membership place)

Practise what you have learned

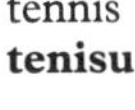

tennis
tenisu

golf
gorufu

jogging
joggingu

skiing
sukii

baseball
beisubooru
(yakyuu)

football
futtobooru
(**Ame-futo =**
American football)

rugby
ragubii

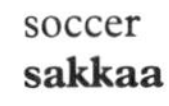

soccer
sakkaa

volleyball
bareebooru

swimming
suimingu

hiking
haikingu

cycling
saikuringu

4

Match the Japanese words on the left with their English counterparts. (Answers p. 188)

(a)	sukii	____	**(1)**	baseball
(b)	beisubooru	____	**(2)**	American football
(c)	Ame-futo	____	**(3)**	jogging
(d)	joggingu	____	**(4)**	skiing

5

Listen to the recording and practise saying the following frequently used phrases. You are already familiar with most of them.

(a)	Do you play some sports?	**Nanika supootsu o shimasu ka?**
(b)	You must be good at it.	**Joozu deshoo.**
(c)	I'm not that great, but...	**Betsu ni joozu ja nain desu kedo...**
(d)	It's interesting, you know.	**Omoshiroi desu yo.**
(e)	I like (it).	**Suki desu.**
(f)	I'm just so-so.	**Maa-maa desu.**

6

Listen to the recording and answer the questions. You will be asked about the sports you played in school. You will also be asked what kind of sports you play now. Answers to the two questions below are on p. 188.

(a) What sport did Miura-san play when he was in school? ____________

(b) What kind of sports does he play now? ____________________

Dialogues

3 *Where do you live?*

Yoshida Anoo, ima doko ni o-sumai desu ka?
Shōda Aa, ima Suginami-ku ni sunde imasu.
Yoshida Aa, Suginami-ku tte yuu to, dokora hen desu ka?
Shōda Ichiban chikai eki ga Ogikubo eki de, soko kara basu de go-fun kurai desu.
Yoshida Aa, soo desu ka.
Shōda Ee...desu kara, chotto fuben nan desu keredomo ne...
Yoshida Go-kazoku to wa go-issho desu ka?
Shōda Anoo, sukoshi mae made wa issho deshita ga, ima wa betsu ni sunde imasu.
Yoshida Demo, Tōkyō de ie o sagasu no wa muzukashiin ja nain desu ka?
Shōda Soo desu ne. Hitori de sagasu no wa taihen na no de, fudoosan'ya-san ni tanonde, sagashite moraimashita.
Yoshida Ie wa hiroi desu ka?
Shōda Ee, yahari Tōkyō desu node, sukoshi semai desu, ne.

o-sumai your home
Suginami-ku Suginami Ward (section of a city)
dokora hen about what area?
kurai about (*eq.* **gurai**)
fuben inconvenient
(go-)kazoku (your) family (*pol.*)
go-issho together (*pol.*)
betsu ni separately
sagasu look for/seek
fudoosan'ya-san estate agent
tanonde/tanomu ask (someone to do something)
hiroi wide/spacious
semai narrow/small (in space)

Suginami-ku tte yuu to... When you say "Suginami Ward"...

Soko kara basu de gofun kurai desu. From there it's about 5 minutes by bus.

Go-kazoku to wa go-issho desu ka? Do you live with your parents? (*pol.*) (*lit.* With your parents, are you together?)

Sukoshi mae made wa issho deshita. We were together until a little while ago (*lit.* until a little before).

Tōkyō de ie o sagasu no wa muzukashii(n) ja nain desu ka? Looking for a house in Tokyo is difficult, isn't it? The word **no** after a verb phrase makes it into a noun phrase. See the Grammar section.

Hitori de sagasu no wa taihen na no de,... Looking (for a house) by myself is awful, so...

Fudoosan'ya-san ni tanonde, I asked an estate agent, and...

Sagashite moraimashita. I had (him) look for me.

hiroi/semai wide/narrow. Instead of "big" or "small", Japanese homes and other spaces (countries, cities, etc.) are spoken of as "wide" or "narrow".

Practise what you have learned

7

Match the English and Japanese phrases below. (Answers p. 188)

(a) Where do you live?	____	**(1)**	Ii tokoro deshoo, ne.
(b) About where is that?	____	**(2)**	Ie o sagasu no wa muzukashii desu ka?
(c) Is it far from here?	____	**(3)**	Doko ni sunde imasu ka?
(d) Is it hard to look for a house?	____	**(4)**	Sore wa dokora hen desu ka?
(e) It must be a nice place.	____	**(5)**	Koko kara tooi desu ka?

8

Listen to the recording and fill in the blanks. (Answers p. 188)

(a) It is a (*small/large*) city. ____________

(b) It is (*near to/far from*) her work.

(c) It takes ____________ minutes by car.

9

Listen to the recording. It will help you have a conversation based on the dialogue you just studied. It would be useful to revise the dialogue and Exercise 7.

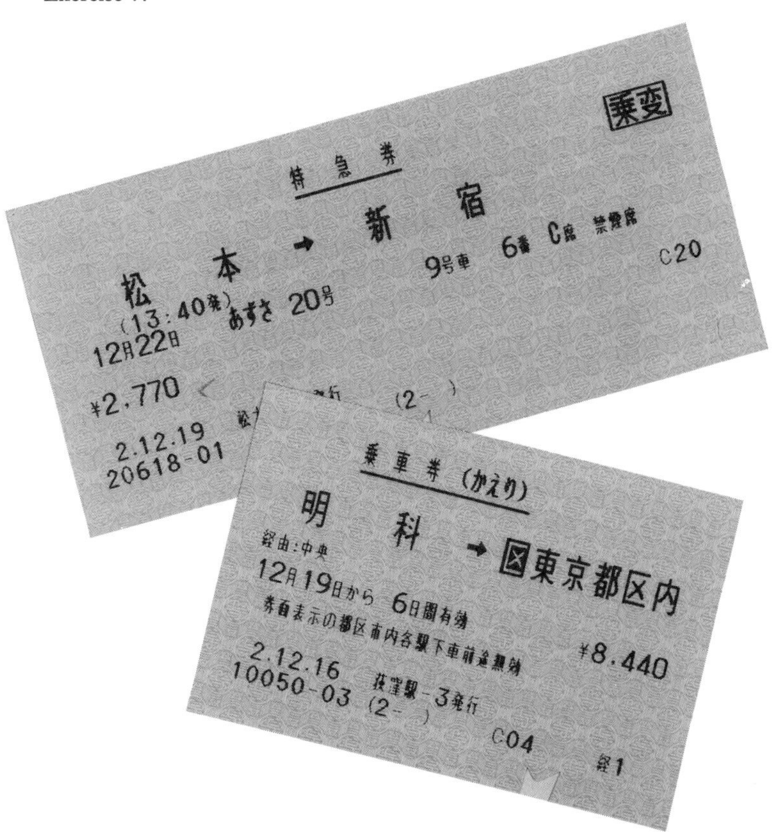

Dialogues

4 *I'm looking for an apartment*

Takada	Anoo...mansuri-manshon o sagashite irun desu keredo kono atari ni nanika arimasu ka?
Estate agent	Watakushi-domo no atsukatte iru apaatomento wa Roppongi ni hitotsu mansuri-manshon ga arun desu keredomo...
Takada	O-nedan wa dono kurai desu ka?
Estate agent	Soo desu ne. Wan-beddo-ruumu kara tsuu-beddo-ruumu made arimashite, maa...daitai nijuu-hachi-man kara, yonjuu-gojuu-man kurai made desu ga...
Takada	Ano, shiitsu ya nanika tsuite imasu?
Estate agent	Hai. Beddo saabisu chaaji to shite, anoo...ryookin ga kakarimasu keredomo...anoo...shiitsu toka, ato...taoru toka tsuite imasu.
Takada	Aa soo desu ka. Anoo, ima aite imasu?
Estate agent	Hai. Ikutsuka no o-heya aite imasu.
Takada	Ja, sore o misete itadakimasu.
Estate agent	Hai.

- ➧ **mansuri-manshon** rented flat (*Eng.* "monthly mansion")
- ➧ **kono atari ni** around here
- **watakushi-domo** we/us (*humb.*) (*eq.* **watakushi-tachi**)
- ➧ **apaatomento** flat (*Eng.*) (*eq.* **apaato**)
- ➧ **dono kurai** about how much? (*eq.* **dono gurai**)
- **Roppongi** a section of Tokyo
- ➧ **(o-)nedan** pricc
- **(wan-/tsuu-) beddoruumu** (one-/two-) bedroom flat (*Eng.*)
- **yonjuu-gojuu-man** 400–500 thousand (yen)
- **shiitsu** sheets (*Eng.*)
- **beddo saabisu chaaji** linen service charge (*Eng.*)
- **taoru** towel (*Eng.*)
- **ikutsuka (no)** some/several

Watakushi-domo no atsukatte iru apaatomento wa... The flats that we are handling...

Wan-beddo-ruumu kara tsuu-beddo-ruumu made arimashite... We have from one- to two-bedroom (flats), and so...

Nijuu-hachi-man kara, yonjuu-gojuu-man kurai made desu. (Rents) are from 280,000 to 400–500,000 (yen).

Shiitsu ya nanika tsuite imasu (ka)? Are sheets and things like that included?

Beddo saabisu chaaji to shite... As a bed service charge...

Ikutsuka no o-heya (ga) aite imasu. Several rooms are open.

Sore o misete itadakimasu. I will have you show them to me. (*humb.*)

Practise what you have learned

10

(1) kagu **(2) shiitsu** **(3) taoru**

(4) daidokoro yoohin **(5) denki** **(6) gasu** **(7) suidoo**

When renting a mansuri manshon, it is important to find out what is included and what there is an additional charge for. Look at the illustrations, listen to the recording, and practise saying the words. Other basic phrases you need when looking for a flat are listed here. Match the Japanese and English phrases below. (Answers p. 188)

(a) Doko desu ka?	____	**(1)** I am looking for a flat.
(b) ____ ga tsuite imasu ka?	____	**(2)** What is included?
(c) Mansuri-manshon o sagashite irun desu keredo...	____	**(3)** Is ____ included?
(d) Jaa, sore o misete kudasai.	____	**(4)** Where is it?
(e) Nani ga tsuite imasu ka?	____	**(5)** About how much is it?
(f) Ikura gurai desu ka?	____	**(6)** Please show it to me.

11

Listen to the recording and find out something about where the woman in the dialogue lives. Put a cross by the correct statement in each pair below. (Answers p. 188)

(1a) **Apaato wa Chiba desu.**
(1b) **Apaato wa Mejiro desu.**

(2a) **Hitori de sunde imasu.**
(2b) **Kazoku to sunde imasu.**

(3a) **Uchi wa shigoto made ichi-jikan.**
(3b) **Uchi wa shigoto made ichi-jikan-han.**

(4a) **Apaato wa benri desu.**
(4b) **Apaato wa chotto fuben desu.**

(5a) **Apaato wa eki kara chikai desu.**
(5b) **Apaato wa eki kara tooi desu.**

12

Working with the recording, describe the **wan-beddo-ruumu mansuri manshon** you heard about in the dialogue—its location, cost, what it includes or does not include, and what you think of it (**takasugimasu, yasui, kirei, suki desu,** etc.).

Key words and phrases

Nanji-goro okimasu ka?	What time do you wake up?
Nyuusu o mitari shinbun o yondari dekimasu.	I can watch news and read papers and such.
Densha no naka de yonde imasu.	I read it in the train.
Kimatte inain desu.	It's not decided.
Urayamashii desu ne!	I envy you!
Supootsu o shimasu ka?	Do you play sports?
(Tenisu) o yoku shimasu.	I play (tennis) a lot.
Kurabu ni haitte imasu ka?	Are you in a club?
Dono gurai joozu desu ka?	How good are you?
Naka-naka umaku narimasen.	No matter what, I don't get any better.
Soko-soko desu.	I'm so-so.
Ie o sagasu no wa muzukashii desu.	Looking for a house is difficult.
Hitori de sagasu no wa taihen desu.	Looking by oneself is awful.
(Shiitsu) ga tsuite imasu ka?	Are (sheets) included?
Ima aite imasu ka?	Is one free now?
Misete itadakimasu.	I will have you show it to me.
(o-)sumai	(your) home
kazoku	family
(Suginami)-ku	(Suginami) Ward
fudoosanya-san	estate agent
nedan	price
hiroi	wide
semai	narrow
fuben	inconvenient
ikutsuka (no)	some/several

Grammar

Adjective + naru

To become (hot, expensive, etc.) is expressed in Japanese by changing the last syllable of an inflectable adjective from **-i** to **-ku** and adding some form of **naru** ("become"). Here are some examples:

(**Takai**) **Nedan wa takakunarimashita.**
The price became high.

(**Umai**) **Naka-naka umakunarimasen.**
No matter what I do, I don't get any better.

(**Samui**) **Ashita samukunaru deshoo.**
Tomorrow it will probably get cold.

A non-inflectable adjective does not change in this form, but the marker **ni** is added before **naru**:

Joozu ni narimashita, ne! He became good (skilful), didn't he?

Making a verb into a noun

When **no** (**wa**) is placed after a verb or verb phrase, it makes it into a noun or noun phrase. Study these examples:

Hitori de tabemasu. I eat alone.
Hitori de taberu no wa iya desu. Eating alone is unpleasant.

Ie o sagashite imasu. I am looking for a house.
Ie o sagasu no wa taihen desu. Looking for a house is awful.

Issho ni ikimashoo. Let's go together.
Issho ni iku no wa ichiban ii to omoimasu. I think going together is best.

Read and understand

1. 公衆電話 **Public phone**

2. 国際電話 **International call**

3. 長距離電話 **Long distance call**

4. 料金相手払い **Collect call**

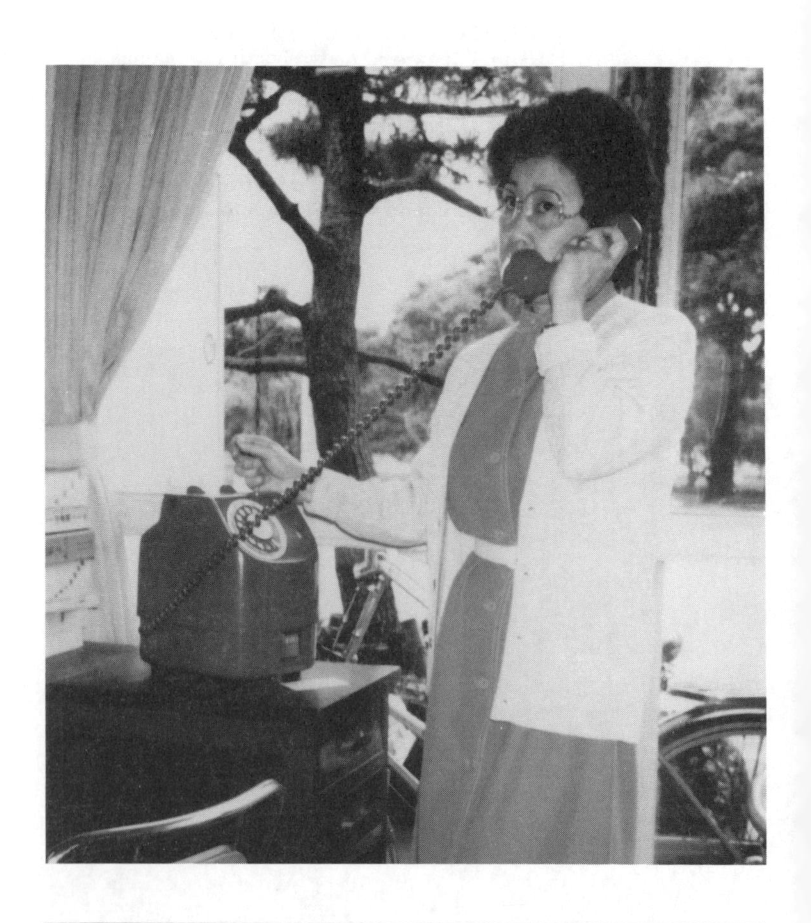

Did you know?

Gestures and body language sometimes speak louder than words. It is not necessary or advisable for non-Japanese to use them, but it is important to know the messages.

- A circle made by the thumb and index finger refers to money—not an "okay" sign.
- A raised thumb refers to one's boss or the "old man"—not a symbol for "Right on!"
- A circling motion with the index finger near one's ear indicates that one thinks the person under discussion is a little bit crazy.
- An index finger pointing at one's own nose means "myself".
- Giving a light tap on one's heart with an open palm means "Leave it up to me. I'll handle it".
- A slight head bob and an open right hand moving up and down with the thumb closer to the nose means "Excuse me".
- A raised right hand with the fingers flapping to indicate "bye bye", is similar to the Japanese sign for "come here". The Western signal for "come here", with a hooked index finger and palm up is a demeaning sign for "come here".
- Gestures used by men to indicate embarrassment, hesitation, awkwardness and dismay:
  Inhaling air audibly through clenched teeth.
  Scratching the back of the head lightly.
  Hitting the forehead lightly with the open palm.
- Moving the open hand in fanning motion in front means "no, no" or "Oh no, not me!"
- Often people nod their heads as they listen to someone speak. Nodding is a signal that the person is listening to what is being said, and not necessarily that he agrees with the speaker.
- Though silence is not a gesture in a strict sense, it needs to be explained. To the Japanese, silence indicates thoughtfulness, intelligence or deep appreciation. A "wise" person in Japan is expected to speak slowly, calmly and with many pauses.

Answers

Practise what you have learned

Exercise **1**	(a) N (b) N (c) N (d) N (e) Y
Exercise **2**	(a) Hayai desu ne (b) Erai desu ne (c) Iie, iie...betsu ni
Exercise **4**	(a) 4 (b) 1 (c) 2 (d) 3
Exercise **6**	(a) None, but he watched rugby (b) He swims every day
Exercise 7	(a) 3 (b) 4 (c) 5 (d) 2 (e) 1
Exercise **8**	(a) small (b) near (c) about 20
Exercise **10**	(a) 4 (b) 3 (c) 1 (d) 6 (e) 2 (f) 5
Exercise **11**	(1) b (2) a (3) a (4) a (5) a

14 STATING YOUR INTENTIONS

You will learn

- how to ask someone his plan for the day
- how to plan a trip to Enoshima
- how to invite someone out for an evening
- how to make travel plans
- something about Kabuki theatre
- about the historical Ueno area
- something about the famous Kamakura area

Study guide

- **Dialogue 1 + Practise what you have learned**
- **Dialogue 2 + Practise what you have learned**
- **Dialogue 3 + Practise what you have learned**
- **Dialogue 4 + Practise what you have learned**
- **Learn: the Key words and phrases**
- **Study: the Grammar section**
- **Read: Read and understand**
- **Read: Did you know?**

Dialogues

1 *What's your plan for the day?*

Miki Kyoo no yotei wa doo natte imasu ka?
Shōda Kyoo wa gogo kara Ueno no bijutsukan ni ikoo to omotte imasu.
Miki Bijutsukan ka... Ii naa. Issho ni itte mo ii desu ka?
Shōda Ee, soo desu ne. Hitori yori mo futari no hoo ga tanoshii desu kara, ne.
Miki Aa, Ueno wa ima sakura ga kirei deshoo, ne.
Shōda Soo desu ne.
Miki Ueno no Bijutsukan wa donna bijutsukan nan desu ka?
Shōda Seiyō Bijutsukan nan desu.
Miki Aa soo desu ka.
Shōda Kitto tanoshii to omoimasu yo.

yotei plan/intention
issho ni together
tanoshii fun/enjoyable
Seiyō Occidental art

Kyoo no yotei wa doo natte imasu ka? What is your plan for the day? (*lit.* How is your plan for the day shaping up?)

Gogo kara in the afternoon (*lit.* from the p.m.)

____ **ni ikoo to omotte imasu.** I'm thinking of going to ____ . See the Grammar section.

Ii naa. That's nice, isn't it? (*m./inf.*) (*eq.* **Ii desu, ne.**)

Issho ni itte mo ii desu ka? Is it okay if we go together? See the Grammar section.

Hitori yori mo futari no hoo ga tanoshii desu. Two (people) are more fun than one (person).

Practise what you have learned

1 Match the following Japanese expressions with their English counterparts. (Answers p. 202)

(a) **bijutsukan** ____ (1) Museum of Western Art

(b) **gogo kara** ____ (2) I think it will be fun.

(c) **Seiyō Bijutsukan** ____ (3) art museum

(d) **Issho ni itte mo ii desu ka?** ____ (4) in the afternoon

(e) **Tanoshii to omoimasu.** ____ (5) May I go with you?

2 Listen to the recording and hear Miura-san and Tanabe-san making plans for the afternoon. Answer the following questions. (Answers p. 202)

(a) What does Tanabe-san want to do tomorrow? ____________________

(b) Is Miura-san going with her? ____________________

(c) Where is the store? (Circle one.) **Ikebukuro** **Shinjuku** **Harajuku** **Shibuya**

(d) How are they going to get there? ____________________

____

3 Suppose you are planning to go to Ueno. Ask a Japanese friend to go with you. (**Ueno e ikimasen ka?**) Suggest going to Ueno by J.R. rather than by taxi. You will be asked to reply. Before you begin, read the "Did you know?" section of this unit to find out more about the area.

____

____

____

____

Dialogues

2 *Where should I go first?*

Yoshida Kondo Enoshima to Kamakura no Hachimangū e iku tsumori nan da kedo...dotchi e saki ni itta hoo ga ii ka na?

Shōda Soo desu ne...Hachimangū wa totemo komu kara, saki ni itta hoo ga ii to omoimasu yo. Sono ato de, Enoshima ni itte mo, Enoshima wa yuuhi ga kirei da shi, ii to omoimasu.

Yoshida Soo ka...Sore jaa, Yokosuka-sen de Kamakura made dete, sore kara Hachimangū ni yotta ato ni, (Ee) Enoden de Enoshima e ikimashoo.

Shōda Soo desu nee.
Tokoro de, kaimono nanka nasaru yotei wa arun desu ka?

Yoshida Soo desu ne. Hachimangū no mae no namiki-michi ni Kamakura-bori no mise ga takusan aru nde, sokora hen no mise o mite arukitai to omotte imasu.

Shōda Sore wa totemo ii to omoimasu.

Enoshima famous tourist spot
Hachimangū Hachiman Shrine
saki ni before/first
komu be crowded
yuuhi setting sun
➧ **ato ni** later (*eq.* **ato de**)
Enoden Enoshima tramcar
➧ **tokoro de** by the way
namiki-michi tree-lined road
Kamakura-bori Kamakura wood carving
sokora hen around there (*eq.* **sono hen**)
mite aruku browse around (*lit.* look and walk)

➧ **Dotchi e saki ni itta hoo ga ii ka na?** Which way would it be best if we went first? (*Cf.* Unit 3, **Tabeta hoo ga ii desu.** "It would be better if we ate".) (*eq.* **Dochira e itta hoo ga ii desu ka?**)

Enoshima ni itte mo... (Even) if you go to Enoshima...

Yuuhi ga kirei da shi... The sunset is pretty, and... Again, **shi** indicates that there are other reasons unstated.

Kamakura made dete... (Go) as far as Kamakura and exit.

Hachimangū ni yotta ato ni... after going by Hachimangū .

Kaimono nasaru yotei wa arun desu ka? Do you plan to go shopping? (*lit.* Do you have plans to do [any] shopping?)

Takusan aru n(o)de... Since there are many...

Practise what you have learned

4

When talking about sequential activities, there are short but useful phrases that will connect sentences and make them flow smoothly.

(a) **saki ni**	before (that)
(b) **hajime ni**	at the beginning; at first
(c) **sono ato**	after that
(d) **sore kara**	and then; afterwards

Read the following sentences and use the above phrases as appropriate to fill the blanks. (Answers p. 202)

Ashita Wada-san to issho ni kankoo suru tsumori nan desu.

____________ **Kōkyo (Imperial Palace) o mimasu.** ____________

Kamakura e ikimasu. ____________ **shokuji o shite,** ____________

Hachimangū e ikimasu.

5

To express a preference, use the following pattern:

Question: (*Noun*) **to** (*noun*) **to dotchi no hoo ga ii desu ka?**

Which do you prefer, ____________ or ____________?

Answer: ____________ **no hoo ga ii desu.**

Now listen to the recording and find out which item in each pair below is preferred. Place a check mark by the preferred item. (Answers p. 202)

(a) ____ washoku / ____ yooshoku
(b) ____ ku-ji / ____ kuji-han
(c) ____ ima / ____ ato
(d) ____ chikatetsu / ____ takushii

6

"**Ko-So-A-Do**" words. The words in the chart below are called **Ko-So-A-Do** words because of their common first syllables. Many have been presented in the dialogues and have been explained independently. Look at them, then listen and work with the recording.

kore	this	**kono** + noun	this + noun
sore	that	**sono** + noun	that + noun
are	that (over there)	**ano** + noun	that + noun over there
dore	which one?	**dono** + noun	which + noun?
koko	here	**kono hen**	around here
soko	there	**sono hen**	around there
asoko	over there	**ano hen**	around (over) there
doko	where?	**dono hen**	around where?
kotchi/kochira	this way		
sotchi/sochira	that way		
atchi/achira	that way (in the distance)		
dotchi/dochira	which way?		

7

Now listen to the recording as Aoki-san guides you in creating sentences using the **Ko-so-a-do** words.

Dialogues

3 *Shall we go to see Kabuki?*

Shōda Tokoro de, Kabuki nanka mi ni ikimasen ka?
Miki Kabuki desu ka.
Shōda Ee.
Miki Mi ni ikitai desu, ne.
Shōda Soo desu ka? Ima totemo ninki no aru dashimono o yatte irun desu keredomo...(Ee.) Ikaga desu ka?
Miki Ee, demo kippu arimasu deshoo ka?
Shōda Aa, mae-uri wa mada katte nain desu keredomo...
Miki Mae-uri ga nai to, toojitsu kaemasu ka ne?
Shōda Soo desu ne...totemo yuumei na hito desu kara, ne. Demo itte miru kachi wa aru to omoimasu yo.
Miki Un, boku mo ichido mitain desu yo.
Shōda Jaa, ikimashoo ka.

- **tokoro de** by the way...
- **Kabuki** Japanese traditional theatre (See "Did You Know?")
  ninki no aru popular
  dashimono performance
- **mae-uri** advance (ticket) (*lit.* previous-sale)
- **toojitsu** same day
- **yuumei na hito** famous person
  kachi wa/ga aru to be worth it/to have value
  ichido onc time/once

Mi ni ikimasen ka? Won't you go and see? In this invitation **mi** is from **miru/mimasu**, meaning "see", "watch", or "look at".

Dashimono o yatte irun desu. They are doing a performance. (*eq.* **...yatte imasu.**)

Mae-uri wa mada katte inain desu. I haven't bought an advance ticket yet.

Mae-uri ga nai to... If there are no advance tickets... **Nai** is an informal form of **arimasen**.

Toojitsu kaemasu ka ne? We can buy one on the same day (of the performance), can't we? **Ka ne** indicates uncertainty, similar to **ka na**.

Itte miru kachi wa aru to omoimasu. I think it would be worth it to go and see.

Practise what you have learned

8 Select the appropriate English words from the box to match the Japanese words. (Answers p. 202)

(a) ichido ____
(b) toojitsu-uri no kippu ____
(c) yuumei na hito ____
(d) ninki no aru hito ____
(e) mae-uri kippu ____

(1)	popular person
(2)	famous person
(3)	advance ticket
(4)	once
(5)	Same-day ticket (bought at the gate)

9 Listen to the recording and answer the following questions. (Answers p. 202)

(a) When are they going to the Kabuki Theatre? ____________________
(b) Did someone buy the tickets already? ____________________
(c) Where are they going to meet? ____________________
(d) At what time? ____________________

10 With Aoki-san's prompting, ask a Japanese friend to go to see Kabuki with you on Tuesday of next week. When your friend worries that tickets might not be available, tell him that you are planning to buy them tomorrow. Before you start, think about how you would say these phrases:

(1) I'm planning to…
(2) Tuesday of next week
(3) Would you like to go…? (polite invitation)
(4) I'm looking forward to it.

Kabuki theatre

Dialogues

4 *I want to plan a trip*

Customer Anoo...Yōroppa-ryokoo o shitain desu kedo ne...hitori de iku tte yuu no wa muri deshoo ka?

Agent Hai. Anoo...o-kyaku-sama wa Yōroppa e o-dekake ni natta koto ga gozaimasu ka?

Customer Iie, nain desu kedo...

Agent Sore demo, daijoobu desu yo. Anoo, pakkeiji-tsuaa ni o-nori ni nareba o-hitori-sama kara, sanka dekimasu.

Customer Soo desu ka? Jitsu wa ne...kurashikku no ongaku ga kikitain desu kedo, doko e ittara ii deshoo?

Agent Soo desu ne. Ōsutorii no Uiin, soshite Doitsu no Myunhen nado wa ikaga de gozaimashoo? Ryokoo wa kugatsu, juugatsu, juuichigatsu ga yokaroo to omoimasu.

▸ **Yōroppa-ryokoo** European travel
muri impossible
sore demo even so
▸ **pakkeiji-tsuaa** package tour (*Eng.*)
o-hitori-sama one person (*pol.*)
sanka participation
Jitsu wa... To tell the truth.../The fact is...
kurashikku no ongaku classical music (*Eng.*)
Ōsutoriya no Uiin Vienna, Austria
Doitsu no Myunhen Munich, Germany
nado and so forth/and like that
yokaroo probably good (*pol.*) (*eq.* **ii deshoo**)

Hitori de iku tte yuu no wa muri deshoo ka? Would such a thing as going alone be impossible?

O-dekake ni natta koto ga gozaimasu ka? Have you ever gone (to Europe)? (*exal.*) (*eq.* **Itta koto ga arimasu ka?**) See the Grammar section.

▸ **Nai(n) desu.** I haven't. (*eq.* **Arimasen.**)

Pakkeiji-tsuaa ni o-nori ni nareba... If you get on a package tour... (*pol.*) (*eq.* **...ni norimasu to...**)

O-hitori-sama kara, sanka dekimasu. You can participate, since you are alone. (*pol.*) (*eq.* **Hitori desu kara,...**)

▸ **Ongaku ga kikitai(n) desu.** I want to listen to music.

Ikaga de gozaimashoo? How would it be? (*exal.*) (*eq.* **Ikaga deshoo ka?**)

Practise what you have learned

11

There are short but very useful phrases to express feelings. Select the appropriate English phrase to match each Japanese phrase below. Some of them are from other units, but they are included here because they are very helpful to know. (Answers p. 202)

(a) **Daijoobu desu.** ____		(1) Can you do it?/Can it be done?
(b) **Ii to omoimasu yo.** ____		(2) Not yet.
(c) **Dekimasu ka?** ____		(3) It is okay.
(d) **Muri desu, ne.** ____		(4) I think it's fine.
(e) **Dame desu, ne.** ____		(5) It can't be done. Impossible.
(f) **Mada desu.** ____		(6) I have. There is.
(g) **Arimasu.** ____		(7) I haven't. There isn't.
(h) **Nain desu.** ____		(8) It's no good. It won't work.

12

Listen to the recording and practise the phrases from Exercise 11.

13

Suppose you wish to extend your trip to Hong Kong. Listen to the recording and work through the phrases with Tanabe-san's help. The following phrases may be helpful.

(a) I would like to go to Hong Kong. Is it all right to travel alone?
(b) Would a package tour be better?
(c) I prefer going alone. (______________ no hoo ga iin desu keredo…)
(d) Do you have a ticket?

Key words and phrases

Yotei wa/ga arimasu ka?	Do you have plans?
Yotei wa nan desu ka?	What are your plans?
Yotei wa doo desu ka?	How are your plans?
(Ik)oo to omotte imasu.	I am thinking about (go)ing.
(It)te mo ii desu ka?	Is it okay if I (go)?
Mi ni ikimasen ka?	Won't you go and see?
(Mae-uri) ga nai to...	If there are no (advance tickets).
(It)ta koto ga arimasu ka?	Have you ever (gone)?
issho ni	together
saki ni	previously
ato ni	afterwards
tokoro de	by the way
sore demo	even so
ichido	one time/once
nado	and so forth/and like that
ninki no aru	popular
kachi ga aru	valuable/worthwhile
muri	impossible
mae-uri	advance ticket
toojitsu	same day

Grammar

"I think I will..."

The verb ending **-oo to omoimasu** indicates that the speaker is thinking about doing something. Look at the following examples:

Kyōto ni ikoo to omoimasu. I think I will go to Kyoto.

Kyōto ni ikoo to omotte imasu. I am thinking that I will go to Kyoto.

Asking/giving permission

To ask permission to do something, the **te-**form of a verb is followed by **mo ii desu ka?** To give permission, simply leave off the marker **ka**. Literally, this form means "If I do it, is it okay/good?" Look at the following examples:

Issho ni itte mo ii desu ka? Is it okay if I go with you?

Mizu o nonde mo ii desu. It's okay to drink the water.

Moo notte mo ii desu ka? Is it okay to board already?

Soko de matte mo ii desu. It's okay to wait over there.

Ta-form + koto ga arimasu

The **Ta-**form of a verb looks like the **Te-**form except for the vowel, but its purpose is totally different. When followed by **koto ga arimasu ka**, it means "Have you ever (done something)?" A simple response to this question would be either **Hai, arimasu** or **Iie, arimasen**. Look at the following examples.

Yōroppa ni itta koto ga arimasu ka? Have you ever gone to Europe?

Washoku o tabeta koto ga arimasen. I have never eaten Japanese food.

Kabuki o mita koto ga arimasen ka? Haven't you ever seen Kabuki?

Hitori de ryokoo shita koto ga arimasu. I have travelled alone.

Read and understand

Warning sings

禁煙	**No smoking**
撮影禁止	**No photography**
水泳禁止	**No swimming**
危険	**Danger**
立入禁止	**Do not enter**
さわるな	**Do not touch**

Did you know?

Kabuki

With three hundred years of tradition, this stage art is still by far the most popular traditional Japanese theatre. When **kabuki** originated in the 17th century, a troupe consisted entirely of women players. However, it was soon prohibited by law, accused of contributing to the deterioration of public morals. **Kabuki** later reestablished itself with all male players, some playing the female roles (**oyama**), and it has developed into a rich and colourful theatrical tradition.

Themes of the **kabuki** plays, which can last as long as six hours, are feudalistic in setting and sentiment. Loyalty, love, sacrifice, revenge, conflicts between clans and individuals are all common themes.

Kabuki attendance is a formal affair. There are avid followers with season tickets, and there are others who will go to **kabuki** once in a lifetime. The play begins in the early afternoon, and a long interval is provided for the audience to enjoy an elaborate box lunch (**Makunouchi bentoo**) sold on the premises. (It is best to place an order before the play and pick it up at the interval.)

The stage setting and costumes are colourful, dramatic and uniquely Japanese. To help foreigners follow story lines, English translation earphones are available for a small fee. Those who wish to have only a taste of **Kabuki** can get tickets to watch only a portion of the performance. In Tokyo the performances are held at the **Kabukiza**, in the east end of the **Ginza**, or at the National Theatre, near the Imperial Palace.

Ueno

Located in the northern section of Tokyo on the J.R. Line, Ueno is a busy hub for railway services heading for northern Japan. The **Tōbu** Line leaves for **Nikkō** from Ueno. It is also near **Asakusa**, the traditional entertainment section of old Tokyo, where people today still come to visit the temples and to enjoy the atmosphere.

Ueno Park (Ueno Kōen)

Ueno Park, adjacent to the station, is famous for its historical significance. The park houses numerous museums—Tokyo National Museum, the Orient Museum, the National Museum of Western Arts, Tokyo Fine Arts Metropolitan Gallery, the Old Tokyo Museum (**Shitamachi**) and the National Science Museum—as well as the zoo. There are also the **Kan'eiji** Temple built in 1625 to protect Edo (old Tokyo), **Tōshōgū** shrine dedicated to the Tokugawa Shogunate in 1627, and **Horyū-ji Hōmotsuden**, the temple museum.

Kamakura

Located one hour from Tokyo by **Yokosuka-sen**, this was once the capital of ancient Japan, and for the past century it has been enjoyed as a quiet seaside resort. Many artists and novelists live there, as did the late **Kawabata Yasunari**, the Nobel Laureate author. In recent years it has become a popular dormitory town for those who commute to work in metropolitan Tokyo. It is also a tourist resort area and, especially for foreign visitors, the Great Buddha (**Daibutsu**) is of particular interest. This bronze sitting figure of **Amida** is 38 feet tall and has been in the open site since 1369. **Tsurugaoka Hachiman-gū** is one of the most popular shrines for New Year's Day shrine visits. The colourful annual festival for this shrine is held on September 15 and 16. In **Kamakura** there are 65 Buddhist temples and 19 Shinto Shrines. **Kamakura** is also a walker's haven, so weekend visits, especially in the summertime, will be very crowded.

Answers

Practise what you have learned

Exercise **1**	(a) 3 (b) 4 (c) 1 (d) 5 (e) 2
Exercise **2**	(a) go to the art exhibition at Sibu Dept. Store (b) yes (c) Ikebukuro (d) By J.R.
Exercise **4**	b, c, a, d or b, d, a, c
Exercise **5**	(a) washoku (b) kuji-han (c) ima (d) chikatetsu
Exercise **8**	(a) 4 (b) 5 (c) 2 (d) 1 (e) 3
Exercise **9**	(a) Saturday (b) yes (c) in front of the Kabuki Theatre (d) 4:00
Exercise **11**	(a) 3 (b) 4 (c) 1 (d) 5 (e) 8 (f) 2 (g) 6 (h) 7

15 TALKING ABOUT THE PAST

You will learn

- how to talk about past events
- how to talk about other foreign language learning experiences
- how to enquire "How was your day?" and to describe your day
- about Japanese customs and behaviour: **omoiyari** and **enryo**
- about "Yes" and "No" in Japanese

Before you begin

This is the last unit of the course. To get the most out of this course, develop a habit of thinking in Japanese. For example, when you step out to go shopping, you notice that it's a hot day and the traffic is heavy. You can immediately make a couple of comments: **Kyoo wa atsui desu ne** or **Konde imasu ne!** After a while, you can begin to develop your own dialogue by asking a question and answering it: **Tenki wa doo desu ka? Samuin desu yo,** and so forth.

Study guide

	Dialogue 1 + Practise what you have learned
	Dialogue 2 + Practise what you have learned
	Dialogue 3 + Practise what you have learned
	Dialogue 4 + Practise what you have learned
	Learn: the Key words and phrases
	Study: the Grammar section
	Read: Did you know? and note the phrases

Dialogues

1 *Have you studied foreign languages?*

Miki Nani-go ga wakarimasu ka?
Shōda Soo desu ne...Eigo wa hanasemasu kedo...demo, ima daredemo Eigo wa wakarimasu kara, ne.
Miki Soo desu ne.
Shōda Donna kotoba o o-hanashi dekimasu ka?
Miki Toruko-go ga sukoshi wakarimasu.
Shōda Toruko-go desu ka? Mezurashii desu nee. (Hai) Doko de benkyoo shitan desu ka?
Miki Toruko ni ryokoo shita toki, benkyoo shimashita.
Shōda Aa, go-jibun de...?
Miki Hai.
Shōda Sugoi desu, ne!
Miki Iie, iie. Anata wa donna kotoba ga wakarimasu ka? Hoka ni wa...?
Shōda Ee, watashi wa Furansu-go ga sukoshi yomemasu.
Miki Aa soo desu ka.

nani-go what language?
Eigo English language
hanasemasu can speak
daredemo anybody
kotoba words/language
Toruko-go Turkish language
sukoshi a little bit
mezurashii unusual/rare
benkyoo study
go-jibun de by yourself (*pol.*)
Sugoi desu, ne. That's impressive!
Furansu-go French language
yomemasu can read

Nanigo ga wakarimasu ka? What language(s) do you understand?

Donna kotoba o o-hanashi dekimasu ka? What kind of languages can you speak? (*pol.*) (*eq.* **Donna kotoba o hanashimasu ka?**)

Doko de benkyoo shitan desu ka? Where did you study? (*eq.* **Doko de benkyoo shimashita ka**?)

Toruko ni ryokoo shita toki, benkyoo shimashita. When I travelled to Turkey, I studied it. See the Grammar section.

Hoka ni wa... Other than (what we've talked about already)...

Practise what you have learned

1 Match the English phrases with their Japanese equivalents. (Answers p. 215)

(a) What language(s) do you understand? ____

(b) Where did you study it? ____

(c) Can you read Japanese? ____

(d) You are good at it! ____

(e) No, I am not good at it yet. ____

(1) Joozu desu ne.
(2) Doko de benkyoo shimashita ka?
(3) Nani-go ga wakarimasu ka?
(4) Iie, iie, mada joozu ja nain desu.
(5) Nihongo ga yomemasu ka?

2 Listen to Miura-san and Tanabe-san talk about their experiences in learning **gaikoku-go** (foreign languages), and answer these questions: (Answers p. 215)

(a) What language(s) has she studied? ______________________________

(b) How many years did she study? ______________________________

(c) What language(s) has he studied? ______________________________

(d) How is his German? ______________________________

3 Talk to a Japanese person about foreign languages. In addition to what has been introduced in this unit, you already know how to say, "I like ______", "It's difficult/easy/interesting", "I want to study", etc. Work through it with Tanabe-san's assistance on the recording.

Dialogues

2 *How was your day?*

Husband Tadaima.
Wife O-kaerinasai.
Husband Kyoo wa daibu tsukareta.
Wife Kyoo wa jimusho ja nakatta no?
Husband Gozen-chuu wa jimusho ni itan da keredomo, gogo wa koojoo no hoo ni itta wake.
Wife Michi wa konde imashita?
Husband Iki wa, maa-maa dattan da keredomo, kaeri wa daibu komimashita.
Wife Kondo wa, koojoo wa itsu iku no?
Husband Raishuu no Kayoobi ni moo ichido ikimasu.
Wife Michi ga suite iru to, ii wa ne.
Husband Tabun Kayoobi wa daijoobu ja nai ka to omotte...

- **Tadaima.** I'm home.
- **O-kaerinasai.** Welcome back.
- **daibu** quite/mostly
- **jimusho** office
- **gogo** afternoon
- **gozen-chuu** during the morning
- **koojoo** factory
- **iki** the trip there/(on) the way there
- **maa-maa** so-so
- **kaeri** the return trip
- **moo ichido** one more time
- **suite iru** is empty

Tadaima./O-kaerinasai. These are standard phrases used when a person returns home or to some other familiar place.

Kyoo wa jimusho ja nakatta no? Weren't you at the office today? (*inf.*) (*lit.* Wasn't it the office today?) (*eq.* **Kyoo wa jimusho dewa arimasen deshita ka?**)

Gozen-chuu wa jimusho ni itan da keredomo... I was at the office in the morning, but...(*inf.*) (*eq.* **...jimusho ni imashita...**)

Gogo wa koojoo no hoo ni itta wake. In the afternoon I went to the plant. **Wake** at the end of this sentence implies "and that's why (I am so tired)".

Maa-maa dattan da... It was so-so. (*inf.*) (*eq.* **Maa-maa deshita.**)

Koojoo wa itsu iku no? When will you go to the factory? (*inf.*) (*eq.* **...itsu ikimasu ka?**)

Michi ga suite iru to, ii wa ne. It'll be nice if the traffic is light, won't it? (*inf.*) (*lit.* If the roads are empty...)

Kayoobi wa daijoobu ja nai ka to omotte (imasu). I'm thinking Tuesday will probably be okay. (*lit.* I'm thinking, "Tuesday is okay, isn't it?")

Practise what you have learned

4 Read the Japanese phrases below and match them with their English equivalents. (Answers p. 215)

(a) Konde imashita.	____	**(1)**	It was so-so.
(b) Kyoo wa suite imashita.	____	**(2)**	Oh, I'm tired.
(c) Aa...tsukaremashita.	____	**(3)**	The traffic was heavy.
(d) Maa-maa deshita.	____	**(4)**	The traffic was light today.

5 **Tadaima** and **O-kaerinasai** are two standard, paired greetings. When a person comes home or returns to an inn, etc., he will say **Tadaima**, and whoever welcomes him back says **O-kaerinasai** and usually adds a phrase equivalent to "How was the day?" (**Doo deshita?**) Read through the following phrases and then listen to and practise with the recording. Some frequently used phrases are listed below. (See also *Did you know?*)

Tadaima.	I'm home.
O-kaerinasai.	Welcome home.
Kyoo wa doo deshita?	How was the day?
Konde imashita?	Was traffic heavy?
Tsukareta deshoo.	You must be tired.
Atsukatta deshoo.	It must have been hot!
Samukatta deshoo.	It must have been cold!
Tookatta deshoo.	It must have been far.

6 Listen to the recording and practise some response phrases. You already know most of these words, but a review might be in order. If you are in agreement with what has been said, say **Ee, daibu...** (Yes, quite a bit...) but if you want to minimize the problem, say **Ee, chotto...** (Yes, a little...) If you want to say, "No, it wasn't so bad", say **Iie, daijoobu deshita**.

Dialogues

3 *The room is too small!*

Shōda Shiriai no gaikoku-jin ga Nihon ni kitan de, bijinesu hoteru, ii tokoro o erande, tanondan desu. Demo, tonikaku, sono semasa ni odoroichatte, konna ni semain ja nimotsu mo okenai tte itchatte... Tada-tada odoroite bakkari nandesu yo. Shiyoo ga nai kara, furonto ni itte, watashi ga kooshoo shite, sagaku o haratte, anoo, futari-yoo no heya ni kaete morattan desu. Maa, watashi nanka dewa, ano heya wa futsuu ni kanjimasu kedo nee...yappari chigau mono nan desu ne.

shiriai an acquaintance
▸ **gaikoku-jin** foreigner
▸ **Nihon** Japan
erande choose (and...) (*dic.* **erabu**)
tonikaku anyhow
semasa narrowness/small size
konna ni this much
▸ **nimotsu** baggage
okenai cannot put down
tada-tada just/absolutely (emphasizer)
▸ **furonto** front desk
▸ **kooshoo** negotiation
▸ **sagaku** difference (monetary)
▸ **haratte** pay (and...) (*dic.* **harau**)
▸ **futari-yoo no heya** a double room
kaete change (and...) (*dic.* **kaeru**)
futsuu normal/ordinary/common
kanjimasu feel/seem (*dic.* **kanjiru**)
yappari/yahari after all
chigau mono something different

Shiriai no gaikoku-jin ga Nihon ni kitan de... A foreign acquaintance came to Japan and...

Ii tokoro o erande, tanondan desu. I chose a good place and asked for (reserved) it.

Sono semasa ni odoroichatte,... Being shocked at its smallness... (*eq.* **...odoroite shimatte** = being completely shocked)

Konna ni semain ja If it's this small... (*eq.* **Konna ni semai to...**)

Nimotsu mo okenai tte itchatte... Saying right out that you can't even put down your bags... (**itchatte = itte shimatte**)

Tada-tada odoroite bakkari nan desu yo. I was just completely surprised!

▸ **Kooshoo shite, sagaku o haratte...** I negotiated and payed the difference...

▸ **Futari-yoo no heya ni kaete morattan desu.** I had them change it to a double room. (*eq.* **...kaete moraimashita**.) See the Grammar section for **-te moraimasu.**

Watashi nanka dewa... As for me...

Ano heya wa futsuu ni kanjimasu kedo... That room feels normal, but...

Yappari chigau mono nan desu. It is, after all, a different thing (for foreigners). The implication here is that a foreigner would be accustomed to more spacious hotel rooms.

Practise what you have learned

7 Frequently sizes, quantities and food portions in Japan are smaller than they are in the West. Accepting that fact, a person can negotiate as we saw done in this dialogue, provided he is willing to pay the difference. Match these useful negotiation phrases: (Answers p. 215)

(a)	It is too small (size).	____	**(1)**	Sagaku o haraimasu.
(b)	I would like to change it.	____	**(2)**	Chotto chiisa-sugimasu.
(c)	It is a little small (narrow).	____	**(3)**	Chotto semai desu.
(d)	I'll pay the difference.	____	**(4)**	Sumimasen ga, kaetain desu.

8 The room that your Japanese friend arranged for you is too small for comfort. Go to the front desk to try to upgrade it. Listen to the recording and, with Miura-san's help, make the necessary arrangements. You will need some of the phrases listed below.

(a) My room is too small. ________________

(b) I want to change it. ________________

(c) Do you have a big(ger) room? ________________

(d) Oh, there isn't? That's a problem. ________________

(e) I will pay the difference. ________________

9 Listen to the recording and, with Tanabe-san's help, elaborate on the previous exercise.

(a) As of when is the larger room available? ________________

(b) What is the difference (in the room charge)? ________________

(c) What is the room number? ________________

Room with a view, Shiroyama Kanko Hotel in Kagoshima

Dialogues

4 *At the noodle shop*

Shōda Kinoo totemo omoshiroi koto ga attan desu yo. Shiriai no gaikoku-jin, raamen'ya-san ni tsurete ittan desu. Menyuu o mite, wakaranai n'de, ichiban futsuu no raamen o tanondan desu, ne.
Raamen ga kitan desu keredomo, o-hashi shika nai deshoo... O-hashi zenzen tsukaenai mono desu kara, o-mise no obasan ni, "Anoo, fooku arimasu ka?" tte kiitan desu. Demo, fooku nanka nakute, moo...kare, taberu no ni, moo...ichi-jikan ijoo kakatchattan desu yo. Nan de nafukin made oite nain da nante yutte tan desu yo. Demo, tabe-owatta toki ni wa, "Totemo oishikatta" tte itte kuremashita.

koto thing (abstract idea)
raamen'ya-san noodle shop
tsurete take along (and...) (*dic.* **tsureru**)
o-hashi chopsticks
zenzen (not) at all
tsukaenai cannot use
mono thing (tangible)
o-mise no obasan woman of the shop
fooku fork (*Eng.*)
ijoo more than
nafukin napkin (*Eng.*)
owatte finish, end (and...) (*dic.* **owaru**)

Raamen'ya-san ni tsurete ittan desu. I took him along to a noodle shop. (*eq.* **...tsurete ikimashita.**)

Ichiban futsuu no raamen o tanondan desu. He asked for the most common noodles. (*eq.* **...tanomimashita.**)

O-hashi shika nai deshoo. There's nothing but chopsticks, you know?

O-hashi zenzen tsukaenai mono desu kara... Chopsticks are something he can't use at all, so...

O-mise no obasan ni...kiitan desu. He asked the woman (*lit.* "aunt") of the shop...(*eq.* **...kikimashita.**)

Fooku nanka nakute There not being such a thing as a fork...

Taberu no ni...ichi-jikan ijoo kakatchattan desu. It took him over an hour to eat. **Taberu no ni** = as for eating. **Kakatchattan desu** = **kakatte shimaimashita**.

Nande nafukin made oite nain da nante yuttetan desu yo. He was saying, "Why, they don't even have napkins!" (*eq.* **Nafukin demo oite inai to itte imashita.**)

Tabe-owatta toki ni... When he finished...(See the Grammar section.)

Itte kuremashita. He said (kindly). **Kuremashita** (*dic.* **kureru**) after the **te**-form of a verb indicates that something is done as a favour out of kindness.

Practise what you have learned

10 Read each conversational phrase and identify whether the sentence is in present or past tense. Remember that the present tense is also used to indicate future intention. (Answers p. 215)

(a) Totemo omoshiroi koto ga arun desu yo. ____

(b) Hoteru no furonto ni tanondan desu. ____

(c) Oishii raamen o tabetan desu. ____

(d) Kamakura ni ikun desu. ____

(e) Fooku ga nakattan desu. ____

11 Listen to the recording. Tanabe-san and Miura-san will change verbs to past tense in two different ways. Practise with the recording.

Example:

	(He) speaks Japanese.	(He) spoke Japanese.
	Nihongo o hanashimasu.	**Nihongo o hanashimashita.**
or	**Nihongo o hanasundesu.**	**Nihongo o hanashitandesu.**

(a) Japan Times o yomimasu. Japan Times o yo ______________

(b) Tenki-yohoo o mimasu. Tenki-yohoo o mi ______________

(c) Hoteru o yoyaku surundesu. Hoteru o yoyaku shi ______________

(d) Yuujin ga kurundesu. Yuujin ga ki ______________

12 Try putting the above phrases into present and past tense conversational forms, as in the example. (Answers p. 215)

Example: (**yomimasu**)

Kyoo hoteru de Japan Times o yomun desu (present)

Kinoo hoteru de Japan Times o yondan desu (past)

(a) (**mimasu**)

Konban heya de tenki-yohoo o ______________ (present)

Kinoo no ban, heya de tenki-yohoo o ______________ (past)

(b) (**shimasu**)

Yuujin ga hoteru o yoyaku ______________ (present)

Kinoo yuujin ga hoteru o yoyaku ______________ (past)

(c) (**kimasu**)

Raishuu yuujin ga ______________ (present)

Kinoo yuujin ga ga ______________ (past)

Now go back to the recording and complete the exercise.

Key words and phrases

Tadaima.	I'm home.
O-kaerinasai.	Welcome back.
Sugoi desu.	That's great!
Nanigo ga wakarimasu ka?	What language(s) do you understand?
Donna kotoba o hanashimasu ka?	What kind of languages do you speak?
Doko de benkyoo shimashita ka?	Where did you study?
Ryokoo shita toki...	When I travelled,...
Tabe-owatta toki ni...	When I finished eating,...
(Kae)te moraimashita.	I had them (change it).
____ **ni tsurete ikimashita.**	I took (him) with me to ____ .
____ **ni kikimashita.**	I asked ____ .
(It)te kuremashita.	(He) kindly (said).
iki	(on) the way there
kaeri	(on) the return trip
koto	thing (abstract idea)
mono	thing (tangible)
nani-go	what language?
Eigo	English
Nihon	Japan
gaikoku-jin	foreigner
o-hashi	chopsticks
zenzen	(not) at all
____ **ijoo**	more than ____
daredemo	anyone
moo ichido	one more time
tonikaku	anyhow
konna ni	to this degree/this much
futsuu	ordinary/usual/common

Grammar

-te morau

-te morau (**-te moraimasu**) to have someone do something

Futari-yoo no heya ni kaete moraimashita.
I had them change it to a double room.

Yuujin ni nimotsu o hakonde moraimasu.
I will have a friend carry the baggage.

Verb + toki

The word **toki** literally means "a point in time". When it follows a verb it can be translated "when", as in the following examples:

Nihon ni sunde ita toki,... When I was living in Japan,...

Eiga ga owatta toki,... When the movie ended,...

Ashita iku toki,... When I go tomorrow,...

-go and -jin

The suffix **-go** after the name of a country refers to the language spoken in that country. The suffix **-jin** indicates a native of that country. Here, for your reference, is a list of some country names, languages and peoples:

Country	*Language*	*People*
Nihon (Japan)	**Nihongo**	**Nihonjin**
Doitsu (Germany)	**Doitsugo**	**Doitsujin**
Supein (Spain)	**Supeingo**	**Supeinjin**
Itariya (Italy)	**Itariyago**	**Itariyajin**
Furansu (France)	**Furansugo**	**Furansujin**
Chuugoku (China)	**Chuugokugo**	**Chuugokujin**
Taiwan (Taiwan)	**Chuugokugo**	**Taiwanjin** *or* **Chuugokujin**
Kankoku (Korea)	**Kankokugo**	**Kankokujin**
Betonamu (Vietnam)	**Betonamugo**	**Betonamujin**
Honkon (Hong Kong)	**Chuugokugo**	**Chuugokujin**
Mekishiko (Mexico)	**Supeingo**	**Mekishikojin**

Some notable exceptions are:

Igirisu *or* **Eikoku** (England)	**Eigo**	**Igirisujin** *or* **Eikokujin**
Beikoku *or* **Amerika**	**Eigo**	**Beikokujin** *or* **Amerikajin**

Did you know?

Omoiyari (lit. consideration)

Omoiyari is an action taken by a person anticipating another's need, and this practice is taught from a young age as a preferred and virtuous act. The Japanese may serve drinks without asking what their guests would like, or they may even call a taxi for a departing business client before one is asked for. When someone returns home, the phrase he usually hears is not the question "How was the day?" but more often, "It must have been a hard day!" or "It must have been hot!"

In Japan compliments on attire and jewelry are often low-key and general: **Ii desu ne. Kirei desu ne.** A gushing remark such as, "Oh, I like it! That's gorgeous!" is out of place and can cause the wearer to take it off and present it to you.

Enryo (lit. reserve)

Somewhat related to **omoiyari** is the Japanese concept of **enryo**, hesitation to express one's needs for fear of imposing on others, which is practised in both business and social life. When someone gives a gift, the receiver may refuse the gift several times before finally, with obvious reluctance, accepting it. When two people are going through a doorway, it is not unusual for each to insist that the other go through first, until one finally breaks down and says, **Ja, o-saki ni shitsurei shimasu** ("Excuse me for going ahead").

In Unit 10 Dialogue 1 the guest is going through the expected formality when tea and cake are served, even though the two women are close friends.

Neither **omoiyari** nor **enryo** is an alien concept in the West, but in Japan they are sometimes taken to what Western cultures might consider extremes.

HAI and IIE

There are instances in Japanese when a simple "yes" or "no" response to a question or comment may require the opposite of what might be expected in English. For example, in answer to the question **Eiga ni ikimasen deshita ka?** ("Didn't you go to the movie?"), the response would be either **Hai, ikimasen deshita**, or **Iie, ikimashita yo.** In other words, a negative question is often treated as if it were true/false. The above question, "Did you *not* go to the movie?" is answered by "Yes, (true) I did not go" or "no, (false) I did go."

Although the Japanese may respond to some negative questions according to sense, as in English, you should be aware of this difference. When someone asks you **Ocha demo nomimasen ka?** ("Won't you have some tea?"), a simple **hai** or **iie** may be the wrong answer. **O-negai shimasu** ("Please") or **Kekkoo desu** ("[No,] thanks") would be better choices for a clear response.

Another important aspect in the use of **hai** and **iie** is the hesitancy of the Japanese to make a clear refusal of an offer or suggestion. Instead of saying an abrupt **iie**, they often will say **Muzukashii desu** ("It's difficult") or **Chotto wakaranain desu** ("I don't really know").

When it comes to receiving compliments, however, a Japanese person will not hesitate to deny his own accomplishments, abilities or qualities, no matter how strongly someone may insist that the compliment is true.

Answers

Practise what you have learned

Exercise **1**	(a) 3 (b) 2 (c) 5 (d) 1 (e) 4
Exercise **2**	(a) Eigo/English (b) juuni-nen gurai/about 12 yrs. (c) Eigo to Doitsu-go/Eng. and German (d) amari joozu ja nain desu./not very good
Exercise **4**	(a) 3 (b) 4 (c) 2 (d) 1
Exercise **7**	(a) 2 (b) 4 (c) 3 (d) 1
Exercise **10**	(a) present (b) past (c) past (d) present (e) past
Exercise **12**	(a) mirun desu; mitan desu (b) surun desu; shitan desu (c) kurun desu; kitan desu

Ja o-genki de.
Ganbatte!

Take care!

Numbers & Counters

Cardinal numbers

0 **zero/rei**	10 **juu**	20 **ni-juu**
1 **ichi**	11 **juu-ichi**	21 **ni-juu-ichi**
2 **ni**	12 **juu-ni**	22 **ni-juu-ni**
3 **san**	13 **juu-san**	23 **ni-juu-san**
4 **shi/yon**	14 **juu-shi/-yon**	24 **ni-juu-shi/-yon**
5 **go**	15 **juu-go**	25 **ni-juu-go**
6 **roku**	16 **juu-roku**	26 **ni-juu-roku**
7 **shichi/nana**	17 **juu-shichi/-nana**	27 **ni-juu-shichi/-nana**
8 **hachi**	18 **juu-hachi**	28 **ni-juu-hachi**
9 **ku/kyuu**	19 **juu-ku/juu-kyuu**	29 **ni-juu-ku/-kyuu**

10 **juu**	100 **hyaku**	1,000 **sen/issen**	10,000 **ichi-man**
20 **ni-juu**	200 **ni-hyaku**	2,000 **ni-sen**	20,000 **ni-man**
30 **san-juu**	300 **san-byaku**	3,000 **san/zen**	30,000 **san-man**
40 **yon-juu**	400 **yon-hyaku**	4,000 **yon-sen**	40,000 **yon-man**
50 **go-juu**	500 **go-hyaku**	5,000 **go-sen**	50,000 **go-man**
60 **roku-juu**	600 **roppyaku**	6,000 **roku-sen**	60,000 **roku-man**
70 **nana-juu**	700 **nana-hyaku**	7,000 **nana-sen**	70,000 **nana-man**
80 **hachi-juu**	800 **happyaku**	8,000 **has-sen**	80,000 **hachi-man**
90 **kyuu-juu**	900 **kyuu-hyaku**	9,000 **kyuu-sen**	90,000 **kyuu-man**

Classic counters (Item counter)

1 (item)	**hitotsu**	6 (items)	**muttsu**
2 (items)	**futatsu**	7 (items)	**nanatsu**
3 (items)	**mittsu**	8 (items)	**yattsu**
4 (items)	**yottsu**	9 (items)	**kokonotsu**
5 (items)	**itsutsu**	10 (items)	**too**

(Above 10 use cardinal numbers)

Days of the week

Monday	**Getsuyoobi**	Friday	**Kin'yoobi**
Tuesday	**Kayoobi**	Saturday	**Doyoobi**
Wednesday	**Suiyoobi**	Sunday	**Nichiyoobi**
Thursday	**Mokuyoobi**		

Months of the year

January	**Ichigatsu**	July	**Shichigatsu**
February	**Nigatsu**	August	**Hachigatsu**
March	**Sangatsu**	September	**Kugatsu**
April	**Shigatsu**	October	**Juugatsu**
May	**Gogatsu**	November	**Juuichigatsu**
June	**Rokugatsu**	December	**Juunigatsu**

Hours (o'clock) and minutes

1:00	**ichi-ji**	1 minute	**ippun**
2:00	**ni-ji**	2 minutes	**nifun**
3:00	**san-ji**	3 minutes	**sanpun**
4:00	**yo-ji**	4 minutes	**yonpun**
5:00	**go-ji**	5 minutes	**gofun**
6:00	**roku-ji**	6 minutes	**roppun/rokufun**
7:00	**shichi-ji**	7 minutes	**nanafun**
8:00	**hachi-ji**	8 minutes	**happun/hachifun**
9:00	**ku-ji**	9 minutes	**kyuufun**
10:00	**juu-ji**	10 minutes	**juppun**
11:00	**juuichi-ji**	(etc., in pattern)	
12:00	**juuni-ji**		

People

1 person	**hitori**	3 people	**sannin**	5 and up	number + **nin**
2 people	**futari**	4 people	**yonin**		

Days of the month

1st	**tsuitachi**	11th	**juuichi-nichi**	21st	**nijuuichi-nichi**
2nd	**futsuka**	12th	**juuni-nichi**	22nd	**nijuuni-nichi**
3rd	**mikka**	13th	**juusan-nichi**	23rd	**nijuusan-nichi**
4th	**yokka**	14th	**juuyokka**	24th	**nijuuyokka**
5th	**itsuka**	15th	**juugo-nichi**	25th	**nijuugo-nichi**
6th	**muika**	16th	**juuroku-nichi**	26th	**nijuuroku-nichi**
7th	**nanoka**	17th	**juushichi-nichi**	27th	**nijuushichi-nichi**
8th	**yooka**	18th	**juuhachi-nichi**	28th	**nijuuhachi-nichi**
9th	**kokonoka**	19th	**juuku-nichi**	29th	**nijuuku-nichi**
10th	**tooka**	20th	**hatsuka**	30th	**sanjuu-nichi**
				31st	**sanjuuichi-nichi**

Ages

1 yr. old	**issai**	11 yrs. old	**juu-issai**	21 yrs. old	**nijuuissai**
2 yrs. old	**ni-sai**	12 yrs. old	**juu-ni-sai**	22 yrs. old	**nijuuni-sai**
3 yrs. old	**san-sai**	13 yrs. old	**juu-san-sai**	23 yrs. old	**nijuusan-sai**
4 yrs. old	**yon-sai**	14 yrs. old	**juu-yon-sai**	24 yrs. old	**nijuuyon-sai**
5 yrs. old	**go-sai**	15 yrs. old	**juu-go-sai**	25 yrs. old	**nijuugo-sai**
6 yrs. old	**roku-sai**	16 yrs. old	**juu-roku-sai**	26 yrs. old	**nijuuroku-sai**
7 yrs. old	**nana-sai**	17 yrs. old	**juu-nana-sai**	27 yrs. old	**nijunana-sai**
8 yrs. old	**hassai**	18 yrs. old	**juu-hassai**	28 yrs. old	**nijuhassai**
9 yrs. old	**kyuu-sai**	19 yrs. old	**juu-kyuu-sai**	29 yrs. old	**nijukyuu-sai**
10 yrs. old	**jussai**	20 yrs. old	**hatachi**	30 yrs. old	**sanjussai**

*Floors**

1st floor	**ikkai**
2nd floor	**ni-kai**
3rd floor	**san-gai**
4th floor	**yon-kai**
5th floor	**go-kai**
6th floor	**rokkai**
7th floor	**nana-kai**
8th floor	**hakkai**
9th floor	**kyuu-kai**
10th floor	**jukkai**

1st = ground floor in Britain
2nd = 1st floor in Britain
etc.

Train tracks

Track 1	**ichi-ban-sen**
Track 2	**ni-ban-sen**
Track 3	**san-ban-sen**
Track 4	**yon-ban-sen**
Track 5	**go-ban-sen**
Track 6	**roku-ban-sen**
Track 7	**nana-ban-sen**
Track 8	**hachi-ban-sen**
Track 9	**kyuu-ban-sen**
Track 10	**juu-ban-sen**

Hotel reservations

Days' stay

1 day	**ichi-nichi**
2 days	**futsuka**
3 days	**mikka**
4 days	**yokka**
5 days	**itsuka**

Nights' stay

1 night	**ippaku**
2 nights	**ni-haku**
3 nights	**san-paku**
4 nights	**yon-haku**
5 nights	**go-haku**

Elapsed time

Weeks

1 week	**isshuukan**
2 weeks	**ni-shuukan**
3 weeks	**san-shuukan**
4 weeks	**yon-shuukan**
etc.	(number + **shuukan**)

Months

1 month	**ikkagetsu**
2 months	**ni-kagetsu**
3 months	**san-kagetsu**
4 months	**yon-kagetsu**
etc.	(number + **kagetsu**)

Hours

1 hour	**ichijikan**
2 hours	**nijikan**
3 hours	**sanjikan**
4 hours	**yojikan**
etc.	(number + **jikan**)

Days

1 day **ichinichi**
2 days and up—same as days of the month

Other counters

flat objects	number + **mai**
ordinal numbers	number + **ban/banme**

Grammar Index

Unit 1

Unit 2

Unit 3

Unit 4

Unit 5

Unit 6

Unit 7

Counters for flat objects (**-mai**), p. 100
Elapsed time counters: months (**-kagetsu**), p. 102
"It is okay if...," p. 103
Comparisons (___ **yori** + adjective), p. 103
___ **toka**, p. 103

Unit 8

Verbs (*Irregular, Type 1, Type 2*) + **-masu**, p. 117
"can" (**-emasu** vs. **-imasu, -raremasu, koraremasu, dekimasu**), p. 117

Unit 9

shika/dake, p. 131
Grammar markers (**ya** ["etc."], **de** ["at/"in"]), p. 131
-te miru, p. 131
-to omou, p. 132

Unit 10

Adjective + **-soo** (**desu**), p. 145
desu/masu form, p. 145

Unit 11

suki vs. **kirei**, p. 150
Standard request (**-te kudasai**) vs. polite request
(**-te kudasaimasen ka**), p. 159
Past and negative of adjectives (**-kunai [desu]/-ku arimasen,**
-kunakatta [desu]/-ku arimasen deshita), p. 160

Unit 12

Adjective + **sugimasu**, p. 173
___ **rashii desu**, p. 173
Verbs that describe nouns, p. 173

Unit 13

Adjective + **naru**, p. 185
Making a verb into a noun (**no**[**wa**]), p. 185

Unit 14

ko-so-a-do words, p. 193
"I think I will..." (**-oo to omoimasu**), p. 199
Asking/giving permission (**-te mo ii desu [ka]**), p. 199
ta-form + **koto ga arimasu**, p. 199

Unit 15

Conversational present vs. past (**yomun desu/yondan desu**), p. 211
-te morau, p. 213
Verb + **toki**, p. 213
-go and **-jin**, p. 213

Vocabulary

A! expression of surprise
A, soo (**desu ka**)? Is that so...?
aakeido arcade (*Eng.*)
abura-e oil painting
achira (*pol.*) that person, that direction
agaru/agarimasu go up, ascend
aisu koohii iced coffee (*Eng.*)
aisu kuriimu ice cream (*Eng.*)
aisu tii ice tea (*Eng.*)
aite iru open
aki autumn
akibare clear sky in autumn
Akihabara a section of Tokyo
amai sweet
amari/anmari (not) too, (not) so
ame rain
ame-futo American football (*Eng.*)
anata you
annai guide, guidance
ano that over there
ano sa... (casual) by the way...
apaato(**mento**) flat, apartment (*Eng.*)
are that over there
arigato/arigatoo thanks
aru/arimasu there is/are; (we) have
aruku/arukimasu walk
asa morning
asatte the day after tomorrow
ashi foot/leg
ashita tomorrow
asoko over there
asu tomorrow
atama head
Atami a resort near Tokyo
atarashii new
atari vicinity
atatakai warm
atchi/achira way over there
ato de later
atsui hot
atsusa heat
au/aimasu meet/see (friends)

baa bar (*Eng.*)
baasudei birthday (*Eng.*)
bakari only, nothing but
ban-/banme ordinal suffix (**go-ban** = number 5/the fifth)
bankoku kyootsuu world-wide standard
basu bus (*Eng.*)
beekon bacon (*Eng.*)
beisubooru baseball (*Eng.*)
benkyoo suru/shimasu study
benri convenient
beru-booi bellboy (*Eng.*) / porter
betsu ni separately
biiru beer (*Eng.*)
bijinesu hoteru business hotel (*Eng.*)
bijutsukan art museum
Bisa Kaado Visa Card (*Eng.*)
boku I (*m./inf.*)
burausu blouse (*Eng.*)
buruu blue (*Eng.*)

-chan diminutive of **-san**
chashuumen noodles with sliced pork
chekku-auto check out (*Eng.*)
chekku-in check in (*Eng.*)
Chekosurobakiya Czechoslovakia
chigau different
chiisai small
chiizu cheese (*Eng.*)
chikadoo underground passage
chikai/chikaku ni near/nearby
chikatetsu underground railway
chikoo gozaimasu It is near (*pol.*)
chintsuu pain reduction
chizu map
choo intestines
chooshoku breakfast
chotto a little bit, a little while
Chūō-Yūbinkyoku Central Post Office
chuu-gurai about the middle, mid-range
chuugakusei junior student
Chuuka-ryoori Chinese cuisine
chuumon order

daibu for the most part
daidokoro yoohin kitchen utensils
daijoobu all right, fine, okay
daikirai dislike very much
dainingu ruumu dining room (*Eng.*)
daisuki like very much
daitai approximately
dakara that's why/consequently
dake only
dame hopeless/no good

dantai-sama tour group (*pol.*)
daredemo anybody
daroo probably is (*eq.* **deshoo**)
dashimono performance
datta informal past tense of **desu**
de by means of ____ (**J.R. de ikimasu.**)
de for the purpose of (**Kankoo de kita**.)
de in/at (for action verbs: **Shinjuku de kaimasu.**)
de then, therefore; (**te-**form of **desu**)
deito date (*Eng.*)
dekakeru/dekakemasu go out
dekiru/dekimasu can do/can be done
demo however/but
demo such a thing as ____
denki electricity
densha train
denwa telephone
denwa bangoo telephone number
deshoo probably is
desu is
Dii-Shii D.C. (Diners Club)
dochira? where?/which?/which way?/who? (*pol.*)
Doitsu Germany
dokka/dokoka somewhere
doko where
doko made? up to where?, how far?
doko made mo as far as possible
dokora hen? in what area? (*eq.* **dono hen?**)
donna? what kind of ____ ?
dono? which?
dono gurai/kurai? about how much?/how long?
doo? how?
doo iu? what kind of?
doo iu yoo na? what kind of?
Doomo Thanks (*inf.*)
Doomo arigatoo (gozaimasu/ Thank you very much. **gozaimashita.)**
Doozo please/go ahead
Doozo go-yukkuri Please have a pleasant stay/Please take your time
dore? which one?
dore kurai/gurai? approximately how long/how much? (*eq.* **dono kurai/gurai?**)
doresu dress (*Eng.*)
dotchi? which way? (*eq.* **dochira?**)
Doyoobi Saturday

e direction marker to/towards (**Tōkyō e ikimasu.**)
ee yes
eeto... let me see.../Uh...
eiga movie
Eigo English language
eki station
en yen (*monetary unit*)
enganbu coastal area
Enoden Enoden Line (*railway*)
Enoshima a sightseeing spot near Kamakura
Enryo shinaide! Please go ahead. Don't hesitate.
enshoo inflammation
erabu/erabimasu choose
erebeitaa lift, elevator (*Eng.*)

fingaa sandoitchi finger sandwich (*Eng.*)
fooku fork (*Eng.*)
fuben inconvenient
fudoosan'ya-san estate agent
-fun/-pun counter for minutes
Furansu France
furonto reception. front desk (*Eng.*)
furu/furimasu fall (rain or snow)
futari two people
futari-yoo no heya a room for two
futatsu two (items)
futsuka 2nd day of the month/2 days
futsuu normal
futtobooru football (*Eng.*) (*eq.* **ame-futo**)
fuukei scenery

ga subject marker (**Heya ga arimasu ka?**)
gaikoku foreign country
gaikoku muki no (kitte) (stamps) for overseas mail
gaikoku-go foreign language
gaikoku-jin foreign person
gakkoo school
gakusei student
gasu gas (*utility*) (*Eng.*)
genetsu fever reduction

geri-dome diarrhoea medicine
Getsuyoobi Monday
Ginza a section of Tokyo ("The Ginza")
go five
go- honorific prefix
-go (*after name of country*) language
Go-chisoo-sama deshita Thank you for the meal
Go-chuui kudasai Please be careful (*pol.*)
Go-gatsu May
gogo p.m.
go-jibun de by yourself (*pol.*)
go-kiboo your preference (*pol.*)
Gomen kudasai Hello (*when entering a shop*); Goodbye (*pol.*)
Gomen nasai I'm sorry
-goo number (of a train)
goro about, approximately (*time*)
gorufu golf (*Eng.*)
Gotanda a section of Tokyo
go-yosan-teki ni to meet your budget
gozaimasu (we) have/there is (*pol.*) (*eq.* **arimasu**); (it) is (*eq.* **desu**)
gozen-chuu during the morning
guramu gram (*Eng.*)
guriin green (*Eng.*)

ha tooth
hachi eight
Hachigatsu August
Hachimangū Hachiman Shrine
hagaki postcard
hahaa... expression of pondering
hai yes (*pol.*)
hairu/hairimasu enter, come in, go in
haitatsu suru/shimasu deliver
haitte imasu is included
hajime ni at the beginning
Hajimemashite How do you do?
Hakone a resort near Mt. Fuji
hamu ham (*Eng.*)
hamu-eggu ham and eggs (*Eng.*)
-han half, the half hour
hana flower
hanakaze head cold (*lit.* nose cold)
hanasu/hanashimasu speak
Hangarii Hungary
hankachi handkerchief (*Eng.*)
Harajuku a section of Tokyo
harau/haraimasu pay
hare clear weather
hareru/haremasu clear up
haru spring
hatachi twenty years old
-hatsu departure: **12-ji-hatsu**
hatsuka 20th day of the month/20 days
hayai fast/early
hayaku quickly, soon, early
heijitsu weekdays
hen vicinity, neighbourhood
hen (na) strange
heya room
heya-dai room charge
hi day
hidari left
hidoi terrible, awful
Higashi-guchi East entrance
Higashi-Yooroppa Eastern Europe
hiitaa heater (*Eng.*)
Hikari a Shinkansen train
hiroi spacious/wide
Hiroki (male) given name
Hiroshima name of a prefecture/city
hiru-gohan noon meal/lunch
hito person
hitomawari gurai about one full size
hitori one person
hitori de by oneself
hitotsu one (*item*)
hiza knee
hodo approximate amount
hoka ni other than that
hoka no other/another
hon book
honjitsu today (*pol.*) (*eq.* **kyoo**)
honkan main building
honto/hontoo true
honto ni really/truly
hon'yaku translation
hoo direction; (*after an adj.*) the; (*adj.*) one
hooboo everywhere/(in) all directions
hoomu station platform (*Eng.*)
hoshii want
hyaku (one) hundred

i-no-mukatsuki nausea
ichi one
ichiban first/no. 1/most (*before an adjective*)

ichigatsu January
ichigo strawberry
ichiji for a while, one o'clock
ichinchi/ichinichi one day
ichioo for the time being
ichooyaku medicine for stomach problem
ie house
ii good/all right/okay
iie no
ijoo in excess of, more than, above
ikaga? how?, how about?
ikahodo? about how much? (*pol.*)
Ikebukuro a section of Tokyo
iki (on the way) going, the trip there
ikkai once/first (ground) floor
iktadaku/itadakimasu partake (*humb.*); (*after* **te-***form verb*) I will have you (do something).
iku/ikimasu go
ikura? how much?
ikutsu? how old?/how many?
ima now
imi purpose, meaning
ippai full
ippaku one night stay
ippan-teki (na) common, general
ippun one minute
Irasshaimase Welcome/Come in
irassharu/irasshaimasu be (in a place), go, come (*exal.*) (*eq.* **iru/imasu, iku/ikimasu, kuru/kimasu**)
ireru/iremasu put in, insert, include
iro colour
iroiro (na)/ironna various
iru/imasu be (in a place) (with person or animal as subject)
isha medical doctor
isogashii busy
issai one year old
issho (ni) together
Itadakimasu (a phrase used before eating) I will partake
itai (desu) hurts, is painful
itami pain
Itariya Italy
itasu/itashimasu do (*humb.*) (*eq.* **suru/shimasu**)
itsu? when?
itsuka sometime
itsuka 5th day of the month/5 days
itsumo always
itsutsu five (items)
Itte irasshai Hurry back
Itte kimasu I'll be back
iya disgusting, unpleasant
iyaa (*expression*) well...

ja then, well...
ja nai(n desu) is not
Ja ne (I'll) see you! (*inf.*)
Jei Shii Bii J.C.B. (*credit card*)
-ji (*counter for hours*) o'clock
jikan time
jiki a certain (period of) time, a season
jimu gym (*Eng.*)
jimusho office, agency
jitsu wa the truth is...; actually...
jiyuu-seki general seating
joggingu jogging (*Eng.*)
joozu good at (an activity), skilful
J.R. Japan Railway system
Junko (female) given name
juu ten
Juugatsu October
Juuichigatsu November
Juunigatsu December
juusho address

-ka counter for days of the month (also **-nichi**)
ka? question marker: **Kankoo desu ka?**
kaado credit card (*Eng.*)
Kabuki Kabuki Theatre
kaeri (on the way) back, the return trip
kaeru/kaemasu change, exchange
-kagetsu counter for months (*elapsed time*)
kagi key
kagu furniture
-kai counter for floors of a building
kaidan stairway
kaigai(ni) overseas
kaigi business meeting
kaiin-sei membership system
kaimono shopping
kaisatsuguchi entry where tickets are punched, turnstile

kaisha office/company
kaisha-in company employee
kakaru/kakarimasu take, require (time *or* money)
kaku/kakimasu write
kakugo determination
kakugo de areba if you're willing to do ____
Kamakura an ancient capital near Tokyo
Kamakura-bori carvings done in Kamakura area
kamo shiremasen (*after a verb or* **soo**) it may be
Kanada Canada
kangofu nurse
kanjiru/kanjimasu feel/seem
kankoo sightseeing
kankoo kyaku tourist
kanojo she
kara from (**Eki kara arukimasu.**); since (**Sanji kara...**); because, so
kare he
karei raisu curried rice (*Eng.*)
karui light-weight
kasan sareru/saremasu be added
Kashikomarimashita I understand; At your service
kashira (*after a verb*) I wonder if...
kata person (*pol.*)
Katō family name
kau/kaimasu buy
Kayoobi Tuesday
kazagusuri medicine for cold
kazoku family
kedo but... (*eq.* **keredomo**)
keeki cake (*Eng.*)
kekkon suru/shimasu be married
kekkoo fine, okay, all right; quite a bit (**Kekkoo furu...**)
keredo(mo) but, however
kibishii stern, severe
kiiro yellow
kikoeru/kikoemasu be able to hear; be audible
kiku/kikimasu hear
Kimatte iru It has been decided
Kin'en-sha non-smoking car
Kin'yoobi Friday
kippu ticket
kirai (desu) dislike
kirasu/kirashimasu be out of stock
kirei beautiful, pretty
kisetsu season
Kita-guchi North entrance
kitte stamps
kitto for certain
kizu-gusuri antiseptic ointment
kochira (*pol.*) here/this person (me)/this way/in this direction
kochira no this one (*pol.*) (*eq.* **kono**)
koko here
kokonoka 9th of the month/9 days
kokonotsu nine (items)
kokunai domestic
Kōkyo Imperial palace
Komarimashita It's a problem./I'm perplexed
komu/komimasu be crowded
Konbanwa Good evening
kondo this time/next time
kongetsu this month
konna ni like this, to this degree
Konnichiwa Hello (*day time*)
kono this
kono mae in front of here/ before
konshuu this week
konshuu-matsu this weekend
kon'ya tonight
koocha black tea
koojoo factory
kookoosei high-school student
kookuubin airmail
koora cola (*Eng.*)
kooshoo negotiation
korareru/koraremasu come (*exal.*)
kore this
koshi lower back
kotchi this one, this way (*eq.* **kochira**)
kotoba language
-ku ward, district (of a metropolis)
kudamono fruit
kudasai give me ____ : *noun* + **(o) kudasai**
kudasai (*after* **te-***form verb*) please do ____ .
Kugatsu September
kumo cloud
kumo ga deyasuku may become cloudy
kuni country/hometown
kurabu club (*Eng.*)

kurashikku no ongaku classical music (*Eng.*)
kureru/kuremasu (*after* **te-***form verb*) Please (do); kindly (do)
kuru/kimasu come
kuruma carriage
kusuri medicine
kusuri o nomu/nomimasu take medicine
kutsushita socks
kuuraa air conditioner (*Eng.*)
kyanseru cancellation (*Eng.*)
kyasshu cash (*Eng.*)
kyoo today
kyoo dooyoo same as today
kyooshi teacher
Kyooshuku de gozaimasu ga... I'm sorry but...(*pol.*)
kyootsuu de for a common purpose
Kyōto ancient city of Kyoto
kyuu nine

ma so, well...
maa-maa so-so
machi town
machi-nami ambience of town
mada still/yet
Mada (desu) Not yet
made until/up to/as far as
mae front/before
mae motte beforehand
mae-uri advance ticket
magaru/magarimasu turn
-mai counter for flat objects
Maiko (female) given name
mairu/mairimasu come/go (*humb.*)
man ten thousand
mannaka middle/centre
manshitsu fully occupied
mansuri-manshon monthly rented flat
massugu straight
-masu normal-polite verb ending
-masu = present positive
-masen = present negative
-mashita = past positive
-masen deshita = past negative
-mashoo = "Let's do..."
-mashoo ka? = "Shall we do...?"
masu goto ni each time ____ is added
Masumoto family name
Masutaa Kaado Master Card (*Eng.*)
mata again
mata wa or
mazu first of all
me eye
Meiji Jingū Meiji Shrine
menyuu menu (*Eng.*)
mezurashii unusual
mi ni iku/ikimasu go and see
michi road/street/path
Midori no Madoguchi Green Window (information service)
migi right
migi-gawa right side
migite right hand
mijikai short
Miki family name
mikka 3rd of the month/3 days
mikkusu sando mixed sandwiches (*Eng.*)
mikomi prediction
mimi ear
Minami-guchi South Entrance
miru/mimasu see, watch, look at/(*after a* **te-***form verb*) try and ____
miruku milk (*Eng.*)
mise shop/store
mise no obasan woman of the shop
Misete itadakimasu I would like to have you show me
mitsukeru/mitsukemasu find
mittsu three (items)
Miura family name
mizu water
mo also, too, as well
mochiron of course
Mokuyoobi Thursday
momiji autumn colours
mono thing
moo already
moo ichido one more time
mooningu kooru wake up call (*Eng.*)
Mooshiwake arimasen (polite) I am sorry
morau/moraimasu (*after* **te-***form verb*) have someone (do something)
Mori family name
moshi if
moshi moshi hello (*telephone*)
motte iku/ikimasu take, carry (with)
motte iru/imasu have, be in possession of

motto more
muika 6th of the month/6 days
mukanai not suitable
muri not possible
mushoku retired/unemployed
musume my daughter
muttsu six (items)
muzukashii difficult
Myunhen Munich

nafukin napkin (*Eng.*)
nagai long
nai(n desu) is not (*inf.*) (*eq.* **arimasen**)
naka in/inside
naka-naka no matter what
Nakagawa family name
Nakayama family name
namae name
namiki-michi tree-lined road
nan/nani? what?
nan no? what kind of?
nana seven
nanatsu seven (items)
nanban? what number?
nangai/nankai? what floor?
nangatsu? what month?
nani-go? what language?
nani-jin? what nationality?
nanika/nanka something
nanimo nothing
nani-ryoori? what kind of cuisine?
nani-sen? what (railway /underground) line?
nanji? what time?
nanjikan? how much time?, how many hours?
nanmai? how many (flat objects)?
nannichi? what day of the month?
nannin? how many people?
nanoka 7th day of the month/7 days
nanpaku? how many nights?
nanpun? how many minutes?
nan'yoobi? what day of the week?
narabu/narabimasu line up
naru/narimasu become, come to
nasaru/nasaimasu do (*exal.*) (*eq.* **suru/shimasu**)
natsu summer
ne? ...isn't it?;...right? (*tag question*)
Ne... Say...
nedan price
nekutai tie (*Eng.*)
Nerima a section of Tokyo
neru/nemasu sleep
ni to/towards (*direction marker:* **Tōkyō ni ikimasu.**)
ni in/at (*location marker:* **ni imasu**.)
ni at (*specific time marker:* **Sanji ni...**)
ni two
-nichi counter for days of the month (*also* **-ka**)
Nichiyoobi Sunday
Nigatsu February
Nihon Japan
nihonshoku Japanese food
nihonshu Japanese rice wine (*eq.* **o-sake**)
nimei-sama two people (*pol.*)
nimotsu luggage
-nin counter for people
ninbun, -ninmae counter for servings of food
ninki no aru popular
nitchuu during the day
niwaka-ame sudden shower
no possessive marker: **watashi no namae**
no (*after a verb*) one (*makes verb phrase into noun phrase*)
noboru/noborimasu climb
nochi later/afterwards
node because, so
nodo throat
-nomi only: **chooshoku nomi** (only breakfast)
nomigusuri medication that is taken orally
nomimono beverage
nomi-sugi over-drinking
nomu/nomimasu drink
noru/norimasu get on (a vehicle)/board
nuudo nude (*Eng.*)
nyuusu newscast (*Eng.*)

o object marker: **Mizu o nomimasu.**
o- honorific prefix: **o-cha**
O-azukari shimasu I shall take care of it (*pol.*)
obasan aunt, old woman
o-cha green tea
o-chazuke hot tea poured over cooked rice
O-dekake desu ka? Are you going out? (*pol.*)

odoroku/odorokimasu be surprised
o-furo bath
Ogikubo a section of Tokyo
o-hashi chopsticks
Ohayoo gazaimasu Good morning
oishii delicious
Okaerinasai Welcome back
o-kaeshi your change (*pol.*)
O-kamai naku Don't trouble yourself
o-kanjoo bill
o-keiko (-goto) (arts/crafts) lesson
okiru/okimasu wake up, get up
o-kosan your children (*pol.*)
oku/okimasu put, place; (*after* **te-***form verb*) do something for a later purpose
okuru/okurimasu send, ship
o-kyaku-sama visitor, guest (*pol.*)
O-matase itashimashita Sorry to have kept you waiting
O-me ni kakarimashoo Let's see each other (again) (*pol.*)
o-mie ni naru/narimasu arrive (*pol.*)
omoi heavy
omoshiroi interesting, funny, amusing
Omotesandō a section of Tokyo
omou/omoimasu think (that), have an opinion
Onaka ga sukimashita I'm hungry (*inf.*: **Onaka suita.**)
Onegai shimasu Please (take care of it)
ongaku music
onna no ko girl
onsen hot spring
oobaa overcoat (*Eng.*)
oobaa suru/shimasu over-book, go over, exceed (*Eng.*)
oodanhodoo pedestrian crossing
oo-eru office lady, female office clerk
ooi many, plentiful
ookii big (*col.* : **okkii**)
oomune mostly
oosugiru/oosugimasu be too much
oriru/orimasu go down, descend, get off (a vehicle)
oru/orimasu (I) am (*humb.*) (*eq.* **imasu**)
o-sake rice wine
o-shiro castle
Osore irimasu ga... I am terribly sorry, but...
o-sumai your home (*pol.*)
Ōsutoriya Austria
o-tachi ni naru/narimasu leave (*pol.*)
o-taku you, your place (*pol.*)
Ōtemachi a section of Tokyo
o-tenki weather
oto sound, noise
otoko no ko boy
o-tomari your stay (*pol.*)
owari the end
o-yasumi-chuu during vacation

paasento percentage (%) (*Eng.*)
paatii party (*Eng.*)
pakkeiji-tsuaa package tour (*Eng.*)
pantaron women's slacks (*Fre.*)
pasupooto nanbaa passport number (*Eng.*)
pikunikku picnic (*Eng.*)
pinku pink (*Eng.*)
pitsa pizza (*Eng.*)
Pōrando Poland (*Eng.*)
poteto sarada potato salad (*Eng.*)
Puraha-joo Prague castle
purezento present, gift (*Eng.*)
puuru swimming pool (*Eng.*)

raamen'ya-san ramen noodle shop
rafu nude art form
raigetsu next month
raishuu next week
raji-kase radio-cassette (*Eng.*)
rajio radio (*Eng.*)
rashii (desu) (*after adj., noun, or verb*) seems, seems to be, seems like ____
remoneido lemonade (*Eng.*)
reshiito receipt (*Eng.*)
resutoran restaurant (*Eng.*)
ribon ribbon (*Eng.*)
roku six
Rokugatsu June
rooka corridor/hallway
roosuto-biifu roast beef (*Eng.*)
Roppongi a section of Tokyo
ruumu saabisu room service (*Eng.*)

ryokoo trip
ryokoo ni deru/demasu go on a trip
ryokoo suru/shimasu travel
ryoohoo both
ryookin charge, fee, fare
ryookin ga kakaru/kakarimasu charge a fee
ryoori cooking, cuisine
ryooshin (both) parents

Saa Well...
saabisu chaaji service charge (*Eng.*)
Saga-Kyūbin Saga Delivery Service
sagaku monetary difference
sagasu/sagashimasu look for
-sai counter for years of age
saikin recently
saikuringu cycling (*Eng.*)
saki e iku/ikimasu go first
saki ni at first, previously
saki no the previous (one)
sakkaa soccer (*Eng.*)
saku/sakimasu bloom/blossom
sakura cherry tree
-sama honorific suffix after a name
samui cold (weather)
san three
-san honorific suffix, after a name
sanbun no ichi one third (1/3)
sando(itchi) sandwich (*Eng.*)
Sangatsu March
sanka participation
sara plate, dish
satoo sugar
sauna sauna (*Eng.*)
Sayonara/Sayoonara Goodbye
sebiro man's suit
seibutsu still-life
Seiyō Bijutsukan Museum of Occidental Art
semai small (space), narrow
semasa smallness (space)
sen thousand
-sen line (*railway/subway*); track (**niban-sen** = track no.2)
sengetsu last month
sensei teacher/instructor
senshuu last week
sentaa-rain centre line (*Eng.*)
sentaku laundry/cleaning
sentaku suru/shimasu do the laundry/cleaning
shake-chazuke salmon **o-chazuke**
shashin photograph
shashin o toru/torimasu take pictures
shi (*after a verb*) and, and so on
shi four
Shibuya a section of Tokyo
shichi seven
Shichigatsu July
Shigatsu April
shigoto work, job
shiharai payment
shiitsu sheets (*Eng.*)
shika only, nothing but
shimau/shimaimasu (*after a* **te**-*form verb*) do completely, finally
shimi spot, stain
shimi nuki spot remover
shinbun newspaper
Shinjuku a section of Tokyo
Shinkan-sen Bullet Train
Shinpai shinaide kudasai Please don't worry
shinpai suru/shimasu worry
shiraberu/shirabemasu check something; look up (in a dictionary)
shiriai acquaintance
shiru/shitte imasu know
shirushi mark/symbol/sign
shita younger (child)/below/underneath/lower
shitagi underwear
shitei-seki reserved seat
shitsurei rude
Shitsurei desu ga... Excuse me but...
Shitsurei shimasu Excuse me
Shiyoo ga nai It can't be helped
Shōda family name
shokuji dinner/meal
shokuji-tsuki meals included
shoohin prize
shoohizei sales tax
shooka-furyoo indigestion
shookai introduction
shookai suru/shimasu introduce
shooto keeki short-cake (*Eng.*)
shufu homemaker, housewife
shumi hobby, special interest
shuppatsu departure
shurui kind, species
-shuukan counter for weeks (*elapsed time*)

soba buckwheat noodles
sochira that direction, that person (*pol.*)
soko there
soko-soko so-so
sokora hen over there, that area (*col.*) (*eq.* **sono hen**)
sonna ni like that, to that degree
sono ____ that ____
sono ato after that
soo so, in that way
Soo desu That's right
-soo desu (*after an adj.*) looks ____ ; (*after a casual verb form*) I hear that...
soo shitara and then; in that case
soo suru to if that's the case, if you do that
soo yuu baai in a case like that
soo yuu no something like that
soogoo de combined
sooseiji sausage (*Eng.*)
sora-moyoo weather, condition of the skies
sore that (one)
sore deshitara in that case, if that's so
sore dewa/sore ja well then...
sore ni besides that
sorede then, therefore, because of that
sorekara after that, then, therefore
soretomo or, or else, otherwise
sorosoro soon, gradually
sotchi that way (*eq.* **sochira**)
soto outside
soto ni deru/demasu go outside
subete altogether, everything
-sugimasu (*after an adj.*) too ____
Suginami-ku Suginami Ward (in Tokyo)
sugoi impressive, great
suidoo water (*utility*)
suimingu swimming (*Eng.*)
suite iru/suite imasu (traffic) is light, (stomach) is empty
Suiyoobi Wednesday
sukaato skirt (*Eng.*)
suki (**desu**) like
sukii skiing (*Eng.*)
sukkari completely
Sumimasen Excuse me
sumu/sumimasu live, reside (**sunde imasu** = be living in a place)
supageti spaghetti (*Eng.*)
Supein Spain
supootsu sports (*Eng.*)
surippa slippers (*Eng.*)
suru/shimasu do
sutokkingu stockings (*Eng.*)
suutsu women's suit (*Eng.*)
suwareru/suwaremasu can be seated
suwaru/suwarimasu be seated, sit down
suzushii cool

tabemasu eat
tabemono foodstuff
tabe-owaru/tabe-owarimasu finish eating
tabun most likely
tada only
tada-tada just (*emphasizer*)
Tadaima I'm back
tadaima right now, just now
-tai(**n desu**) (*after a verb*) want to (do something)
taifuu typhoon
taihen difficult/terrible
taizai stay, sojourn (*pol.*)
takai expensive
Takarabe family name
takusan a lot
takushii taxi (*Eng.*)
tamago egg
tame purpose (____ **no tame** = for the purpose of ____ , for the ____)
Tanaka family name
tanjoobi birthday
tanomu/tanomimasu please take care (of it)./ask for/request
tanoshii pleasant, fun
Tanoshimi ni shite imasu I'm looking forward to it
tanuki udon noodles with fried bean curd
taoru towel (*Eng.*)
tasu/tashimasu add
tatemono building
te hand
tegami letter
tehai arrangements/preparations
teikyuu-bi store's regular day off
ten'in shop assistant
tenisu tennis (*Eng.*)

tenki-yohoo weather forecast
terebi television (*Eng.*)
to and
-to mooshimasu I am called ____.
to omou/omoimasu (*after a verb*) I think that...
Tochigi-ken Tochigi prefecture
toire toilet (*Eng.*)
toka (*after a noun*) for example; and others
toki point in time/(*after a verb*) when (one does)
toki doki once in a while
tokoro place
tokoro de by the way
tokoro ni yotte depending on the area
toku ni especially
Tōkyō Capital of Japan
Tōkyō Tawā Tokyo Tower
tomaru/tomarimasu stay (over)
tomato juusu tomato juice (*Eng.*)
tomodachi friend
tonikaku anyhow
tonkatsu pork cutlet
too ten
toojitsu on the same day
tooka 10th of the month/10 days
tooroku registration
toosuto toast (*Eng.*)
Toranomon a section of Tokyo
toreru/toremasu can be removed
toriaezu first of all, in the meantime
toriatsukau/toriatsukaimasu handle, deal with
tori-no-kara-age deep-fried chicken
Toruko Turkey
totemo very/quite
tsuika an addition
tsuika ryookin additional charge
tsuika suru/shimasu add to
tsuin twin room/bed (*Eng.*)
tsuitachi first of the month
tsuite iru/tsuite imasu be included
tsukareru/tsukaremasu become tired
tsukau/tsukaimasu use
tsukeru/tsukemasu put on; turn on (elec. appliance)
tsukiatari dead end
tsukiataru/tsukiatarimasu come to a dead end or T-junction
tsukimi soba buckwheat noodles with an egg
tsuku/tsukimasu arrive
tsumetai cold (to the touch)
tsumori (desu) (*after a verb*) intend to (do something)
tsurete iku/ikimasu take (someone) along
tsutomeru/tsutomemasu work, have a job
tsutsumu/tsutsumimasu wrap
Tsuyoshi (male) given name
tsuyu rainy season
tte They said/I heard that...(*inf.*)
tte yuu to... when you say ____,...

uchi our place/home
udon noodles
ue above/top/over/older (child)
Ueno a section of Tokyo
Uīn Vienna
ume-chazuke plum **o-chazuke**
un (*casual*) yes
urayamashii enviable
urusai noisy, bothersome
uwagi man's sport coat
uzu-uzu suru/shimasu be frustrating

wa topic marker: **Kyoo wa samui desu.**
waishatsu man's dress shirt
wakaru/wakarimasu I understand
wake reason
wan-beddo-ruumu one-bed-room (*Eng.*)
wariai to rather
warui bad
washoku Japanese cuisine
watakushi/watashi I
watakushi-domo we (*humb.*)
watakushi-tachi we
wataru/watarimasu cross, cross over
watasu/watashimasu (I) will give to (you)

yahari/yappari as expected, after all
Yamada family name
Yamamoto family name

yasai vegetable
yasui inexpensive
yasu-uri-shoppu discount store
yattsu eight (items)
yo emphasis marker: **Soo desu yo.**
yoi good (*eq.* **ii**)
yokaroo probably good/(*pol.*) (*eq.* **ii deshoo**)
Yokatta desu It turned out all right.; Thank goodness
yoku often, well
yomu/yomimasu read
yoohin utensils/paraphernalia
yooi preparations
yooka 8th of the month/8 days
yooshoku Western cuisine
yori (mo) exceeding, in excess of
Yōroppa Europe
yoroshii good (*pol.*) (*eq.* **yoi**)
Yoroshiku (onegai shimasu) I'm happy to meet you/Please take care of it
Yoroshuu gozaimashoo ka? Will that be all right? (*pol.*) (*eq.* **Ii desu ka?**)
Yoshida family name
Yoshiko (female) given name
yotei schedule, plan
Yotte kudasai Please call
yottsu four (items)
yoyaku reservation
yuki snow
yukkuri leisurely (*time spent*)
yuubin mail
yuubin o dasu/dashimasu mail a letter
yuubinkyoku post office
yuuhi sunset
yuujin friend
yuumei(na) famous

Zannen desu It is disappointing/too bad
zehi by all means
zenbu de altogether
zenkan entire building
zenzen not at all
zero zero (*Eng.*)
zubon men's slacks (*Fre.*)
zuibun quite a bit
-zutsu each (**hyaku-en zutsu** = 100 yen each)
zutto all the way

Index

Breakthrough Language Packs

Complete self-study courses

Each Breakthrough Language Pack is designed as a complete self-study course using audio cassettes and a course book. Each Pack contains:

* Three 60- or 90-minute audio cassettes
* The course book

Breakthrough Language Packs available:

Breakthrough Arabic	ISBN 0–333–56692–0
Breakthrough French	ISBN 0–333–58511–9
Breakthrough German	ISBN 0–333–56730–7
Breakthrough Greek	ISBN 0–333–48714–1
Breakthrough Italian	ISBN 0–333–48179–8
Breakthrough Russian	ISBN 0–333–55726–3
Breakthrough Spanish	ISBN 0–333–57105–3
Breakthrough Further French	ISBN 0–333–48193–3
Breakthrough Further German	ISBN 0–333–48189–5
Breakthrough Further Spanish	ISBN 0–333–48185–2
Breakthrough Business French	ISBN 0–333–54398–X
Breakthrough Business German	ISBN 0–333–54401–3
Breakthrough Business Spanish	ISBN 0–333–54404–8

* CD Packs are also now available for:

Breakthrough French	ISBN 0–333–58513–5
Breakthrough German	ISBN 0–333–57870–8
Breakthrough Spanish	ISBN 0–333–57874–0

£8.50 net